About the editors

Kees Koonings is Associate Professor of Development Studies at the Faculty of Social Sciences of Utrecht University. He has published on development issues, ethnicity, the military, democracy and violence in Latin America.

Dirk Kruijt is Honorary Professor of Development Studies at the Faculty of Social Sciences of Utrecht University. He has published on poverty and informality, military governments, and war and peace in Latin America.

MEGACITIES

The politics of urban exclusion and violence in the global South

EDITED BY KEES KOONINGS
AND DIRK KRUIJT

Zed Books
LONDON | NEW YORK

Megacities: the politics of urban exclusion and violence in the global South
was first published in 2009 by Zed Books Ltd, 7 Cynthia Street, London
N1 9JF, UK and Room 400, 175 Fifth Avenue, New York, NY 10010, USA.

www.zedbooks.co.uk

Set in OurType Arnhem and Futura Bold by Ewan Smith, London
Index: ed.emery@thefreeuniversity.net
Cover designed by Rogue Four Design
Printed and bound in Great Britain by GPI Antony Rowe, Chippenham and
Eastbourne

Distributed in the USA exclusively by Palgrave Macmillan, a division of
St Martin's Press, LLC, 175 Fifth Avenue, New York, NY 10010, USA

A catalogue record for this book is available from the British Library
Library of Congress Cataloging in Publication Data available

ISBN 978 1 84813 295 5 hb
ISBN 978 1 84813 296 2 pb
ISBN 978 1 84813 490 4 eb

Contents

Figures and tables

Acknowledgements

The chapters in this book were originally presented as draft papers at the conference 'The politics of urban poverty, exclusion and violence: comparative analysis and policy insights', organized in The Hague on 27 and 28 September 2007. The intention of the conveners of the conference that eventually resulted in this book was to analyse in academic terms emerging development problems that until then had not received explicit attention in the donor community. The conference was jointly organized by the Department of Cultural Anthropology and Sociology of Utrecht University and the Directorate for Effectiveness and Quality of International Development Cooperation of the Dutch Ministry of Foreign Affairs (DEK). The scholarly and policy meeting was part of a multi-year collaboration programme started in 2006 – called Academy of International Cooperation (Internationale Samenwerking in Dutch) – between the ministry and Utrecht University in the field of poverty alleviation and good governance.

We are grateful to our colleagues at the ministry, Maarten Brouwer, Jan Waltmans, Bert Vermaat and Rob Visser, for their active interest and support. Invaluable substantial and logistic support before and during the conference was provided by our research assistant Sara Koenders, and also by Tessa Dipholt and Suzan van der Wilt.

The authors responded generously to our suggestions for revision of their papers. We are particularly grateful for their willingness to give us the necessary leeway in moulding the texts into their eventual chapter form. Sara Koenders offered key support to the process of editing.

We are grateful to the anonymous reviewer for incisive yet supportive criticism of the draft manuscript.

Finally, we owe a debt of gratitude to the editors at Zed Books, Ellen Hallsworth and her successor Ken Barlow, for guiding us through the project, being flexible on deadlines and supportive with everything else.

About the authors

Mariano Aguirre is director of the Norwegian Peacebuilding Centre (NOREF), Oslo. He holds a master's degree in Peace Studies from Trinity College, Dublin. He is author, co-author and editor of several books on international relations, and contributes to international media. Previously he was programme officer at the Ford Foundation in New York and director of peace and security studies at the Spanish think tank FRIDE.

Sérgio Baierle is a political scientist and member of the board of directors of Cidade (Centro de Assessoria e Estudos Urbanos – Porto Alegre, Brazil). Cidade is an NGO that researches, and advises civil organizations on, access to information to stimulate new ways of producing knowledge on urban issues.

Asef Bayat is the academic director of ISIM and holds the ISIM chair at Leiden University. His publications include work on the politics of the urban poor, labour movements, development NGOs, everyday cosmopolitanism, comparative Islamisms and Muslim youth cultural politics, primarily in Iran and Egypt.

Jo Beall is Professor of Development Studies in the Development Studies Institute (DESTIN) at the London School of Economics (LSE). She is a renowned specialist on the theme of urban development and urban governance and politics, and has extensive research experience in South Africa and West Asia.

Owen Crankshaw is Professor of Sociology in the Department of Sociology at the University of Cape Town. He has published extensively on urban poverty and urban problems as well on the changing relationship between racial and class inequality.

Robert Gay is Professor of Sociology and director of the Toor Cummings Center for International Studies and the Liberal Arts at Connecticut College. He is the author of several books and numerous articles on democratization, civil society, clientelism and violence in Brazil.

Caroline Moser is Professor of Urban Development and head of the Global Urban Research Centre at the University of Manchester. She has published extensively on urban development, urban violence and insecurity.

Susan Parnell is an urban geographer in the Department of Environmental and Geographical Sciences at the University of Cape Town. She has published numerous articles and edited volumes on urban historical geography, local government, poverty reduction and urban environmental justice.

Janice Perlman is the founder and president of the Mega-Cities Project, a global non-profit organization working in nineteen of the world's largest cities to seek and share innovative solutions. She is affiliated with the New School in New York City and has recently completed her latest book, *FAVELA*, a reworking of her *Myth of Marginality*.

Introduction

KEES KOONINGS AND DIRK KRUIJT

There is no doubt that the twenty-first century is the critical stage for the overall urbanization of the world's population. Depending on the definition of 'urban' (threshold number of inhabitants of compact built environments), somewhere between last year (2008) and next year (2010) UN worldwide demographic projections expect the size of the rapidly increasing urban population to overtake that of the stagnant rural population. Between 2005 and 2030, the urban population is expected to grow from less than 50 per cent to almost 60 per cent of the global population. In 2030, the urban population in developing countries will be the prime site of rapid demographic expansion worldwide.

As a consequence, global trends of poverty and social exclusion will have a predominantly urban face in the present century. Particularly, the so-called megacities around the world are rapidly becoming the scene of deprivation and exclusion, especially in what has come to be called the global South. In such large-scale yet concentrated and integrated social environments, a complex set of relationships links poverty and exclusion to urban politics, power relations and public policy. Conventionally, cities in developing countries have been particularly important for the interface between politics and 'the poor'. Cities have been places where poverty has become directly visible in structural articulation and close daily proximity to 'development' and 'relative affluence', and where the poor have found many ways to develop 'agency'. In cities, the poor exert pressure on the state and demand that their short- and sometimes even long-term interests be met. In democracies, the urban poor form an increasingly important part of the electorate and therefore are directly relevant to political strategies and calculations. As a consequence, urban public policies are of direct importance in a broad range of issues related to poverty alleviation and social inclusion.

A particular element of growing importance and concern is the expansion of urban social-territorial spaces where formal or effective governance is absent. In concrete terms this means that there is no effective presence of state power and public institutions in parts of cities that are seen as poor or marginal. In such urban spaces, an uncivil logic of coercion and violence

1

takes over, and these zones become synonymous with violence and insecurity. Recent scholarship has moved beyond the superficial equation of poverty, marginality and violence to unravel the connections between deprivation, exclusion and contending forms of power and control. Violence brokers are not merely operating in the atomized and anomic world left to itself by the state and formal institutions; violence has become the basis for alternative, 'parallel' forms of order, control, resource distribution, legitimacy and identity. In many cases, the local state is drawn into a perverse spiral of escalating violence, crime and arbitrary conduct that is transforming the cityscape into a theatre of low-intensity warfare. Violent actors seek to build upon de facto power in strategies that seek access to urban politics and policy-making. The urban poor are faced with the challenge of charting pathways in their 'encounters with violence' (Moser and McIlwaine 2004). Local politicians, administrators, grassroots leaders and NGO officials are faced with the puzzle of how to restore effective non-violent institutions, legitimate governance and citizen security.

The point of departure adopted in this volume is that poverty, exclusion and violence in so-called megacities (usually defined on the basis of their population size, with 5 million inhabitants as the most commonly used lower threshold), but more generally in any urban environment, are increasingly intertwined in such a way that conventional distinctions between a formal, legal, institutional, peaceful (in short 'ordered') city and its counterpoint (informal, illegal, non-institutional or 'disordered') more and more fail to have analytical and practical meaning. This has of course been acknowledged for quite some time by scholars and practitioners in the case of livelihood strategies of poor urban individuals and households (viz. the lively debate on the 'informal sector' since the early 1970s). But it is also becoming increasingly manifest in more socially and politically circumscribed domains of urban life: the reproduction of social capital, social mobilization and grassroots urban civil society, and political participation. The rise, during the 1990s and early 2000s, of the discourse of 'good governance' prioritized 'formal' institutions, practices and cultures within civil and political society. This approach was part of a post-Washington Consensus framework focusing on Western- (or liberal-) styled legal-political institutions. Although presented as 'objective' conceptualization, in fact the good governance approach had clear subjectivist and voluntaristic connotations. The nominal spread, since the 1980s, of Third Wave democracy and its urban corollary, decentralization, has not by itself solved the political problem of urban exclusion and violence. The adoption of this discourse by much of the international cooperation community has contributed to a widening gap between 'real' conditions and mechanisms for the agency of the urban excluded and the paradigms sponsored by experts and donors.

Urban violence, fear and insecurity are arguably the domain where this gap is most visible. In increasingly violent megacities, the urban excluded face the brunt of what in many cases seems like low-intensity urban warfare. From their perspective, little difference exists between the forces of the 'law' and non-state criminal, violent or armed actors who benefit from the frag-mentation of protective capabilities to establish de facto spheres of control in urban social spaces. Institutional approaches to the conundrum of urban violence (such as security sector reform) alone, therefore, have mostly fallen short of the mark.

These complex problems are further conceptualized and contextualized in our opening chapter, and subsequently addressed by the contributors to this volume. As we argue in the first chapter, the concept of megacities used throughout this book is not in the first instance based on the absolute demographic size of the conurbation. Rather, we consider urban spaces to constitute a megacity if their size reflects a certain pattern of social and economic problems. While the forerunner megacities have been expanding to dwarf the population of a great many small and medium-sized countries, many cities that used to be considered secondary cities in the recent past are now displaying megacity size and symptoms. In addition, while some chapters deal with a particular urban case, other chapters take a thematic, national or regional starting point.

Part One focuses on the social dynamics of exclusion and violence in megacities in this broader sense. It contains three chapters on Latin Ameri-can megacity cases, two of which discuss different aspects of exclusion and violence in the paradigmatically unequal and violent megacity Rio de Janeiro, and one on the less well-known case of Ecuador's largest city, Guayaquil. All three studies offer a unique longitudinal perspective made possible by the authors' long-term research strategy and diachronic data collection.

Robert Gay shows in Chapter 2 how different violent actors in Rio de Janeiro have been interlocked in what could be called a 'fatal escalation' of violence and counter-violence in which the police are definitely part of the problem. He highlights the dramatic historical chain of events that turned 'favelas of hope', where vibrant grassroots organizations were poised to put their mark on post-authoritarian urban politics, to 'favelas of despair', where extralegal armed actors (including the police, given the nature of their opera-tions) spread terror and mistrust across the shanty towns and low-income neighbourhoods, contributing to the exclusion and stigmatization of the *favelados* at large.

In Chapter 3, Janice Perlman used data from her extensive reworking of her original *favela* research in the late 1960s and 1970s to demonstrate that, while material conditions may have improved, conditions of insecurity and violence worsened dramatically, turning the 'myth of marginality' into the 'reality of insecurity and violence' from the perspective of *favela* inhabitants. The violence of the *favelas*, embedded in a number of historical and structural factors highlighted in the chapter, has undermined, in absolute terms, the prospects for social mobilization and empowerment that were very much alive twenty-five years ago, when military rule gave way to democratic politics.

Caroline Moser shows in Chapter 4 that Guayaquil has also seen the presence and impact of organized (gang) crime increase over the past generation, although not to the degree experienced by Rio de Janeiro. In the poor neighbourhood of Indio Guayas, ordinary citizens have succeeded in improving their material conditions over the past generation or so. Just as in Rio and in many other megacities, a certain degree of economic progress is certainly not absent in most shanty towns (a fact belying the catastrophic imagery of authors like M. Davis 2006 and Neuwirth 2005). In Guayaquil, Moser shows, exclusion takes on other forms, such as spatial segregation, stigmatization and, above all, violence. The local state has also tended to respond in a repressive way. The dénouement of the violent case presented in Moser's chapter shows, therefore, not only that the inhabitants of Indio Guayas have their own quite coherent moral and practical concepts of 'law', 'order' and 'justice', which deviates from the formal order supposedly upheld by the authorities, but also that their lack of trust in these same authorities combined with the degree of power and prestige enjoyed by grassroots organizations and their (female!) leadership allows for an 'informal conflict resolution' approach to harassment by local gangsters.

This part is concluded by an authoritative survey by Asef Bayat on collective social responses to rapid urbanization and urban poverty and exclusion in the Middle East. This region shares certain patterns of post-colonial urbanization with Latin America, as well as a legacy, in a number of countries, of national-popular or developmentalist regimes prior to the onset of neoliberal globalization. Asef Bayat demonstrates in Chapter 5, however, that across the board, Middle Eastern megacities were much less affected by neoliberal globalization than their Latin American counterparts. Social movements and collective action took on a variety of forms, of which the autonomous role of social Islamism, the reluctance to address the state directly within a 'rights and citizenship' framework (as exists in Latin America), and the relative absence of non-state urban armed actors rooted in territorially organized violent crime are perhaps the three most notable elements. Bayat has coined the concept of 'quiet encroachment' to label the largely unobtrusive forms of entitlement claiming pursued by the urban excluded in this region.

Part Two addresses political and policy dimensions of urban exclusion and violence. The four chapters included in this part move between local, national and transnational levels of politics and policy-making pertinent to urban issues in general and exclusion and violence in particular.

In Chapter 6, Jo Beall lays the conceptual groundwork for an understanding of urban politics. She argues that social movements of the urban poor and excluded have often thrived on the overall 'creative potential' in cities. If urban movements manage to articulate their demands and address the state in non-violent ways, very often outcomes can contribute positively to social struggles against exclusion. Urban movements, through their enormous variation of issues, goals, strategies and mobilizational forms, thus add to the 'creative tension' of non-violent conflict in cities, a tension that may well bolster inclusive, participatory models of urban governance. It is when violence kicks in that this potential is rapidly destroyed, especially given the repressive reflex of most urban administrations and the post-9/11 associations between 'urban fragility' (a euphemism for social exclusion) and national and international militarization of approaches to urban security.

In Chapter 7, Sérgio Baierle analyses what has perhaps been one of the most famous recent cases of 'creative potential' of cities: the participatory budgeting system (or process) in the Brazilian city of Porto Alegre. Baierle has been a long-term observer and activist in this process, being at the same time a scholar and the leader of the Porto Alegre-based urban think tank and research NGO Cidade. Therefore, he chooses to take a somewhat more partisan approach that is understandably critical of the changes in the participatory budget of Porto Alegre brought about by the centre-right municipal administration in power since 2005. He shows how the participatory budgeting process, introduced by the first municipal administration led by the Workers' Party (PT) in 1989, evolved from a social-movement-based effort of the PT to counter the powerful populist and corporatist interests at the city's grass roots, to an administration-led format for neighbourhood participation and expansion of citizenship. The participatory budgeting process is a good example of the blurring of formal and informal spaces of governance; it also shows that democratic politics by themselves do not guarantee the continuity of proven mechanisms of empowerment of the urban excluded. The defeat of the local

5

PT in 2004, after four terms of mayoral office, brought new stakeholders to power with a more pro-business, technocratic and clientelistic take on the participatory budget. The fact that the 'right' cannot ignore the issue of popular participation in urban governance, however, may also be seen as proof of the headway made by such participatory notions as part of the long-term convergence of popular activism and decentralized democratic urban administration in cities like Porto Alegre and others (Koonings 2009). At the very least, spaces for non-violent contestation in the city are preserved and mainstreamed within the political arena.

The key points brought up by Jo Beall are confirmed by Mariano Aguirre, who in Chapter 8 takes on the nexus between fragile states and urban violence from a (global) security discourse perspective. He argues that, with the appearance of 'fragile states' in a globally interconnected system, cities are increasingly the site where global mechanisms of inclusion and exclusion, security and insecurity are defined and acted upon. He criticizes the framing of urban violence in a conventional 'state security frame', enhanced by the 'war on terror' discourse of the previous US administration. Instead, he points at the interconnections between poverty, exclusion, stigmatization and violence in global megacities. A human security framework offers a more cogent and promising paradigm for addressing urban insecurity and violence.

The importance of the level of the nation-state and especially national transitional politics for the framing of urban policies affecting megacities is clearly brought out by the discussion of South African urban and regional policies by Susan Parnell and Owen Crankshaw. In Chapter 9, they show how the canon of post-apartheid reconstruction and development policies was determined by strong notions of the patterns and logic of racial social exclusion during the apartheid regime. These notions emphasized the rural nature of poverty and racial exclusion, and overlooked the increasingly urban patterns of inequality and exclusion in South Africa. While this may in part be explained by the configurations of regional and ethnic political power within the ruling party (ANC), Parnell and Crankshaw demonstrate that these 'follies', as they call them, eventually lead to inadequate policies against urban exclusion and extreme violence, a legacy of apartheid one might expect a democratic South Africa would want to remove at all costs.

In the conclusions, we draw together the main arguments of each chapter and link them to the framework set out in Chapter 1: the blurring of formal and informal urban spaces, and its impact on the pattern of urban exclusion and violence and the agency of urban stakeholders in the domains of livelihood, social mobilization and violence. We will look at the political and policy implications suggested by our analysis, pointing at the limitations of conventional 'good governance' approaches that have been dominant during the past two decades.

(Utrecht/Bogotá/Berlin/Rio de Janeiro, April–June 2009)

1 | The rise of megacities and the urbanization of informality, exclusion and violence

DIRK KRUIJT AND KEES KOONINGS

In 2008, for the first time in history, the world population became urban, the result of a rapid process of urbanization that started in the second half of the twentieth century. In 2008, 75 per cent of the population in the developed countries and 44 per cent of the population in Third World countries were living in cities. UN estimates for 2050 predict that 86 per cent of the population in the more developed countries and 67 per cent of the population in the less developed countries will be urban. Moreover, 10 per cent of the entire urban world population will be living in megacities of 10 million inhabitants or more. Those living in metropolitan areas of one million or more city dwellers will constitute 40 per cent of the urban world population (UN 2008b: 220, Table A17). Population growth will be decisively an urban phenomenon (Kruijt 2008a).

This staggering pattern of urban explosion, the expansion of megacities and of secondary metropolitan areas, will largely materialize in developing countries. Between 2010 and 2050, cities and not the rural areas will absorb most of the population growth. Moreover, in this period the rural population is expected to decrease, in absolute numbers as well as proportionately. In 2050 the number of rural inhabitants of the world is expected to be 600 million less than that of today (UN 2008a: 1). In 2050 the world population is expected to be 9.2 billion. By then the population of urban areas will probably be around 6.4 billion, or 70 per cent of the world population (ibid.: 4).

The second consequence of this urbanization process is that the global pattern of world poverty, informality and exclusion will definitively acquire an urban face. The concentration of large segments of urban poor and excluded in capital cities and metropolitan areas but also in so-called 'secondary cities' (many of which will grow considerably in size) will have fundamental socio-economic and political consequences and will involve the possibility of destabilization of the economic, social and political order.

In this opening chapter we will first analyse the consequences of the process of urbanization, informalization, exclusion and violence that has taken place, especially in Latin America, where urbanization has been well documented over the last few decades. Subsequently we will turn to an overview of key issues in research and scholarly debate on urban poverty and exclusion from the 1970s to the present. Our analytical framework is that urban exclusion and social, political and violent responses to it are embedded in an overlapping set of grey zones in which commonly held distinctions between legal and illegal, formal and informal, peaceful and violent, legitimate and illegitimate are disappearing. Finally, we will assess the current patterns of exclusion in three urban fields within these grey zones: livelihood, mobilization and participation, and violence and insecurity. The expansion of informality, the potential but also the limitations for empowerment of the urban poor through social movements and political participation, and, most of all, the apparent proliferation of urban violence and insecurity, can be understood from the perspective of this blurring of societal domains. This is posing serious challenges to political and policy approaches towards urban poverty and exclusion. We will take up this theme in the conclusion of the book. But first we'll take a brief look at the emergence of so-called megacities.

Megacities

Among the less developed regions there are remarkable differences between Africa, Asia and Latin America and the Caribbean. In Latin America, and to a lesser degree the Caribbean, a spectacular process of sustained urbanization has taken place between the 1950s and the present: Latin America's urban population in 2008 was 78 per cent, comparable to or even higher than that of western and eastern Europe. In its early concentration of large poor, informal and excluded population segments in urban areas, and its parallel process of increasing urban violence, the region is a forerunner of both Asia and Africa. In fact, Africa and Asia are experiencing a similar urbanization process to that of Latin America in previous decades. It is expected that in 2050 most of the urban world population will live in Asia (54 per cent) and in Africa (19 per cent). Between 2010 and 2050 the African urban population is likely to treble and in Asia it will more than double. Moreover, the growth of the urban world population will be concentrated in a few countries. China and India will account for about a third of the total increase. They will be followed by Congo and Nigeria in Africa, Bangladesh, Indonesia, Pakistan and the Philippines in Asia, and Brazil and Mexico in Latin America, surpassing a population increase of 2–3 per cent per year (UN 2008a: 6, 7).

Explosive urbanization and, consequently, an enormous process of rural–urban migration and of informalization of the urban labour markets are at present characteristics of Africa and Asia. The process started later there than it did in Latin America but the same phenomenon of slum rings around the former city centres, the eroding formal order and the volatile pattern of informalization of the economy, society and the political system are evocatively expressed in the title of a recent study by Mike Davis (2006): *Planet of Slums*. (We will come back to Davis's argument below.) As we will also suggest, patterns of informalization, exclusion and violence that we are familiar with from the Latin American experience are currently being reproduced in many of the megacities in Africa and Asia.

As part of this process the pattern of configuration of the world's megacities is to be transformed. In 2025, of the fifteen largest cities in the world, thirteen will be located in Asia, Africa and Latin America: Bombay (26 million), Delhi (23 million), Dhaka (22 million), São Paulo (21 million), Mexico City (21 million), Calcutta (21 million), Shanghai (19 million), Karachi (19 million), Kinshasa (17 million), Lagos (16 million), Cairo (16 million), Manila (15 million), and Beijing (14 million) (UN 2008b: 167, Table A11). These projections should not distract us, however, from the expectation that the boosting of the urbanization and informalization process will take place in the 'secondary' metropolitan areas, the cities of between 1 million and 10 million inhabitants (those, indeed, attaining the size of the megacities of the previous generation).

At this point, it will be useful to take a brief look at the concept of 'megacities'. As a rule, megacities are defined on the basis of their population size, with 5 million inhabitants as the most commonly used lower threshold.[1] In addition, megacities are depicted as the most extreme variety of 'overurbanization' (D. Davis 2005; M. Davis 2006). They are 'big but not powerful [...] attract[ing] other forms of theoretical fascination: with the dark and disturbing side of urbanization' (Robinson 2002: 540). Yet many of the manifest characteristics of this type of urbanization are visible in all cities in the developing world (or the 'global South'), irrespective of their size. Therefore, we need to choose a qualitative definition of the urban phenomenon of the megacity. Megacities, then, are large cities (in absolute terms or in relation to the country in which they are situated) in which geographic and demographic size are just one out of many factors that shape a certain kind of urban pathology: a systematic disjuncture between opportunity structures for livelihood, service provision, security and overall urban planning and regulation, on the one hand, and the size and composition of the urban population on the other. Inequality, exclusion, segregation, violence and insecurity are apparently endemic features of megacities. The fault lines of urban exclusion are drawn by class, caste, race, ethnicity and religion. To the extent that these fault lines contribute to the disarticulation of urban systems, megacities can be considered 'fragile'. Yet, as we will argue below and as will be shown in the other chapters in this book, they are also the stage for important and sometimes innovative spaces for social mobilization, urban politics and policy-making.

Patterns of urbanization: the forerunner case of Latin America[2]

Latin America's urban growth process was a sustained development over more than fifty years. In addition, the peak period of massive urbanization (from the late 1970s to the 1990s) coincided with a severe transformation of the economic and political order. The most substantial political change of the decade of the 1980s was, without doubt, the replacement of military dictatorships by democratic governments in the majority of the Latin American countries. Tragically, the democratic transition process coincided with a severe economic crisis with long-term consequences. The mainstream model of economic adjustment programmes in the 1980s and 1990s induced impoverishment and instability in the economy and society. The evident failure of governments to expand the urban labour markets and to provide basic public services such as education, health and security produced a rather restricted integration of the incessant migration stream from the rural hinterland. This precarious integration is related to a transgenerational process of informalization and social exclusion in the urban, and particularly the metropolitan, environments. This development is reflected in high and persistent inequality in the distribution of urban income and wealth, in the expansion of slums and the deterioration of popular neighbourhoods over the past two or three decades. Latin America has, according to the yearly World Bank and UNDP reports, the most skewed income distribution in the world, more out of line than that of China, India or Russia.

No Latin American country can pride itself on having won the struggle against poverty. No national government could reincorporate the masses of population that had previously slipped away into informality, or reinsert the vulnerable categories (including the indigenous and Afro-Latin populations) that have suffered the stigma of being second-class citizens. The development of Latin America's informality is astounding. The informal economy and society are composed not only of owners of micro-enterprises and their employees; the vast majority is formed by the self-employed, whose economic activity is a vehicle for day-to-day survival. Latin America's informality has an ethnic face as well, with ethnicity a stratifying factor. Mechanisms for survival predominate: ties of ethnicity, religion, real or symbolic family relationships, closeness to the place of birth, local neighbourhood relations. In another publication, on the dynamics of urban poverty, informality and social exclusion in

Latin America (Kruijt et al. 2002), we introduced the notion of 'informal citizenship', or the precarious implantation of (urban) second-class citizenship. An important UNDP (2004) report coined the terms 'low-intensity citizenship' and 'low-intensity democracy', typifying the post-dictatorship democracy in the region. Latin America has thus become a continent where, in most of its countries, a significant segment of the population is, simultaneously, poor, informal and excluded.

This river of poverty and exclusion bursting its banks and generating a new basin of informality and second-class citizenship has been described in terms of the decline of the institutional pillars of traditional Latin American society, overwhelmed by the mushrooming of the slum cities, and its consequences in terms of the emergence of a qualitatively new urban society. A characteristic of this new class structure is the implicit duality of the formal and informal economy and society (Portes 1985; Portes and Hoffman 2003). Recent ILO data emphasize a consolidation of the informality in Latin America and the Caribbean: 55 per cent of the region's employment is informal and in some smaller economies (Bolivia, Guatemala, Nicaragua, Peru) the informal labour market surpasses 70 per cent. Originally interpreted as a short-term under- and unemployment phenomenon, employment in the informal economy is at present clearly consolidated. The informal economy in turn shapes a kind of informal society, partially inserted in the formal order and partially forming a parallel social structure with its own internal social hierarchies.

There are some marked changes within the Latin American urban class structures. The chronically poor are now joined by the 'new poor', descending from the former strata of the middle and industrial working classes. Old and new poor converge as informal entrepreneurs and self-employed in search of survival and livelihood strategies. The decomposition of the formerly substantive working classes has led not only to the formation of a new edifice of social stratification but also to changes in the size and composition of poor households' family structures. The traditional role of men as heads of families is ebbing away with the enlarged number of female-headed households in the popular neighbourhoods and slum cities. Furthermore, the informal economy and society even generate hidden migration cycles, demographic breakdowns and cleavages within the family structure.

Urban second-class citizenship is also citizenship with a violent face. In the 1970s and 1980s, the 'divided', 'fragmented' or 'fractured' cities were mostly typified in terms of urban misery or social exclusion. Mostly they were described in terms of the dichotomy between elites and well-to-do middle classes in the affluent urban centres and high-income neighbourhoods versus the 'forgotten' slum dwellers in the ever vaster expanses of the urban periphery. More recently, the dynamics of social exclusion and the proliferation of violence have acquired different social, cultural and spatial dimensions. Exclusion has increasingly become 'segregation', in which geographical distance as such is less important than the boundaries drawn by social, political and symbolic attributions. Urban segregation refers not only to the geographical distribution of poverty but also to the territorial and social division of cities in 'go' and 'no-go' areas, from the perspective of the local public administration, even the police. The slums and shanty towns come to be seen as genuine enclaves that obey a different set of rules and codes of conduct.

The case of Brazil, whose poverty-stricken and crime-ridden *favelas* are synonymous with 'no-go areas' within the metropolitan boundaries, acquired a depressing reputation among researchers and authors dealing with urban violence. A similar relation between the increase of poverty and violence can be found in Argentina (Greater Buenos Aires) and Colombia, where urban social exclusion, crime and violence became part of the amalgam of drug-based organized crime and political violence. In particular it ignited in the capital cities of post-war Central America (Guatemala City, San Salvador, Tegucigalpa) and of Jamaica (Kingston), Mexico and Venezuela (Caracas). Moser and McIlwaine (2004) published the results of a systematic and comparative study on urban violence as perceived by the urban poor. It is remarkable to observe the strong coincidence between perceptions of the poor and the factual analysis of researchers and government reports about violence and the perpetrators of violence.

It is interesting to note that, in the context of permeating violence and fluctuating mini-wars in specific urban territories, the armed forces usually do not play a significant role. Since the 1990s, the armed forces have been leaving direct confrontation with non-state violent actors to the police and the special police forces, more adapted to urban aggression and explicitly trained in counter-aggression. In Rio de Janeiro in the early 1990s and in Medellín in the early 2000s the military engaged in brief incursions into the shanty towns dominated by heavily armed drug gangs or gang-based leftist militias. These campaigns proved either ineffective (in Rio de Janeiro) or paved the way for the takeover of the shanty towns of Medellín (the *comunas*) by paramilitary units that adapted the local gang structure to their strategy of territorial control (Rozema 2008). Alongside an increasingly militarized and repressive police in many Latin American cities we can observe the proliferation of 'private vigilantism': the array of private police, privately paid street guardians in the middle-class and even popular metropolitan districts, citizens' private police,

13

private protection squads, extralegal task forces, paramilitary commandos, death squads, etc.

In the shanty towns and low-income neighbourhoods themselves there are the new armed actors as the local boss or trafficker is invested with de facto authority with regard to law and order, at the same time being the benefactor of local development, the local churches and local NGOs. Usually, the local population has to choose between the formal police force (frequently absent or extremely violent) and the de facto guardians of the informal local order (Arias and Davis Rodrigues 2006). In terms of urban territories involved, maybe 25 per cent of the urban space in metropolitan Rio de Janeiro, São Paulo, Buenos Aires, Bogotá, Medellín, Mexico City, Guadalajara and other important agglomerations are 'disputed areas'. Local chiefs of armed actors represent the local parallel law and justice. Sometimes they impose taxes, in other cases they act as financiers of local development. In some cases they negotiate with the local social, political and religious leadership, which has learned how to survive in terms of peaceful coexistence. A considerable segment of the youth in the marginalized neighbourhoods is unemployed and not even employable. They find a certain status, even identity and belonging, in the youth gangs, a fact that explains the relative popularity of gang membership as a lifestyle in Argentina, Brazil, Colombia, Central America, Mexico and Venezuela.

The many urban mini-wars and the proliferation of the (urban) armed actors involved are related to the phenomenon of local governance voids (Kruijt and Koonings 1999). Governance voids exist where the legal authorities and the representatives of law and order are absent and, consequently, a local vacuum of 'regular' law and order is created. In this vacuum a kind of osmotic symbiosis emerges between the state (the police, the judiciary) and 'common' criminality and criminalized former members of the armed forces, the police, paramilitary units and sometimes guerrilla combatants. In these violence enclaves, informal or 'parallel' structures arise (Leeds 1996), seeking various forms of confrontation or accommodation with the legitimate authorities and with civil society. The new urban warlords of local violence – the chiefs of the local drug traffickers, the leaders of the youth gangs in the slums of Central America, the monopoly holders of local illegal (albeit accepted) violence – are the new enforcers of customary justice. The paradox is that most Latin American governments, as many local popular leaders and church authorities previously did, have accepted a de facto coexistence with the violent non-state actors, as long as they do not constitute a challenge to the national political order. Zero tolerance or 'urban counter-insurgency' strategies on the part of security forces mainly respond to requirements of political image-making and generally fail to provide an effective strategy for 'law and order'.

The shifting debate on poverty, inequality and social exclusion in megacities

Research and scholarly debate on urban poverty and exclusion passed an important first watershed in the 1970s. Building on then recently advanced notions of the urban 'informal sector' (Hart 1973) and critiques of prevailing approaches based on classical dualist concepts, urban research and theory started to look at the way in which urban poverty and inequality were integrated into patterns of unbalanced urbanization. Janice Perlman's (1976) seminal study on the *favelados* (slum dwellers) of Rio de Janeiro made clear that their economic and social position, their personal and collective histories, survival strategies and forms of collective action did not fit the prevailing images of 'tradition', 'marginality' or 'culture of poverty'. Poor slum dwellers were not marginal at all, in the sense of being separated from mainstream, formal, modern urban society; they appeared to be actively tracing 'pathways of survival', trying to connect the city of affluence to the city of poverty. Urban poverty henceforward was recognized as a systematic or structural aspect of urbanization in developing countries, and indeed as an increasingly sprawling phenomenon – sometimes called 'overurbanization' (D. Davis 2005: 96). In addition, urban poverty was no longer seen only in terms of income poverty, caused by insufficient jobs and low wages, but also as lack of access to basic needs and public goods and services.

Castells's (1977) influential treatise on the logic of urban class struggle in (dependent) capitalism therefore emphasized 'collective consumption' by the urban poor as the predominant mode of social (or class) struggle in the city. The urban poor, as slum dwellers, shared living conditions rather than experience in the workplace. Social movements organized around the neighbourhood articulated demands for collective consumption (Castells's structuralist Marxist version of basic needs or public and collective goods and services) and so became the principal social force shaping urban development 'from below'. Castells's work subsequently took the so-called 'agency' and 'cultural' turn with the publication of *The City and the Grassroots* in 1983. This work of breathtaking ambition and scope set the stage for a subsequent focus on 'action' and 'strategy' by the poor and excluded within critical urban studies.[3] The so-called 'cultural turn' was visible in the rapidly growing literature on 'new (urban) social movements', especially in Latin America (Eckstein 2001; Escobar and Alvarez 1992). This literature increasingly identified urban communal, ethnic or religious identity as grounding urban collective action in the 1980s and beyond. Urban development studies had definitely moved beyond the old dualism of modernization (which held that 'urban is modern', urban poverty and informality are transitory, and the urban poor are trapped in a 'culture of poverty').

As a result, urban research and debate in developing countries during the 1980s and (early) 1990s focused on informal livelihood strategies and collective action and social movement issues (Portes 1989). The underlying frame shifted from a 'developmentalist' model for urban development to neoliberal globalization (Walton 1998). The model for social and political incorporation of the urban poor changed from an authoritarian and corporatist framework to a citizenship-based script of liberal democracy, decentralization and (participatory) empowerment, not only in Latin America but also in sub-Saharan Africa and South and South-East Asia. From the 1980s onwards, urban policy tended to become more technocratic, in line with dominant ideas of market reform, structural adjustment and trimming down of the state and the public sector. In this neoliberal version, the poor became consumers, citizens became clients of efficient local governments and non-governmental service providers, and grassroots social activists were supposed to enter into public–private partnerships to balance their interests with those of other urban stakeholders, such as urban planners, corporations and middle-class constituencies. The contrast between post-Marxist and neoliberal approaches to urban issues in the 1980s and 1990s was most visible in studies on the informal sector. While authors like Portes (1985, 1989; also Portes and Hoffman 2003) defined informality as the new foundation of the urban proletariat, inspiring new social movements demanding social inclusion, authors like De Soto (1986) saw the informal micro-entrepreneurs as the new individuals, harbingers of a popular capitalist revolution that would challenge and overcome the clientelist state and so bring urban poverty and exclusion to an end.

A second watershed in the debate emerged in the course of the 1990s around the concept of the 'global' or 'world city'. Inspired by Sassen (1991; also 2000, 2002) and others, global urban studies sought to analyse and explain the consequences of globalization for newly emerging forms of urbanization, urban social relations and urban politics and public policy. Although according to some this in fact implied a declining interest in urban development issues (D. Davis 2005: 97), the new globalization paradigm did yield a number of insights that are helpful even today. Yet world city or global city research was primarily interested in unveiling and explaining the consequences of the uplinking of cities to worldwide processes of economic transformation.

Economic globalization meant an unprecedented increase in interconnectivity of production (commodity chains), finance, marketing and consumption. Since the regulatory power of conventional nation-states was fading away, (large) cities took over the role of 'command and control' centres of the global economy. This meant that cities rather than states became the nodal points of communication and control, through hosting the central offices of transnational manufacturers, financial corporations and a host of (post-) industrial service providers employing high levels of skill and sophistication (business consultants, marketeers, R&D outfits, advertising agencies).

From a globalization or 'world system' perspective, this research led to the identification of 'world city hierarchies'. From the point of view of urban poverty and exclusion, the global city approach proposed that, increasingly, world cities are developing a juxtaposition between fancy and wealthy city centres (central business districts) harbouring the global command-and-control centres, as well as related residential areas of the well-to-do (including the new class of well-educated urban professionals), and increasingly run-down lower-class areas of urbanites excluded from the job and consumer markets of global capitalism. As a corollary to market exclusion, urban politics and city planning were driven by stakeholders aspiring to boost the city's position in the global economy, thereby reducing or closing spaces of political influence and urban policy formulation that would benefit the urban poor (Robinson 2002; Shatkin 2007).

The global city approach has provoked various types of criticism. For the purposes of this chapter, it is less important to review the critique that this approach tends to highlight only a limited number of large cities (which can be classified as 'global', hence 'powerful', and mostly located in the post-industrial core of the global system) and therefore takes the majority of cities, in the words of Robinson (2002), 'off the map' of scholarly attention, especially in developing countries. Robinson objects to the idea that the global city approach makes most cities in the world irrelevant, rather like defining 'megacities' as large but insignificant, loaded with urban dysfunctionalities (ibid.: 538, 540). More pertinent are the objections against the limited conception of globalization and the neglect of the variety of social and political processes as part of the dynamics of urbanization within cities, large or small (Gugler 2003, 2004; Robinson 2002; Shatkin 2007).

Indeed, most cities are affected in some way or another by globalization. The world of global corporate finance and specialized services is, however, not the only dimension of globalization that has been shaping urbanization during the past two decades. National or local private businesses catering for national markets, export processing zones for manufacturing, the booming of natural resource exploitation, tourism, and even the incorporation of cities into global networks of development interventions and poverty alleviation schemes through donor agencies and NGOs (Maputo, Mozambique, or Managua, Nicaragua, being good examples), also pattern urban societies – and especially inequality and exclusion – in specific ways. And that is without even mentioning the illicit and criminal sides of globalization whereby the involvement in, for instance, the drugs and arms trades, and the resulting influx of wealth, restyles otherwise 'forgotten' cities and towns in places such as the Colombian Costa Atlántica or small West African countries.

Likewise, local social and political processes have a greater impact on cities than the global city model suggests. Poor and excluded urbanites are not passive recipients of the urban policies dictated by the stakeholders of globalization. Indeed, the rise of democracy and the advance of canons of good governance – admittedly problematic in many places – contributed to the opening up of spaces for contestation and participation 'from below'. Gugler (2003) therefore concludes that 'poor country' world cities are diverse owing to both the multiplicity of globalization and the impact of the role of the state and social movements. Shatkin (2007) offers a lucid and systematic alternative to the study of cities in the era of globalization in which the specificity of historical, cultural and institutional settings and the diverse dynamics of agency and mobilization interact with dimensions of globalization. As far as urban inequality is concerned, the latter are visible in three main ways: growing income inequality and labour flexibility; the growing impact of 'private' urban planning and management favouring elite agendas; and the increasingly visible socio-spatial segregation in cities and towns around the globe. This framework accords with Gugler's (2003: 708) assessment that there is increasing 'elite entrenchment' in city centres and that a variety of globalizing mechanisms have reproduced and enlarged urban inequality (Lemanski 2007). Still, inequality and exclusion are bound to be challenged; the 'distributional outcomes' of urbanization are to a considerable degree formed by popular contestation and by local political elites and administrative agents that respond to the lures of globalization, the protests from below and their own scripts for urban 'improvement' (Marques and Bichir 2003).

These subtleties have to a considerable degree been lost on the third and most recent watershed in urban studies regarding poverty, inequality and exclusion. We dub this approach 'neo-dualist' because it seems to return to a simple juxtaposition of 'rich' and 'poor' city dwellers in which the latter occupy ever growing amorphous and anomic slums. The key protagonist of this approach is Mike Davis (2006), whose *Planet of Slums* draws an apocalyptic view of sprawling urban poverty at the margins of neoliberal globalization (see also Neuwirth 2005). This imagery elaborates on previous notions of 'over-urbanization' and by and large accepts the proposition of the global city literature that this new dualism is the outflow of neoliberal capitalism and its one-track-minded urban planners. The implication drawn by Davis is that a growing majority of urban denizens in developing countries have turned into a huge surplus population and that the shanty towns they inhabit represent a true Armageddon of abandonment and despair. Local governments and NGOs are doing nothing but contributing to poverty and exclusion through pro-elite policies and self-serving, opportunistic and clientelistic attitudes. In the end, the slum proletariat has no option but to respond with violence to the exclusion and oppression they are facing.

The work of Davis and Neuwirth is highly evocative, but also heavily criticized (Angotti 2006; Satterthwaite 2006). According to these critics, their approach denies the variation in livelihood conditions in many shanty towns, and the diversity, the agency and the politics of the urban excluded, as well as the less than monotonic political and institutional responses of urban authorities. Merrifield (2002) calls this 'dialectical urbanism', picking up on Castells's (1977) structuralist Marxist reasoning. Similarly, Angotti (2006) argues that cities are a set of social relations that bridge the positive and the negative. In other words, neo-dualist and apocalyptic views ignore the key question of power and the multiple, mostly overlapping, urban domains in which the urban poor play out their social and political strategies. And Rao (2006: 232) states: '"Slum as theory" thus becomes an important point of departure precisely because it is located in the interstices of a whole range of mutations whose specificity is no longer locatable within singular frameworks.' In the next section we will look at the multiple framework of urban exclusion (of which the notion of 'slum' is a telling proxy) in which economic, social and political responses to exclusion are embedded.

The 'grey zones' of urban exclusion

Urban poverty was analysed, in the 1980s and 1990s, in terms of formal and informal labour markets and survival strategies of the poor and the excluded. In the 2000s, however, analysts and scholars tend to choose a more multidimensional approach, emphasizing a continuum between formality and informality with regard not only to labour markets but also to the social order. The concept of an informal economy thus also implies the concept of an informal society. Moreover, the quality of (urban) citizenship is affected by

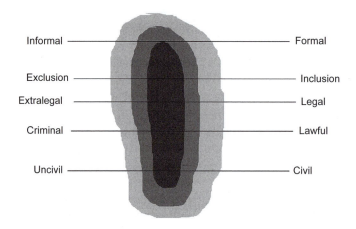

Informal ———————————————————— Formal

Exclusion ———————————————————— Inclusion

Extralegal ———————————————————— Legal

Criminal ———————————————————— Lawful

Uncivil ———————————————————— Civil

The continuums within the larger white field represent the conventional articulated distinctions between the formal-institutional and the informal city. In this field the formal city is dominant and the informal city is subaltern, from the point of view of the principles of social organization and regulation. The shaded fields represent the increasing blurring of these separations in different socio-spatial domains of urban life. Additionally and more specifically, the darkening of the fields indicates increasingly weak or absent protective and regulatory functions of the formal and accountable state.

FIGURE 1.1 Grey areas of urban exclusion and contestation

actors not only in the formal and informal economy and formal and informal society, but also in the formal and informal political order. In addition, the formal–informal divide leads to other dichotomies as well: inclusion and exclusion, legal and extralegal (a-legal, illegal), lawful and criminal, civil and uncivil. To complicate our analysis even more: there is a gradual expansion of a 'grey zone' between the order of inclusion (formality, legality, lawfulness and civility) and the order of exclusion (illegality, criminality and the 'uncivil' society and political arena) (see Figure 1.1).

Within these grey zones, various forms of unclear and sometimes precarious articulations materialize: around the margins of decency and criminality, regarding the peaceful coexistence of actors on both sides of the law, about arrangements that involve 'informal' and 'irregular' solutions for everyday problems. These arrangements may vary from 'innovative' economic exploitation, such as subcontracting by government institutions, to 'cooperatives' of self-employed people headed by rough employers, to brutal and extremely violent solutions by mafia-style gangs, drug lords, vigilante bosses, and social cleansing of petty thieves, street gang members or nasty street children. Sometimes 'twilight institutions', apparently 'clean' organizations operating within the strict margins of the law but contaminated by its 'informal culture' of extralegal efficiency – police officers participating in death squads, slum leadership participating in 'popular justice' applied to petty local criminals – produce an 'extralegal' role expansion. This erosion of the formal order is accelerated in the case of weak or 'failed states', states with a minimal social infrastructure, war-torn societies or states in a post-war transition with a weak civil service or a public sector trying to abandon its militarized legacy (Young 2004).

In studies of informality and exclusion in the urban context, the impact of violence and crime was obscured until the last decade. Violence and crime are at present widespread in all countries all over the world, affecting particularly the poor and the marginalized. Violent crimes (or at least the registration of violent crimes) increased between 1990 and 2000 from 6 to 8.8 per 100,000 persons. According to UN statistical data, between 2001 and 2006, 60 per cent of all urban residents were victims of crime, with 70 per cent in Latin America and Africa. The strong incidence of violence and crime in Africa and Latin America is still not completely explained. The prevalence of homicides and police-recorded robberies is, however, consistently high in urban Latin America (Central and South America) and Africa (sub-Saharan and southern Africa) (UN-Habitat 2007: 10, 54–5). Asia has the highest burglary indicators. Worldwide estimates of the number of street children vary widely from tens of millions to 100 million. Their number is reportedly asssociated with the pace of urbanization. Street children tend to turn to crime as a survival mechanism, can become an easy target for membership of youth gangs and are, otherwise, an easy victim of paramilitary and para-police forces and other twilight institutions aiming at 'cleansing' practices. Police violence against street children is consistently reported in Brazil, Guatemala, India and Kenya.

In a recent study on urban safety and security worldwide – the already quoted UN-Habitat (2007) report – many of the characteristics of the Latin American situation we have described are replicated in Africa and Asia. The UN-Habitat study mentions a series of more individual country studies and some comparative studies between countries and continents. In all these studies a correlation exists between poverty, inequality, exclusion (be it by gender, race, ethnicity or religious differences), youth unemployment and living in slum cities, the incidence of violence and crime and the possibility of victimization by state and non-state armed actors. The quality of urban planning and urban management – in fact, the quality of the municipal government and the local authorities and institutions – also contributes to the victimization rates of vulnerable population segments: the poor, the excluded, the young, minorities, women and children.

Against the background of these grey areas we will conclude by briefly recapitulating three pivotal fields of urban poverty, inequality and exclusion on which recent urban research has been converging.

Livelihood, mobilization, violence

Three pivotal fields define the patterns of urban poverty, inequality and exclusion, particularly in megacities. These fields both shape the mechanisms of deprivation and exclusion and the strategies for contestation: assets and livelihood strategies; social mobilization and political participation; insecurity and violence. Another element of convergence is that this pattern is increasingly visible in the various regions of the so-called global South. Whereas Latin America has long been the forerunner in issues and studies of urban development, poverty, exclusion and contestation, in recent years South and East Asia (notably China), and even Africa, have become more visible in terms of the 'urban question'. Rao (2006) even speaks of an urban turn in South Asian studies. There are even clear parallels with trends in the cities of the North, where Wacquant (2007) discerns a process of what he calls 'advanced marginality' in the low-income areas of cities in the USA, France, Germany and the Netherlands.

Livelihood Over the past decade or so, the concept of poverty has been broadened to include not only private or household income and consumption and available productive assets, but also other 'capabilities', human, social, political, cultural and protective (DAC 2001). For the issue of urban poverty this means that we have to look at a broad array of resources and capabilities that determine the livelihood perspectives of individuals, households and even urban communities such as neighbourhoods. Livelihood strategies combine the use of key capitals (physical, financial) and skills, divisions of labour within and beyond households, access to common pool resources and public goods and services ('collective consumption') and social capital (defined as the set of social relations that underpin the reproduction of economic success, or in this case, livelihood – see Putnam 1993a; Portes 1998). Here the micro-level of everyday survival connects critically to the macro-level of the so-called 'opportunity structure' in which crucial variables are set, such as access to employment, to markets for informally produced goods and services, and to infrastructure, education and healthcare.

In terms of this opportunity structure, over the past two decades a model of 'structural heterogeneity', in which growth in formal sector employment was accompanied by gradually expanding informal livelihood opportunities, has been replaced by a duality of more confined – from the perspective of the urban poor – employment opportunities in the formal market (Roberts 2005). At the same time, the informal sector has been losing its elasticity in terms of providing livelihood options. As has been demonstrated by, for example, González de la Rocha and Grinspun (2001) and Mitlin (2005), the 'erosion of work' on all fronts has made livelihood perspectives of the urban poor more precarious in Latin America, Africa and Asia. Even in China, the current global economic downturn has led to the loss of millions of jobs in export manufacturing, making the livelihoods of a large number of migratory workers uncertain. Assets of the urban poor working as micro-entrepreneurs or of those self-employed are structurally vulnerable (Moser 1998). In many African countries, urban survival depends on maintaining links with a food-producing and excess-labour-absorbing rural hinterland (Frayne 2004). In Latin America, South and South-East Asia, many households (mainly urban but also rural) take refuge in the international migration of household members to add foreign wage income to the household budget. At the same time, new models for public service provision (more strictly targeted, conditional safety nets, or NGO assistance) have made access to resources for human capabilities less certain. As a result, González de la Rocha et al. (2004) speak of the 'new poverty' in Latin American cities. Mitlin (2005) sees urban poverty in developing countries as a transgenerational reproduction of low income, asset vulnerability and lack of human capabilities. Since all this is set within social relations and constructions of meaning, precarious livelihood at the same time means 'symbolic' exclusion and polarization: being stigmatized for doing the wrong kind of work, living in the wrong part of the city, belonging to the wrong class, caste or ethnic group (ibid.: 8).

Mobilization and participation As we have already argued, the unmistakable global trend of urban social polarization and social and spatial segregation does not mean that the urban poor are an anomic mass of human derelicts, as M. Davis (2006) suggests (echoing Fanon's famous 'wretched of the Earth'). Urbanization has brought a long and rich history of social movements, not only in the erstwhile heartlands of urban-industrial development since the nineteenth century, but especially also in the developing world, first in Latin America, later elsewhere. Here, social mobilization is closely linked to the question of political participation, the nature and beneficiaries of urban public policy, and, ultimately, urban politics and empowerment. In this domain, the importance of agency in shaping urban development, as argued by Shatkin (2007), is clear. Social and political agency is a field where diversity reigns: historical, institutional and cultural frames combine with specific resource dynamics to produce a wide variety of scenarios. As argued by Satterthwaite (2008), the urban setting generates propitious conditions for the identification of common goals, collective strategies and shared identities; social movements find it relatively easy to engage the state – either in protest or in cooperation – owing to their high visibility and the immediate political impact of urban issues (see also Jo Beall's argument in Chapter 6 of this volume).

It is beyond the scope of this chapter to give anything approaching a complete overview. We therefore mention only some notable recent trends. In Latin America, the urban movements for survival in the 1970s and for political change in the 1980s have entered a new cycle in which access to services and access to political decision-making has been linked to demands for recognition as being part of the city. The overarching framework has been one of citizenship (Roberts 1996; Hochstetler 2000), which, as pointed out by Holston (2008), has often to be attained by non-conventional, extralegal means. In many Latin American cities, this has been echoed by experiments (in some cases solid practices; see Koonings 2004) of participatory governance (Avritzer 2002; Melo and Baiocchi 2006); but almost as often, these pathways of empowerment have been punctured by violence and insecurity (see below).

In Africa, urban social movements tend to be more closely linked to political factionalism and ethnic allegiances. The decomposition of the post-colonial state in a number of African countries (Young 2004), the widespread violence and, as for instance in the case of Zimbabwe, the entrenchment of authoritarian and arbitrary regimes, makes the environment for empowerment through urban mobilization more complicated. In South Asian cities, as argued by Appadurai (2002), urban claim-making lies outside the conventional scripts of (national) citizenship: formally 'illegal' actions of the urban poor (such as squatting) are directed at the state, while a more conventional middle-class civil society has developed with the neoliberalization of Indian cities. Urban mobilization is often punctured by caste or by ethnic and religious conflicts, such as in the recent violence in Ahmedabad (Chandhoke 2008). In the Middle East, Bayat (this volume) notes a similar process of 'quiet encroachment', which amounts to an informal strategy of 'faits accomplis' vis-à-vis the urban authorities. At the same time, religion has been offering a powerful frame for urban mobilization in countries such as Egypt, Iran, Palestine and Lebanon. In China, urban mobilization is very incipient, and seems to be spearheaded by the urban middle classes which make specific demands of the state. The peculiar status that many of the million urban poor have, namely that of transit workers who are formally residents of rural communities with no collective entitlements at all in the cities where they work, creates fundamental obstacles to collective claim-making in spite of the very gradual opening up of the Chinese regime to demands from below (Friedmann 2003; Zhang 2001). In the end, the effectiveness of urban movements anywhere depends on their ability to encroach upon, or change, existing hierarchies of power and privilege. This ability depends to a significant degree on the nature of political institutions and strategies within urban political arenas. In the most extreme of situations, violence and insecurity can destroy the efforts of urban social movements and create a situation of absolute disempowerment, as in the case of Rio de Janeiro.

Violence and insecurity As we have already mentioned, whereas 'war is the continuation of politics by other means', urban violence transforms urban politics and limits the scope for empowerment of the urban excluded. In view of the fragile protective capabilities of the state, access to guns becomes part of the package of organizational capabilities needed to advance claims. Yet urban violence does not seem to herald the uprising of the masses living in the 'planet of slums' against the oppression of neoliberal global capitalism. Neither is urban violence a sign of growing anomie within a context of increasing urban decomposition. Urban or 'slum' wars (Beall 2006; Rodgers 2009) or 'low intensity' urban warfare (Koonings and Veenstra 2007) do indeed appear to be part and parcel of urban exclusion across the Global South, not just in Latin America (Rotker 2002; Koonings and Kruijt 2007) but also in South Africa, Nigeria, India, the Philippines, etc. Indian cities are landscapes of conflict and violence (Rao 2006); South African cities are part of a country 'at war with itself' (Altbeker 2007). Although we should be careful not to fall into the temptation of drawing an apocalyptic picture of generalized urban violence in poor megacities, there are clearly discernible mechanisms that, in combination, lead to urban violence as an endemic feature of urban exclusion. Those without access to the means of violence – that is to say, the overwhelming majority of the urban poor – suffer a process of disempowerment through the erosion of grassroots civil organizations and urban political institutions. As Jo Beall (this volume) puts it: 'Politically violence undermines creative contestation in cities.'

One of the striking findings of Janice Perlman's (this volume) new study of the *favelas* of Rio de Janeiro is that the 'myth of marginality' has changed into the 'reality' of exclusion and violence. As we have already noted above, we have been using the notion of 'governance voids' (Kruijt and Koonings 1999: 12) to delineate the domains in which urban violence can take hold, but we would repeat that this is not to be understood as an absence of the state in

25

any absolute sense. It rather means that the state (in this case the authorities formally responsible for urban order, law enforcement and security) has lost the capability (or political will) to guarantee protective capabilities or 'citizen security' (Koonings and Kruijt 2007). Typically this has been the case where the effective violence monopoly of the state has crumbled, so that alternative armed actors and violence brokers have been able to carve out spaces of social and territorial control. Here, they use violence to secure access to key (illicit) resources, including weapons, and to inspire a combination of loyalty and fear among the urban residents. Lack of non-violent prospects for social advancement, or in other words the social exclusion of, especially, young males, provides a permanent recruiting ground for urban armed actors such as criminal gangs, militias or vigilante groups (Cruz 2007). In a city like Rio de Janeiro, successive generations of gang leaders (*donos*), 'soldiers' and 'auxiliaries' (who generally start at a very young age) have been recycling the low-intensity urban war against each other and the police since the 1980s (Gay, this volume; Perlman, this volume; Leeds 1996, 2007; Zaluar 2004b).

The case of Rio de Janeiro also demonstrates that gang violence and its corollary, police 'urban counter-insurgency', is embedded within a wider framework of political interests, what Arias (2006) calls 'criminal networks'. These networks link powerful economic interests in the city and the electoral agendas of politicians (who may sponsor zero tolerance towards a middle-class constituency in combination with clientelistic ties to criminal gang leaders in the *favelas*) to violence and insecurity in the shanty towns reproduced by the perverse logic of urban politics. Something similar has been noted in Mumbai (Bombay), where mafia-style real estate brokers and land speculators use violence to consolidate their control of the slums but at the same time maintain links to globalized corporate capital, city authorities and the police (Weinstein 2008). Well known also are Kingston's (Jamaica) garrison communities, where local gang leaders ('dons') are powerful brokers between the neighbourhoods and political society (Henry-Lee 2005; Clarke 2006). Indeed, this is the continuation of politics by other means.

Notes

1 See the Mega-Cities Project, founded and directed by Janice Perlman (www. megacitiesproject.org). For the population size definition see Planet Earth/Earth Sciences for Society's brochure no. 7, *Mega-cities – our global urban future* (December 2005, available at www.yearofplanetearth. org/content/downloads/Megacities.pdf).

2 Here we draw on Koonings and Kruijt (2004, 2007).

3 See Castells (2006), Mayer (2006), Miller (2006), Staeheli (2006) and Ward and McCann (2006) for interesting recent retrospectives on Castells's work.

ONE | The social dynamics of exclusion and violence in megacities

2 | From popular movements to drug gangs to militias: an anatomy of violence in Rio de Janeiro

ROBERT GAY

On 27 June 2007, 1,350 troops from the civil and military police and the recently constituted National Security Force invaded the conglomeration of *favelas* known as the Complexo de Alemão, in Rio de Janeiro's northern zone. By the time the operation had ended, nineteen civilians lay dead. The authorities claimed they were members of the Comando Vermelho (Red Command), the oldest and – until recently – most powerful of Rio's organized crime factions. The invasion brought to a head a two-month-long campaign to break the power of the Comando Vermelho by shutting down the drug trade, a confrontation that had already cost twenty-five lives. The invasion of the Complexo de Alemão was swiftly and loudly condemned by human rights groups, which accused the government of provoking the conflict and of killing and injuring scores of innocent and already marginalized victims.[1] The newly installed governor of Rio, Sérgio Cabral, responded by pronouncing that it was time to take back the city and that the state was at war with criminal elements, a war that could not be won without bloodshed.[2]

The events that I have described above represent a recent example of a series of confrontations, some more deadly than others, that have punctuated the lives of the residents of Rio de Janeiro over the course of the past two decades and produced levels of violence that exceed those in war zones.[3] In this chapter, I examine the historical origins of such confrontations and their consequences. I argue that competition for the massive profits to be made from the drug trade in the 1980s provoked a war between rival gang factions and the police, who quickly became involved. And that, as the level of violence increased, the police proved incapable of doing, or unwilling to do, anything about it, a situation that prompted elements in civil society to take security matters into their own hands. Unfortunately, the losers in all this have been the residents of Rio's eight hundred or so *favelas*, who, having barely tasted the fruits of democracy, are caught in what is an increasingly deadly crossfire and, more significantly, have become the focus of calls for hard-line policies to incarcerate and punish those suspected of being perpetrators of violence.[4]

How violent?

Since the transition to democracy in the mid-1980s, Brazil has experienced a sudden and dramatic increase in violent crime.[5] Between 1980 and 2005, for example, the number of homicides increased from 13,910 to 48,374 per year and the homicide rate almost tripled from 11 to 27 per 100,000 people. Furthermore, Brazil now ranks second in the world – to Venezuela – in terms of death rates by firearms and fourth in terms of homicide rates for young persons between the ages of fifteen and twenty-four. In fact, it is the increase in homicide rates among Brazilian youth which, more than anything else, accounts for the dramatic increase in the homicide rate for the country as a whole.[6]

The state of Rio de Janeiro ranks third in the nation in terms of homicides, with a rate of 49.2 per 100,000 people, close behind the states of Espírito Santo (49.4) and Pernambuco (50.7). Rio also ranks first in the country in terms of death rates by firearms (43.3) and first in terms of homicide rates for young Brazilians between the ages of fifteen and twenty-four (102.8). The vast majority of these homicides take place in the more heavily populated and urbanized areas of the state, not only in the municipality of Rio de Janeiro, but also in those that immediately surround it. Indeed, the five suburban municipalities of Macaé, Itaguaí, Itaboraí, Duque de Caxias and Nova Iguaçu are among the twenty-five most violent municipalities in all of Brazil.[7]

Homicides, of course, are only one manifestation of increasing violence in Rio.[8] In recent years, there have also been high incidences of civilians being hit by stray bullets, car robberies, carjackings, residential break-ins, bank robberies and assaults on pedestrians, including tourists (*O Globo*, 23 May 2007). And then there are the more dramatic and high-profile events involving heavily armed gangs attacking government buildings and police stations, ordering schools and entire commercial districts to close their doors for business, holding up and robbing buses and then burning them to the ground – occasionally with the passengers still inside – and posing as police officers and holding up traffic on Rio's major roads and highways.[9]

Taken together, these incidences of violence have created a sense of extreme public insecurity and the perception – right or wrong – that there has been a complete breakdown in public law and order. As a consequence, many residents of Rio have chosen to dramatically change the way they go about their lives. Fewer people go out at night, for example, and if they do they tend to stay close to home or frequent shopping malls and specially created 'gastronomic poles' that are patrolled by private security guards. It is also common for middle- and upper-class residents of Rio to carry bags of unimportant and, therefore, disposable items that can be handed over if they are robbed, and they are far more likely than in the past to use taxis instead of their own vehicles.

There has also been a rapid rise in the number of cars in Rio that are specially reinforced to withstand gunfire, and more and more middle- and upper-class residences are barricaded in by high steel gates and fences and monitored twenty-four hours by closed-circuit TVs.[10] There are also restrictions on how much money residents of Rio can withdraw from ATM machines at a time, to prevent robbers from kidnapping victims and forcing them to empty out their bank accounts. And finally, there has been a proliferation of private security agencies whose employees stand guard in front of residencies, restaurants, hotels, stores and schools and whose ranks now far outnumber the local civil and military police.

Slums of hope

The early 1980s was a time of great hope and optimism in Brazil. The military was in the (long) process of returning to barracks and handing over power to elected civilian authorities. Democratization was also accompanied by waves of mobilization and protest by a variety of popular groups and organizations, including, among others, labour unions, Christian base communities and professional and neighbourhood associations. Together these various groups and organizations pushed to establish their collective political and social rights and to build a new and very different constituency of political actors that could challenge the power of what had, until then, been a decidedly authoritarian and tutelary state. In fact, such was the energy and dynamism of the popular sector that many described the period as one of the 'resurrection of civil society' (Escobar and Alvarez 1992).

In Rio de Janeiro, the *favelas* were very much a part of this process. Beginning in the late 1970s, the statewide *favela* federation, the Federação das Associações das Favelas do Estado do Rio de Janeiro (FAFERJ), reorganized itself and, in doing so, began to challenge and transform its relationship with the local state. Instead of supporting politicians in return for what were represented as 'favours', a system of political exchange otherwise known as clientelism, the leadership of the *favelas* began to demand things instead as 'rights'. This meant that instead of voting on the basis of a new set of shirts for the local football team, or a truckload of roof tiles for the neighbourhood association, the leadership of the *favela* movement began focusing on much broader issues and collective demands, such as the legalization of tenure, the provision of water, electricity and sewerage, and improved access to transport,

31

healthcare and education (Gay 1994: 25–34). What this meant, effectively, was that politicians in Rio had to work much harder to deliver votes from such areas, and that instead of being able to negotiate with – and pick off – *favelas* on an individual basis, they were forced to confront and deal with a relatively well-organized, combative and vocal collective body. Indeed, such was the strength of the *favela* movement in the early to mid-1980s that most of the candidates for the executive offices of governor and mayor of Rio de Janeiro felt obliged to meet with representatives of the *favela* movement and address their various demands.

The high point of the popular movement's success in Rio was the election in 1985 of the Partido Democrático Trabalhista (PDT) candidate for mayor, Saturnino Braga. Braga's running mate and eventual vice was Jó Resende, the former president of the Federação das Associações de Moradores do Estado do Rio de Janeiro (FAMERJ). FAMERJ was the statewide federation that brought together neighbourhood associations that were not part of FAFERJ. And while the neighbourhoods that were affiliated with FAMERJ were – on average – of higher socio-economic status, the decision by Saturnino Braga to choose a political outsider from the ranks of the popular movement as a running mate spoke volumes about the movement's strength and political capacity at that time.

Unfortunately, the Braga administration proved to be a disaster, in that the city was forced to declare bankruptcy in his final year in office. It was, nevertheless, an administration that welcomed the input and participation of representatives of the popular movement, including many presidents of *favela* neighbourhood associations, in a way that foreshadowed the process of participatory budgeting that subsequently became the flagship of the Partido de Trabalhadores (PT) in the south of Brazil in subsequent years.

Slums of despair

In late December 1986, I was in the process of finishing up my fieldwork in the *favela* of Vidigal, in Rio de Janeiro's southern zone. The leadership of the *favela* was very much involved in the restructuring of the *favela* movement in the late 1970s and early 1980s and worked closely with the Pastoral de Favelas, which was, at the time, one of the strongest advocates for poor communities' rights. I had just interviewed the president of the neighbourhood association at his house and he was giving me a ride to the bottom of the hill. Halfway down, he pointed out the ten or so armed men who were standing guard in the expectation of a retaliatory strike by a rival gang. I asked him how the presence of a heavily armed drug gang affected his work in the community.

Looking up at the soldiers, he told me that as long as he and his colleagues were in control of the neighbourhood association, everything would be all right. It would be another thirteen years before the drug gang in Vidigal took over, but the process was well under way.

Drug gangs and drug gang factions in Rio's *favelas* can be traced back to criminal organizations that emerged from inside the walls of the state's penitentiaries. Between 1969 and 1975, the military punished those who took up arms against the dictatorship by locking them up with common criminals in a prison on the island of Ilha Grande, to the south-west of the city of Rio.[11] These political prisoners impressed upon a small group of common criminal detainees the advantages of organization, loyalty and discipline and instructed them in the art of urban guerrilla warfare. The product of this unlikely encounter was the Comando Vermelho (Amorim 1993: 61–102).

Initially, the Comando Vermelho sought to impose its control over Ilha Grande and other prisons in the system. It took out members of rival factions, introduced strict codes of prisoner conduct and negotiated for improved conditions with suddenly besieged prison officials. Eventually, however, the reach of the Comando Vermelho extended beyond the prison system's walls to well-organized and clandestine cells that conducted bank robberies and, later on, kidnappings to finance the purchase of guns and ammunition and the often spectacular escapes of their incarcerated colleagues. Then, around 1982, the decision was made to finance the Comando Vermelho's activities by means of the drug trade (ibid.: 142).

Brazil is not (yet) a major producer of illegal drugs, although marijuana is grown fairly extensively in the interior of the north-east and the country has become an important exporter of precursor chemicals such as acetone and ether for illegal drug manufacture.[12] Over the past three decades or so, however, Brazil has become an important trans-shipment point for cocaine, which is cultivated and processed in the neighbouring countries of Bolivia, Peru and Colombia, in particular, and exported – increasingly via Africa – to expanding drug markets in Europe.[13] More significantly, approximately 20 per cent of the cocaine that finds its way into Brazil is sold locally (NEPAD and CLAVES 2000). In fact, it is now estimated that Brazil is the second-largest consumer of cocaine in the world, behind the USA.[14]

The Comando Vermelho's decision to move in on the drug trade led to a period of intense and bloody warfare for territorial control of Rio's *favelas*, where most of the distribution and selling points for drugs continue to be located. Many of the leaders and rank-and-file members of the Comando Vermelho were from the *favelas*, and so the relationship between these areas and drug trafficking naturally followed. Furthermore, the illegal, haphazard and impenetrable nature of most *favela* neighbourhoods in Rio provided the perfect terrain for drug gang operations. All drug gangs had to do was to arrange for shipments of drugs to be made from neighbouring countries and states. The gangs would then mix the cocaine with some sort of filler or cocaine-like substance, repackage it and sell it to wealthy clients in surrounding neighbourhoods or, increasingly, to users and addicts in their own communities.[15]

The ability of the Comando Vermelho to operate the drug trade in Rio's *favelas* depended, fundamentally, on the relationship between each drug gang and the community within which it was embedded. Drug gangs rely on the local population to provide new recruits for the various gang roles and positions and, more generally, to provide cover for their activities and protect them from the police. It became increasingly common, therefore, for drug gangs to generate goodwill by providing an increasingly wide variety of social services, such as transportation to and from hospitals and clinics, and financing public works such as day-care centres and recreational facilities.[16] It also became increasingly common for drug gangs to take advantage of the absence and widespread mistrust of public authorities to lay down the law (their law) and punish those who disobeyed orders or who caused trouble. Thus, while the emergence of heavily armed gangs in Rio's *favelas* was met with a fair degree of fear and trepidation, it meant that residents of such areas had a means to resolve personal disputes and could enjoy a measure of personal security.[17]

Over the course of time, the Comando Vermelho split into various loosely organized factions, the most significant being the Terceiro Comando and the more recently established Amigos dos Amigos. These factions then proceeded to compete militarily – literally by invading each other's territory – for a share of the drug market in Rio, which brings in millions of dollars in profit each week.[18] And it is this competition between armies of an estimated 10,000 men which – more than anything else – has transformed, not just a select few neighbourhoods, but almost an entire city into a war zone.[19]

The other major consequence of the emergence and consolidation of drug gangs and drug gang factions in Rio has been the effective demise of the *favela* movement. At first, drug gangs and neighbourhood associations coexisted fairly peacefully, as they did in Vidigal throughout the 1980s and early 1990s. Eventually, however, drug gangs sought control of neighbourhood associations as a means to represent their interests and to communicate and negotiate with the outside world. Politically, this meant that the democratic window of opportunity that was opened by the military's withdrawal in the mid-1980s was now closed. This did not mean that 'politics' and 'electoral procedures' failed to operate in such areas, far from it. What it meant, however, was that democracy began to serve a very different set of interests.[20]

In some *favelas*, this transfer of power meant that the leadership of the neighbourhood association stayed put as long as it acted in the gang or faction's interests. In others it meant that leaders were forcibly removed or replaced. Either way, the position of president of a neighbourhood association became an extremely precarious and often short-lived proposition. Indeed, according to one study, 400 neighbourhood association leaders were executed and another 450 expelled in Rio between 1992 and 2002 (*Jornal do Brasil*, 16 June 2002 and 27 March 2005). Many community leaders simply withdrew from public life. Others found themselves working for NGOs that proliferated in the *favelas* during this period. The vast majority of these NGOs focused on narrow and specific tasks, such as teaching computer literacy, or promoting self-awareness and identity through Afro-Brazilian music and dance. Few of them challenged the power of gangs, however, or could be considered transformative in the broader political sense of the word (Pandolfi and Grynszpan 2003; Zaluar 2004b).

This is not to say, of course, that *all* violence in Rio de Janeiro can be attributed to drug trafficking and the competition between rival drug gang factions for increased market share. The relationship between the emergence of Rio as a trans-shipment point for Andean cocaine and the increase in homicides is clear, however. Indeed, one study of police inquiries and court cases in Rio in 1991 revealed that 57 per cent of homicides in the city that year were linked in some way to drug trafficking. And, as violence spreads beyond the confines of metropolitan Rio, to the once bucolic mountain resorts of Teresópolis, Petrópolis and Nova Friburgo, for example, it is always drug trafficking and associated gun-related deaths which lead the way (*Jornal do Brasil*, 14 August 2007).

Police violence

The police force in Rio has quickly established a reputation as one of the most lethal in the nation and has responded to the recent increase in violence in the region by killing, on average, one thousand civilians each year for the past few years. Most police victims have no criminal record or involvement with crime. They are simply the wrong type of person – in other words, young, male, dark-skinned, uneducated and poor – caught at the wrong place and the wrong time. Occasionally, as in the case of the Candelária Cathedral and

35

Vigário Geral massacres, both in Rio de Janeiro in 1993, international outrage over police brutality in Rio forces state authorities to intervene. The effect of this has always been temporary, however, and it is not long before the number of civilian deaths at the hands of the police begins to rise again.[21]

There are a number of factors that have made the prevention of police homicides difficult in Brazil. The first is that the initial investigation of the crime scene is in the hands of the police. In other words, the first people to arrive on the scene are more often than not often the perpetrators of the crime itself. The second is that the police always claim that they are acting in self-defence, or in defence of others, and that extrajudicial killings are, in fact, the outcome of shoot-outs with dangerous and well-armed criminals. It is clear, however, that in many cases claims of 'self-defence' cover for police executions. A study of police killings between 1993 and 1996, for example, found that half the victims had four or more bullet wounds and more than half had at least one gunshot wound from behind or to the head (Cano 1997). The third factor has to do with the widespread use of unregistered and unauthorized guns. It has been common practice for the police in Brazil to plant guns on their already deceased victims to corroborate claims of a shoot-out. And, finally, bodies are often removed to local hospitals to create the impression that the police tried to assist their victims and to compromise investigations of the crime scene.

There have also been institutional factors that have made the investigation and prevention of police homicides difficult. Until recently, the military police in Brazil were encouraged by their superiors to eliminate – as opposed to detain – criminal suspects. And in the mid- to late 1990s the military police in Rio de Janeiro were given pay rises and promotions for acts of 'special merit' and 'bravery', which, in essence, meant killing urban youth (Human Rights Watch 1997: 13). Also until recently, military police tribunals were responsible for investigating crimes committed by the military police and could be counted on to determine that civilians were, in fact, killed in acts of self-defence (Zaverucha 1999).

In 1996, the situation appeared to change somewhat with the implementation of Brazil's first Human Rights Plan, which transferred oversight and jurisdiction of police homicides to civilian authorities. Even so, it is up to the police to determine what is and what isn't a homicide and the military police retain the right to 'oversee' such cases. Furthermore, civilian witnesses of police brutality are routinely threatened and discouraged from testifying, and few prosecutors have the time, resources or political will to conduct their own investigations.[22] For many, the execution of criminal suspects by the police is simply not a priority. And, because the judicial system in Brazil is so overburdened and inefficient, changes in the oversight and processing of police crimes have had little effect.[23]

Most significantly, there is also widespread support for extrajudicial police action among the general population (Pandolfi 1999). Death squads comprising of off-duty and former policemen are often hired by local merchants to clear the streets of 'undesirables' and are responsible for killing a large number of Brazilian youths each year (Human Rights Watch/Americas Final Justice 1994; Huggins 1998). This should in no way be seen as an endorsement of the police, however. Few Brazilians make use of the police, who are perceived, quite rightly, as untrustworthy and violent.[24] It is more an indication of how far the situation has deteriorated and the insecurity and fear of violence experienced by the residents of, not just Rio, but many of Brazil's major cities.[25] The problem is that in recent years violence, and in particular drug-related violence, has spilled out beyond the *favelas* into all areas of city life, such that there are few safe havens in Rio.[26] And it is within this context of generalized violence and fear and the breakdown of public law and order that calls for the extension of human rights to police victims have fallen on deaf ears.[27]

Many people will tell you, for instance, that they blame Rio's first post-authoritarian governor, Leonel Brizola, for preventing the police from rooting out the Comando Vermelho in the first place. Brizola was a long-time opponent of the military in Brazil, and his surprise election as governor of Rio in 1982 was seen, at the time, as a victory for democracy and the forces of the left.[28] It is somewhat ironic, therefore, that his pro-human rights stance is believed to have handcuffed the police and enabled drug gangs to become established in the *favelas*, a belief that has provided popular justification for hard-line policies ever since.

Whether the above claim is true is hard to say. What is clear, however, is that the police in Rio are incapable of dealing with the situation, as it currently exists. And this is in no small part because of the nature of the force(s).[29] The police in Brazil are extremely poorly trained. Few receive instruction in the basics of criminal investigation or human rights and, as a consequence, the few cases that are solved are solved because the perpetrator happens to be caught in the act, a witness agrees to testify or, more likely, a confession is literally beaten out of a suspect. Thus, despite a 1997 anti-torture law, a recent report by the United Nations claims that it is still the case that the 'police routinely beat and torture criminal suspects to extract information, confessions or money', and that 'the problem of police brutality, at the time of arrest or during interrogation, [is] reportedly endemic'.[30]

The police in Brazil are also badly equipped. There are an estimated 17.3 million firearms in Brazil. The authorities, including the armed forces, account for only 1.7 million. The remaining 15.6 million are in the hands of civilians. Fewer than half of these guns are registered and, therefore, legal, and an estimated four million are in the hands of criminals (*O Globo*, 18 March 2005). The vast majority of the guns that are held by criminals are manufactured legally in Brazil and bought – or stolen – from private citizens, the military or the police.[31] Alternatively, they are sold to dealers in other countries and then smuggled back in. Whatever their origin, press reports estimate that drug gangs in Rio possess an arsenal of 1,500 rifles and machine guns that include the FAL 762, FAL 556, SIG-Sauer, H&K G3, M16, AR-15, AK-47 and Browning .30 (*Jornal do Brasil*, 13 May 2007). And in one raid in August 2004 the police in Rio came across a stockpile of mines, grenades and gun cartridges in one *favela* worth an estimated 500,000 reais (*O Globo*, 19 August 2004).

Finally, the police in Brazil are also extremely badly paid. Many of the 75,000 or so military and civil police in Rio supplement their incomes by working second shifts, more often than not as private security guards.[32] Thus, while a career in the police provides certain elements of the population with opportunities for advancement, it is – in general – an unattractive and last-resort proposition.[33] As I have already mentioned, the police are subject to widespread mistrust and hatred and policemen and women who live in drug-gang-dominated neighbourhoods are often forced to disguise what they do for a living. Otherwise they are likely to be expelled or, worse still, executed.[34] Drug gangs have also been known to place bounties of as much as 15,000 reais on a single policeman's head, and, in recent years, police officers have been attacked and executed for their guns and ammunition while sitting in their patrol cars.[35]

Police corruption and violence

While it may appear, on the face of it, that the police in Rio have been waging war against the drug trade in order to shut it down, nothing could be farther from the truth. The police have profited from drug trafficking from the very beginning and are involved at every level.[36] When the police go into a *favela*, for example, they are more likely to be after a share of the spoils than to be after the individual members of a drug gang. And, when they do manage to apprehend someone, they often have no intention of making a formal arrest. They are simply out to make money by holding a particular drug gang member hostage. In fact, there have even been reports in the local press that military police recruits are *trained* in the art of extortion, or what's known locally as *mineiração* or 'mining' (*Jornal do Brasil*, 13 March 2002).

When the drug trade is going well, there is enough money to go around. In fact, drug gangs often budget for the amount of money they need – each week – to pay off the police. The system breaks down, however, when drug deals go sour or insufficient money is being made and the police go after what they perceive as their fair share.[37] It is also very common for drug gangs to pay the police to provide them with information and protection. As a consequence, police operations that target particular drug gangs or drug gang leaders often come up empty because the individual or individuals involved have been warned well in advance. One of the most notorious instances of this occurred following the brutal murder of *O Globo* reporter Tim Lopes in June 2002. Lopes was kidnapped, tortured and killed because of an article he published on open-air drug fairs and research he was conducting on public sex acts in the *favelas* involving minors. It took months for the police to capture Lopes's killer, Elias Maluco, despite the fact that they had a very good idea where he was hiding out. The State Secretary for Security in Rio attributed the delay to the fact that Maluco paid the police to protect him and reported that, on one occasion, he had handed over 600,000 reais to be released from police custody.

Occasionally, as in the case of police violence, steps are taken to reform and clean up the police. And, in recent years, the establishment of an anonymous hotline and the appointment of an independent police ombudsman have meant that police operations are subject to much closer public scrutiny (Leeds 2007). The phone line, 'Disque-Denuncia', which was originally created to combat kidnappings, receives on average 10,000 calls per month, of which 30–35 per cent have to do with information about drug trafficking. The phone line is supposed to be secure and anonymous. Many people refuse to use it, however, for fear of being overheard or turned over to the police under investigation, or to drug traffickers.[38] Furthermore, very few of the literally thousands of complaints that have been lodged against the police have resulted in punishment, dismissal or prosecution. And the overwhelming majority of those who have been punished have not been officers, but low-level recruits (*Jornal do Brasil*, 26 November 2002).

Corruption also plagues the state prison system and has, until recently, undermined any attempt to break the power of prison-based criminal organizations. In 1988, a brand-new maximum-security facility, modelled on prisons in the USA, was opened in the neighbourhood of Bangu in Rio's Zona Oeste to house and isolate the leaders of the Comando Vermelho, Terceiro Comando and Amigos dos Amigos who were transferred from Ilha Grande. All three organizations continued to function and thrive, however, as orders for drug and weapons transactions, the invasion of enemy territory, the torture and execution of debtors and informants, and threats and attempts to extort money from innocent civilians continued to be made from the inside.[39]

Orders from the inside are delivered in a number of different ways. Sometimes friends and family pass them along. Sometimes inmates' lawyers, or those who represent themselves as inmates' lawyers, pass them along.[40] Most of the time, however, they are made directly from the outside via cellphone.[41] And, until now, the prison authorities have been unable to cut off either the supply of cellphones or cellphone transmissions, despite the enormous amount of money that has been invested in cellphone-blocking technology.[42] Many of the cellphones, weapons, explosives, drugs and other materials are smuggled in by visitors.[43] The majority, however, are smuggled in and sold to inmates by prison workers and guards. Prison workers and guards have also been known to accept money to facilitate escapes and even the murder of prisoners from rival gang factions.[44] The problem is that it is often difficult – and dangerous – for prison guards and workers to do otherwise.[45] In September 2000, for example, the director of the Bangu prison complex in Rio was executed on her front doorstep by what were rumoured to be either drug gang faction members or the police. The director had been attempting to clamp down on the use of cellphones in Bangu and a system of bribes and kickbacks that totalled an estimated one million reais per month.[46]

Recent attempts at reform (and their violent consequences)

On 11 September 2002, a drug trafficker by the name of Fernandinho Beira-Mar led a rebellion of inmates associated with the Comando Vermelho in one of the maximum-security prisons in the Bangu complex. With the obvious assistance of someone on the inside, Beira-Mar and his associates overcame two guards, passed through three steel doors, crossed a corridor, opened three other doors and took out four drug gang members from a rival faction. Beira-Mar's men all had guns and they had keys to all of the doors in the prison, even though a thorough search had been conducted only twenty-four hours earlier. Apparently, a prison guard had been paid 40,000 reais to smuggle in the guns and make copies of the keys.

Incidents such as these prompted the state government in Rio to make a renewed and concerted effort to break the power of prison-based criminal organizations by placing their leaders in strict isolation, cutting back on visitation rights and other such privileges and redoubling efforts to prevent messages from getting in and orders from reaching the outside.[47] And while these measures failed, for the most part, to rid the prison system of warring gangs and factions, they did make it more difficult for the leaders in Bangu to manage the drug trade.[48] As a consequence, the measures themselves were met with fierce resistance in the form of widespread prison riots, waves of coordinated attacks on public buses, government buildings and the police in Rio and the assassination of prison officials and employees.[49]

More significantly, the crackdown on prison-based criminal organizations broke long-standing and effective chains of command between criminal organization leaders on the inside and their lieutenants and foot soldiers on the outside and sparked a new round of territorial disputes for control of Rio's *favelas*. And, as a consequence, it led to the emergence of a new generation of drug gang members who are younger, less disciplined, less accountable and far more violent and cruel, both in their dealings with the police and with members of the communities in which they happen to be embedded.[50]

The most obvious manifestation of this new reality was the attack on the *favela* of Rocinha, the largest in Rio, by a heavily armed convoy of sixty men that set out from the neighbouring *favela* of Vidigal on 9 April 2004. The attack marked an attempt by the Comando Vermelho to regain control of the *favela* on behalf of its former head, or *dono*. The *dono* had been serving time for nine years for homicide and drug trafficking. On 12 January 2004, however, he was granted permission by a judge to spend his daytime hours with family. So, five days later, on the first day that he was eligible, he walked out of the prison and never came back. According to tradition, *donos* who are released or escape from prison are entitled to reassume control of their communities. In this particular case, however, the *dono* who had taken his place in Rocinha refused to comply. Everyone knew that an attack was imminent.[51] The authorities were powerless to do anything about it, however, demonstrating – once again – that they had effectively lost control of large parts of the city.[52]

The attack on Rocinha, which was launched in broad daylight, and the general state of open warfare between rival factions at that time, prompted the authorities to hunt down and apprehend local gang leaders and to call in the military and special operation police units. This was not the first time that the authorities in Rio had called in the military to combat drug trafficking. In 1994, for example, the military had occupied dozens of *favelas* in an attempt to quell an outbreak of drug-gang-related violence. And in February 2003, the Brazilian military deployed three thousand troops in twenty-five different locations in Rio to keep the city 'safe' for tourists during carnival, a practice that has continued to this day whenever there is a special event, such as the Pan American games, for example.[53]

The attack on Rocinha also prompted the authorities to try to suffocate the drug trade by surrounding and occasionally occupying particularly strategic or problematic *favelas*. This policy was supported at the federal level by efforts to expand and strengthen police presence at the country's borders and international airports and by discouraging the trans-shipment of drugs via Brazilian airspace. With that in mind, on 16 July 2004 President Lula signed decree no. 5144 that granted the Brazilian Air Force permission to shoot down unregistered planes from outside the country that refuse to respond to orders to land. The Brazilian government claims that this change in policy alone resulted in a 60 per cent decline in unauthorized flights over the country between 2003 and 2004, although there are still vast areas of Brazilian airspace that are effectively unmonitored and there is a strong suspicion that drug traffickers are finding other ways to bring their merchandise into the country.[54] There is evidence, for instance, that Colombian cocaine is now being transported by FARC intermediaries through Bolivia to Paraguay, where it is delivered into the hands of Brazilian traffickers in exchange for dollars and munitions (*O Globo*, 10 April 2005; *Jornal do Brasil*, 1 April 2007).[55]

There is little doubt that measures to restrict the movement of drugs have squeezed *favela*-based gangs in Rio, although recent evidence suggests that the Comando Vermelho continues to take in about three million reais each month.[56] That does not mean, however, that their power has been undermined or diminished. Indeed, there is evidence that, in the absence of money to be made from drugs, gangs are moving to control and profit from other activities and enterprises. It is estimated, for example, that in 20 per cent of Rio's *favelas*, gangs charge a mark-up of up to eight reais for a tank of cooking gas, bringing in as much as 20,000 reais per month, and siphon off a portion of neighbourhood association dues and charges for the provision of water (*O Globo*, 20 February 2005). Also, in many *favelas* gangs charge residents to park on the street and impose a surcharge on van and motor taxi services that ferry residents around internally. And in some *favelas* gangs have even been known to impose curfews and to fine residents for coming home late (*Jornal do Brasil*, 3 September 2004). Finally, it is also very likely that the crackdown on drug sales explains the recent increase in many other crimes such as robberies and assaults on buses (*O Globo*, 23 May 2007).

In addition, it should be kept in mind that the effectiveness of all of these attempts to suffocate the drug trade and reduce drug-gang-related violence continues to be compromised by corruption. In May 2003, former governor and presidential hopeful Antonio Garotinho assumed the position of State Secretary for Public Security in Rio and – in a bold but ultimately failed attempt to further his political career – pledged to reduce violent crime in the city, which, in his own words, had got 'out of control' (*Jornal do Brasil*, 8 May 2003). A few months later, however, he was forced to admit publicly that his efforts were being undermined by widespread police corruption and involvement in crimes.

The police in Rio have been involved in almost every conceivable illegal activity, including charging motorists for improper paperwork during blitzes, laundering drug money, robbing apartments, extorting money from tourists, stealing cars, kidnapping civilians, apprehending high-profile drug dealers and then extorting money for their release, drug trafficking, drug dealing, prostitution and the sexual exploitation of minors, providing security for drug traffickers, leaking and selling information about police activities, and training drug gang members in the art of urban warfare.[57] Indeed, the situation has reached the point at which the police often do not tell their own men where and when they are going on an operation until the very last moment (*O Globo*, 11 April 2005). And there have even been instances, in particularly sensitive situations, when the police have relied on hand-picked teams of evangelicals (*Jornal do Brasil*, 28 November 2004).

Unfortunately, despite numerous crackdowns on illegal police behaviour and the large number of legal proceedings that have been brought against the police, it is still proving extremely difficult to purge criminal and corrupt elements.[58] A recent analysis of cases brought against the police in the six years and nine months of the existence of the office of police ombudsman in Rio, for example, revealed that of 8,330 military and civil policemen and -women who have been caught participating in one type of crime or another, only sixteen have been expelled from the force (*O Globo*, 3 February 2006). Of course, the police claim that they are taking measures to clean up the force and that more and more policemen and -women are being expelled each year, including, in one particularly high-profile case in December 2006, an entire military police battalion – along with its commanding officer – for involvement with organized crime.[59]

The question is, is it simply a matter of rooting out the occasional bad element? Or are the police so intimately involved with organized crime – and dependent on violence for their livelihood – that nothing short of a complete dismantling and rebuilding of the force will suffice? The circumstances surrounding the latest police massacre in Rio, in the notoriously violent Baixada Fluminense, would suggest the latter. On 31 March 2005, a group of military

43

policemen indiscriminately shot and killed twenty-nine innocent victims in the neighbourhoods of Nova Iguaçu and Queimados. The massacre was a reaction by the police to hard-line measures that had been imposed by a new battalion commander who had been sent in to clean up the force.[60]

The other question is, what happens to the police when they are expelled? Many, it turns out, are reinstated and go on to commit more crimes.[61] Others end up in the pay of drug gangs, often as military advisers. Alternatively, they join forces with the estimated six hundred to a thousand firemen, prison workers, active-duty and retired policemen who constitute the militias that are gradually and inexorably – it would seem – taking over the *favelas* of Rio's Zona Oeste (*O Globo*, 19 August 2007). These militias, otherwise known as *polícia mineira*, act much like the gangs they aim to replace in that they promote parties and cultural events and provide legal and medical services via each community's neighbourhood association. They also charge protection fees and make money from the sale of cooking gas and from taxes levied on real estate transactions and moneylending. The only difference between the militias and the gangs they replace is that they kill or expel and confiscate the property of anyone suspected of being associated with drug trafficking.[62]

Many of the residents of these areas express relief to be out from under the control of drug gangs. They are acutely aware, however, that they have traded one authoritarian and unaccountable force for another. And to be honest, they have little or no choice in the matter. As one policeman who offered such services said: 'We are a necessary evil. The residents oftentimes don't want us here, but end up agreeing because they need to free themselves of violence' (*O Globo*, 21 March 2005). Unfortunately, however, it is not always the case that areas under the control of militias are free of violence. In fact, a recent study commissioned by the newspaper *O Globo* found that the rates of violent crime in such areas are as high as rates in *favelas* dominated by drug gangs.

The emergence of private militias, which are known to be linked to death squads, is part and parcel of the broader process of the privatization of public security in Rio, which is – in itself – an indication of the general lack of faith in the capacity of public authorities.[63] According to the Sindicato dos Vigilantes do Rio, there are approximately 130,000 men working as private security guards in Rio, only 30,000 of whom were officially registered (*O Globo*, 5 August 2004). One reason for this is that as many as 60,000 police and firemen work clandestinely in this sector because, by law, they are not allowed to work a second shift, or *bico*. Furthermore, an estimated 80 per cent of the illegal private security firms in Rio are in fact controlled if not owned by police (*O Globo*, 29 May 2005).

The question is, if the uniformed and on-duty police can get away with killing, on average, one thousand civilians each year, what possibility or mechanism is there for controlling and overseeing what is becoming the extralegal arm of an already deadly public security force? As in other countries of Latin America, there is the strong suspicion that militias operate with the implicit approval, if not the support, of public authorities. After all, the ninety or so neighbourhoods that are currently under the control of militias in Rio are never subject to the type of incursion that is typical of police operations in *favelas* dominated by the organized gang factions, despite the similarities between them, leading some to suggest that what we are seeing here is a military-inspired campaign to retake and hold, by whatever means necessary, territories that have been lost to the state.

Marginality and violence

A few days after the police invaded the Complexo de Alemão, the federal government announced plans to invest 3.8 billion reais in the state of Rio, including 1.6 billion that was earmarked for Rio's *favelas* (*O Globo*, 3 July 2007). Then, a few weeks later, the federal government unveiled plans for a National Programme of Public Security and Citizenship (Pronasci), which will spend 6.7 billion reais over the next five years on 650,000 individual grants of between 100 and 300 reais. Modelled on the highly regarded social assistance programme Bolsa Família, these grants will be distributed to at-risk youth, low-paid policemen and women, prison workers, army reservists and ex-reservists, and women in positions of leadership in areas of high conflict (*O Globo*, 5 August 2007). Both programmes represent an explicit attempt to extend the reach and influence of the state and to compete with organized crime.

To what extent will these programmes be successful? This is by no means the first attempt to urbanize the *favelas* of Rio. Indeed, since the transition to democracy in the early 1980s, there have been any number of programmes designed to improve the infrastructure of such areas. And, as a result, the majority of the inhabitants of all but the most recently settled *favelas* in Rio now have access to running water, sewerage and electricity. This does not mean, however, that the *favelas* have been integrated into mainstream city life or that the distinction between the worlds of the *asfalto* (asphalt – indicates middle-class neighbourhoods) and the *morro* (hill – most *favelas* are built on hills) has been abolished, far from it. People who live in a *favela* still have to lie about their address in order to get a job, and most middle- and upper-class residents of Rio wouldn't dream of setting foot in such places. Furthermore, and perhaps more importantly, programmes that invest resources in drug-gang-dominated areas of the city do not effectively 'compete' with organized crime, in the sense of there being two parallel universes. In fact, they are far more than likely to be 'captured' by criminal elements and used to consolidate their hold over such areas.[64]

It is also highly questionable whether a programme of small grants – which may be effective in raising the incomes of the truly disadvantaged – will stem the flow of former military and police personnel and poor youth, in particular, into the ranks of organized crime. A 2006 study of 235 *favelas* in Rio by the Instituto Brasileiro de Inovações em Saûde Social (IBISS) revealed that 8,583 youths between the ages of eight and eighteen were working in some capacity or another for drug gangs. This represents a 27.5 per cent increase over figures that were obtained for 2002, and means that the drug trade in Rio has been the largest employer of children and adolescents for the fourth year in a row. In reality, until there is a public education system in place which provides real possibilities for social advancement and formal sector jobs that pay decent wages there will be little to persuade poor teenagers in Rio to stay the course. In fact, it is amazing how so few youths join the ranks of organized crime given the conditions of slave labour and outright discrimination that they face.

Sadly, while the number of Brazilians who are enrolled in primary school has increased dramatically since the mid-1980s, the public education system remains – by the government's own admission – a national disaster.[65] And while the Brazilian economy has performed fairly well since the reforms of the mid-1990s, in terms of controlling inflation and overall macroeconomic stability, it has produced almost no growth.[66] According to the Instituto de Pesquisa Econômico Aplicada (IPEA), the percentage of formal sector workers in Brazil increased only slightly from 37.5 per cent in 1993 to 38.4 per cent in 2002 (IPEA 2005: 105). This means that more than half the workforce is not only low paid, but also lacks the legal protections, guarantees and potential benefits associated with a signed work card, or *carteira assinada*.[67] More importantly, it also means that they have been largely unaffected by recent increases in social spending that have been absorbed by programmes such as pensions and social security that tend not to extend to informal sector workers (*O Globo*, 3 May 2005).[68]

In comparative terms, Rio de Janeiro remains one of the wealthiest and most developed states in the country. The recessions and financial crises of the 1980s and early 1990s hit Rio particularly hard, however, and accelerated what has been a long process of decline from its former position as the country's commercial and political capital.[69] In fact, over the course of the past twenty years or so, Rio de Janeiro's economic performance has been worse than that of any other state in Brazil, despite the lucrative presence of the oil industry, and has resulted in a sharp decline in the state's contribution to the national economy and real wages.[70] The situation has also been exacerbated by the fact that the state of Rio de Janeiro itself invests less than half the average for Brazil in general in public services and infrastructure and less than any other state except Maranhão, the state with the lowest Human Development Index in the federation (*O Globo*, 6 August 2006).

Notes

1 Human Rights Watch demanded an immediate investigation into the deaths, citing strong evidence of summary execution. Unicef also condemned the invasion, comparing the situation to that of areas of Afghanistan and Iraq. In response, the State Secretary for Security and the head of the Civil Police in Rio claimed that human rights organizations were being manipulated by drug traffickers (*O Globo,* 30 June and 5 July 2007).

2 See, for example, the interview with Cabral in *O Globo*, 1 July 2007.

3 A 2005 UNESCO publication in Brazil entitled 'Deaths by gunfire in Brazil 1979–2003' revealed that the number of deaths by gunfire in Brazil during the last decade surpasses that of victims of other armed conflicts in the world, such as the Gulf War and the Palestine–Israel conflict.

4 Although my focus in this chapter is the population of Rio's *favelas*, similar problems plague the population of low-income neighbourhoods and public housing projects.

5 Most of the statistics in this section are from Waiselfisz (2007).

6 Between 1980 and 2004 the homicide rate for those between the ages of fifteen and twenty-four increased from 30 to 51.7 per 100,000 people, while homicide rates for the remainder of the population over the same period decreased slightly from 21.3 to 20.8.

7 Until recently, it has generally been the case that high homicide rates have characterized Brazil's largest cities and most densely populated metropolitan areas. More recently, however, homicide rates have been on the increase in parts of the interior in the wake of economic development and social change, such that some of the highest rates in the country can now be found in the states of Rondônia, Alagoas and Mato Grosso, for example.

8 Recorded homicides are also an imperfect measure of homicides in Rio. A recent study by the Centro de Estudos de Segurança e Cidadania da Universidade Candido Mendes (Cesec-Ucam) found that the number of missing persons in Rio almost doubled from 2,473 in 1993 to 4,800 in 2003. Most of these missing persons are males between the ages of eighteen and twenty-six years of age and 70 per cent are drug related (*O Globo*, 1 May 2004).

9 According to the Federação das Empresas de Transportes de Passageiros do Estado do Rio de Janeiro (Fetranspor), between 1999 and 2004, 639 buses were burned or laid to waste in Rio at a cost of 50 million reais (*Jornal do Brasil*, 18 July 2004).

10 Of the 30,200 armoured cars produced in Brazil between 1995 and 2006, 4,200 or 14 per cent have been delivered to Rio (*O Globo*, 5 November 2006). For gated communities in Brazil, see Caldeira (2000).

11 For an account of prison conditions through the eyes of a foreign ethnographer, see Goldstein (2003: 137–42).

12 In recent years, however, the

47

police in Rio have discovered small laboratories that produce LSD and refine coca paste, which is obtained in exchange for stolen cars in Paraguay (*Jornal do Brasil*, 24 August 2004).

13 According to some estimates, the 'Atlantic route' through Brazil, Venezuela and Guyana now accounts for half of the cocaine leaving Colombia (*Financial Times*, 31 October 2003). For the origins of the drug trade in Brazil, see Geffray (2002).

14 Drug culture in Brazil is by no means confined to marijuana and cocaine, however. According to the 5th Levantamento Nacional sobre Consumo de Drogas entre Estudantes, which polled 48,000 people, Brazilian students of between thirteen and fifteen consume more solvents, among other things, than any other country in the world (*Jornal do Brasil*, 1 June 2005).

15 It is often claimed that the 'drug problem' in Brazil is confined to what is referred to as the 'White Republic' of Rio. There is evidence, however, that in terms of sheer volume São Paulo is the far larger market. In the past, there have been significant differences between the two. The market in Rio has been dominated by cocaine, as opposed to crack cocaine, and has been far more organized and violent. Recent events suggest, however, that the situation in both cities is changing. For the case of São Paulo, see Mingardi and Goulart (2002).

16 For the relationship between drug gangs and the surrounding community, see Alvito (2001: 152); Leeds (1996); Ventura (1994: 103–104); and Zaluar (1994).

17 There is, however, a tendency to exaggerate the degree to which local residents support as opposed to fear drug gangs. Marcos Alvito makes what I think is a useful distinction between drug gang leaders in the past who were cruel but fair and a new generation who are not respected because they torture and kill for the sake of it (2001: 152).

18 By way of illustration, the police in Rio recently estimated that the drug gangs that dominate the four Zona Sul *favelas* of Rocinha, Vidigal, Pavão-Pavãozinho and Cantagalo take in approximately 4.5 million reais, or US$2 million, each week.

19 It was estimated in 2002 that 10,000 men dominated the lives of 1 million people in 800 communities in Rio (*Jornal do Brasil*, 16 June 2002). See also de Souza (2002).

20 Essentially, it was drug gangs which now forged relationships with politicians and gave them permission to campaign, whereas previously it had been the leadership of the neighbourhood association. For an illustration of how this worked, see Gay (2005: 71–3).

21 The civil and military police in Rio killed 397 civilians in acts of so-called 'self-defence' in 1998, 453 in 1999, 483 in 2000, 514 in 2001, 834 in 2002, 1,195 in 2003, 983 in 2004 and 1,098 in 2005.

22 Approximately 40 per cent of those enrolled in witness protection programmes in Rio are being protected from the police. Another 40 per cent are involved in drug-related crimes, including protection from death squads, which also involve the police (*Jornal do Brasil*, 2 July 2004).

23 For problems associated with the Brazilian judiciary, see Pinheiro (2000) and Brinks (2002).

24 See, for example, Neto (1999).

25 Jorge Balán (2002) argues that in cities of Latin America, 'Fear is now as much a threat to democracy as violence itself, since it may justify repression, emergency policies that circumvent the constitutional rule, and, more broadly, alienation from the democratic political process.'

26 Even the international airport has been closed because of shoot-outs in nearby warring *favelas*.

27 See also Caldeira and Holston (1999).

28 At the time of his election, Brizola was vilified by the PT for his habit of forging alliances with the right wing and for populist forms of electioneering, both of

which the PT has become exceptionally skilled at.

29 The police in Brazil are organized and operate at the state level. There is a small federal force that monitors interstate and international drug trafficking along Brazil's porous and remote 9,000-mile border. The vast majority of the 500,000 or so policemen and women, however, serve in the civil and military police forces. The military police are essentially reserve units of the army that patrol the streets, maintain the peace and respond to and investigate crimes in progress. The civil police investigate crimes that have already been committed and oversee the operation of police precincts.

30 *Jornal do Brasil Online*, www.jb. com.br/destaques/1006tortura/tortura. html (accessed 7 February 2006).

31 In 2001, the police apprehended 16,796 firearms in Rio. Only 1,149 were manufactured abroad. And between 1998 and 2001 there were eighty-one reported incidences of firearms going missing from military establishments in Brazil (*Jornal do Brasil*, 26 April 2004). See also Dowdney (2003: 100).

32 This figure also involves firefighters.

33 The police force has provided rare and significant opportunities for Afro-Brazilians.

34 See, for example, *Jornal do Brasil* (23 March 2003).

35 See, for example, *O Globo* (16 October 2004) and *Jornal do Brasil* (20 January 2005).

36 For police involvement with the drug trade, see Leeds (1996). For police corruption in general, see Blat and Saraiva (2000).

37 For a discussion of the different kinds of relationship between drug gangs and the police, see Alvito (2001: 105) and Ventura (1994: 67).

38 Traffickers tell people that the telephones are bugged to discourage informants. They have also been responsible for destroying a lot of public

telephones from where – obviously – these calls are made (*O Globo*, 22 August 2004).

39 It is common for drug gang leaders in prison to order torture sessions and executions by phone. See, for example, *Jornal do Brasil* (6 September 2002).

40 In 2000, the Department for State Prisons (Desipe) sent the Brazilian Lawyers Association a list of 130 lawyers who were suspected of being involved with drug trafficking. It turned out that only fifteen of them were actual lawyers. The other 115 had all obtained false documents (*Jornal do Brasil*, 16 April 2001). For an interview with the attorney of the drug trafficker Fernandinho Beira-Mar, see *Jornal do Brasil* (28 March 2003).

41 The police have discovered digital and satellite-operated phone banks that can transfer calls to and from prison without revealing the identity of the caller and software that can clone privately owned cellphones and change their numbers up to twenty times per day. The equipment for this type of operation is extremely sophisticated and expensive, costing up to US$40,000, and is similar to technology that is used by guerrilla outfits in Colombia (*Jornal do Brasil*, 9 August 2002).

42 On 5 August 2002, for example, the prison authorities confiscated 114 cellphones and 135 cellphone chargers in the Bangu prison complex in Rio (*Jornal do Brasil*, 6 August 2002).

43 Most prisons in Brazil have generous visitation policies, including conjugal visits for male inmates and their wives and partners. Visitation rights are often used as a disciplinary tool, however, and the visitors themselves have to stand for hours in line and be subjected to humiliating and intrusive searches by prison guards.

44 In 1998, the drug gang member known as Celso de Vintém paid 90,000 reais to escape through the front door of a prison hospital. Inmates also escape on a regular basis through tunnels that

are dug by inmates on the inside or, alternatively, by teams of paid workmen on the outside.

45 See, for example, *Jornal do Brasil* (20 March 2003).

46 The Ministry of Justice calculated that 25 per cent out of every million dollars generated by the drug trade is invested in the corruption of the authorities (*Veja*, 18 September 2002).

47 Law no. 7.120 – signed by President Lula – altered the Lei de Execucão Penal and introduced the Regime Disciplinar Diferenciado which states that inmates who threaten the social order within prisons can be held in individual cells with limited access to visits and the open air for up to a year. The law has been criticized by the Conselho Nacional de Política Criminal e Penitenciária as inhumane (*Jornal do Brasil*, 20 August 2004). For a description of the new prison regulations, see *Jornal do Brasil* (19 November 2003).

48 In May 2004, thirty inmates were killed in a prison rebellion in Rio, and some decapitated and burnt, because of an attempt by the authorities to 'mix' gang members. A subsequent investigation revealed that prisoners are routinely asked to sign forms releasing the prison authorities from any responsibility for their safety (*Jornal do Brasil*, 1 June 2004 and 3 June 2005).

49 Between 2001 and 2005, sixty-seven prison workers were assassinated in Rio. Some of these individuals were executed because they were responsible for imposing harsh measures. Others were executed because they refused to take bribes or because they backed out of agreements to facilitate escapes. See, for example, *Jornal do Brasil* (5, 9 and 10 March 2004 and 19 December 2005).

50 This refers to the fact that, increasingly, drug gang members are not from the communities where they operate, which is also a function of this period of increased rivalry and conflict.

51 I was told, before it happened, that all the *donos* associated with the

Comando Vermelho in Rio had signed a document approving the attack.

52 The attack on Rocinha prompted calls to build a wall around the *favela*.

53 This policy has met with limited success. In October 2004 a bus full of German tourists was held up on its way from the international airport to the Zona Sul by carloads of *traficantes* who boarded the bus. The Germans, apparently, were so nonplussed that they thought it was some sort of pageant put on for their entertainment! (*O Globo*, 26 October 2004).

54 The Sistema de Vigilância da Amazônia (Sivam), which cost US$1.3 billion to put in place and is supposed to monitor unregistered air traffic in the Amazon region, is – by all accounts – completely ineffective (*O Globo*, 30 July 2007).

55 There is also evidence that other drugs, such as crack cocaine, ecstasy and heroin, are becoming increasingly common. The federal police seized 27.4 kilos of heroin in 2001, 56.6 kilos in 2002, 66.2 kilos in 2003 and 50.1 kilos in 2004. The shift towards heroin production in Latin America is attributed to the fact that it is easy to cultivate poppies at high altitudes and on scattered plots that are more difficult to detect and eradicate than lowland crops such as cocaine (*Jornal do Brasil*, 15 January 2003 and 18 January 2004). See also *New York Times* (8 June 2003).

56 In May 2007, the police came across eight pieces of paper during an operation in the *favela* of Vila Cruzeiro which detailed the Comando Vermelho's income and outlays for the previous December. The papers revealed that each *favela* affiliated with the Comando Vermelho passed along 5 per cent of its takings each month to a central reserve fund amounting to 94,519 reais. It also revealed that in December the faction had spent money to buy guns and ammunition, to repair guns it already possessed, to pay a bribe to someone to facilitate an escape from prison, to get

a message to an incarcerated colleague, and to copy a circular informing allies that attacks on military targets were imminent (*Jornal do Brasil*, 9 May 2007).

57 The last time the *favela* of Rocinha was invaded by rival gang members in February 2006, the forty or so armed men possessed sophisticated maps and detailed instructions, were divided into four coordinated assault units and wore black uniforms similar to those of the elite units of the Rio police.

58 For more on this issue, see Lembruger et al. (2003) and Amar (2003).

59 See, for example, the interviews about police corruption with the head of the military police in Rio and the State Secretary for Security (*O Globo*, 17 September 2006 and 14 January 2007).

60 Eleven policemen were denounced for the crime. Only five went to trial and only one has – as yet – been sentenced.

61 One of the policemen from the battalion that carried out the massacre in Queimados and Nova Iguaçu tried to cover for one of the suspects and was subsequently expelled from the force. A short while later he was reinstated and went on to orchestrate the massacre of five people (*Jornal do Brasil*, 30 March 2007).

62 For evidence on this point from elsewhere, see D. Davis (2006) and Call (2003).

63 See also the various articles in Koonings and Kruijt (2004).

64 For an excellent analysis of this situation with regard to neighbourhood associations in the *favelas* of Rio, see Arias (2006).

65 As enrolment has increased, the number of students who quit school before completing primary school has also increased. For comments made by President Lula about the declining quality of public education, see *O Globo* (16 March 2007).

66 In this sense, I disagree with those who blame the recent increase in violence in Brazil on neoliberalism. Neoliberalism came late in Brazil and did not lead to a dismantling of social protection programmes or an increase in inequality, quite the opposite in fact. For this perspective, see Wacquant (2003); Portes and Hoffman (2003); and Godoy (2006: 161–2). For a review of recent research on the Brazilian economy, see Cason (2007).

67 A *carteira assinada* is a signed work card that defines an employee's function and guarantees them rights. When an employer signs a work card he or she has to pay approximately 8 per cent of the employee's salary into the federal social security system. It also costs the employee a portion of his or her salary.

68 The exceptions are, of course, the recent increase in the minimum wage and Bolsa Família.

69 Two events, in particular, accelerated this process. The first was the establishment of the port of Santos, which provided a coastal outlet for the emerging economy of the city of São Paulo. The second was the transfer of the nation's capital from Rio to the purpose-built city of Brasília in the interior in 1960.

70 GDP per capita in metropolitan Rio de Janeiro shrank 20 per cent between 1996 and 2002, and income per capita by 5.3 per cent (*O Globo*, 29 July 2006).

3 | Megacity's violence and its consequences in Rio de Janeiro[1]

JANICE PERLMAN

The 'Marvellous City' as a violent city

Rio de Janeiro is one of the most violent cities in the world. Its homicide rate is among the highest for all Brazilian cities. In 2006 the rate was 37.7 per 100,000 (an absolute number of 2,273 people) with São Paulo second at 23.7 per 100,000. The rates of violence were so bad in 2004 before the Pan American games that the government proposed building a high, impenetrable wall around all the *favelas* – literally creating a walled fortress within the city, to 'protect' it. It was even worse in 2002, according to one source who quoted a then murder rate of 62.8 cases per 100,000 residents. In both Rio and São Paulo the homicide rate dropped between 2002 and 2006, but, to give a sense of the death rate in Rio, imagine what it was like to lose almost 50,000 people (more than the total population of many Brazilian municipalities) to homicides between 1978 and 2000.[2] The Greater Rio Metropolitan area is no better. As of 2007, the homicide rate of the metropolitan area was close to eighty victims per week, with the majority dying by assassination, assault or stray bullets. In the same year, Rio State had 39 murders per 100,000 – four times the rate in the São Paulo Metropolitan Area, the second-most violent area.

The most dramatic and devastating change for Rio's poor in the last forty years has been the growth of lethal violence. In 1969, the poor living in *favelas* feared that their homes and communities would be demolished by the government. Today, they fear for their lives. They are afraid that they will be caught in the crossfire of the turf wars among rival drug gangs or that they will be in the wrong place during a police raid. They are terrified that their children will not return alive at the end of the school day or that their baby will be shot while playing on the front steps.

Violence follows poverty.[3] The *traficantes* or *bandidos*, as the drug dealers are called, began entering the *favelas* in the mid-1980s, and their presence spread quickly to the shacks. Now the dealers are becoming a problem in the poor neighbourhoods to which the *favela* residents have fled. In some ways, the traffickers managed to do what no state authority had ever been able to do – reduce the population of the *favelas*. Although only a small fraction of *favela* residents are involved in the arms or drug traffic, the drug trade and police response have been responsible for the deaths of thousands of innocent people in the *favelas*, barrios and *conjuntos* (apartment blocks). The violence has made Rio's most vulnerable population fearful of going about their daily lives, reduced their chances of getting jobs, lowered the value of their homes, weakened the trust and solidarity that has held the community together, and co-opted home-grown community organizations. Especially during the last ten years, increasing numbers of communities have been taken over by one of the three 'factions' (drug gangs): Commando Vermelho (CV or Red Command), the Terceiro Commando (TC or Third Command) or the Amigos dos Amigos (ADA or Friends of Friends).

If the greatest change in Rio's *favelas* from the 1970s to 2000 was the entrance of and takeover by drug gangs, the greatest change since 2005 has been the rise of armed militias. These self-appointed, off-duty or retired policemen take 'law and order' into their own hands – sometimes in opposition to 'the traffic' (drugs trade), sometimes in complicity with it. In the past five years I have witnessed an increase in the number of *favelas* controlled by militias, now said to be nearly one hundred of the eight hundred *favelas* in Rio. These vigilante groups purport to expel the drug gangs and offer 'protection' to the community. The 'security' they provide the residents comes at a steep price. The militias impose stiff fees on the residents for many aspects of their daily lives, including entering and exiting, getting a taxi or motorbike up to the homes, and delivering the propane canisters used for cooking. It is a tax that the poor can ill afford to pay, yet they have no choice.

Once again, the slum dwellers have traded one fear for another. Where fear of removal had been replaced by fear of the drug traffic, now fear of the drug traffic has been replaced by fear of the militias. This is what I mean when I say that *marginality has gone from a myth to a reality*: whatever freedom Rio's poor had is brutally curtailed as they find themselves trapped between the police, the dealers and the vigilantes.

The police: the violent face of the state in the *favelas*

The state has lost control. It has abdicated its responsibility as protector of the physical safety of its urban citizens, especially the poor. In my estimation, only about fifty of the eight hundred *favelas* in Rio have succeeded in remaining independent. The *favelas* that had participated in the large-scale government-sponsored improvement project called Favela-Bairro prided themselves on their autonomy, and their leaders held monthly meetings for a time. But at the last of these meetings, which I attended, in mid-2004, there were only a handful of discouraged people, afraid to take any initiative or collective action that would draw attention to them.

The police are the face of the state in the *favelas*. They are the only government employees present in these communities, and they contribute to the problem by their own violent behaviour and unwarranted use of lethal force or extrajudicial violence, as it is officially called. Community residents generally consider the police worse than the traffickers or the militias because the police enter the *favelas* prepared to kill anything that moves – even entering people's homes and shooting them in front of their own children.

The two types of police who play a role in *favelas* are the Policia Civil (civil police) and the Policia Militar (military police). Both the civil and the military police report to the governor of the state. The civil police are responsible for investigative functions in criminal justice. The military police are part of Brazil's national defence apparatus. They are heavily armed and can apprehend suspects, whom they then turn over to the civil police for investigation. Both the civil and military police have elite squads: BOPE, Batalhão de Operações Policias Especiais (Special Police Operations Battalion) in the military police and CORE, Comando de Operações de Recursos Especiais (Special Resources Operations Command) in the civil police. Most of the police violence in *favelas* is committed by the military police, but both BOPE and CORE are specially trained for violent confrontations and well known for their brutality.

The *favelas* and other poor communities have become the front lines of Brazil's drug wars. If the victims had been from the upper-class neighbourhoods of Ipanema, Leblon, Lagoa or Gavea in the South Zone, their deaths would have created a scandal, and the response would have been immediate and decisive. The lives of the poor are seen as less valuable. In Rio de Janeiro, an epidemic of violence has erupted in the last decade. And like any epidemic, this one does not strike all segments of the population equally. The highest homicide rates are among young males (fifteen to twenty-four years old) living in large cities.[4]

The police, rather than controlling the violence, contribute to it. *Favela* residents tell me that the police are more violent than the drug dealers, and the statistics of Brazil's Institute of Public Safety report from January 2007 corroborate these opinions, showing that in the first half of the year there were 694 'acts of resistance resulting in death of the opponent' (their code word for killing).[5] I assume that the true figures could easily be twice as high since the deaths of *favela* residents are under-reported by both the police and the government.

When police enter the *favelas* on raids, they barge into people's homes, break down their doors, knock the people around, and destroy their possessions, all under the pretext of searching for a hiding gang member. The gang members provoke this by forcing residents to hide them, often putting a gun to a resident's head and saying, 'Hide me here in your home or I will blow your brains out.' Being the sole presence of the state in the *favelas*, the police are free to behave as they wish, showing no respect for the residents. Their approach is 'shoot first, ask questions later'. In 2003, police killed 1,195 'suspects' during police raids, up from 596 and 897 deaths in 2001 and 2002 respectively.[6] Cano et al. (2004: 15–16) report that the intention of many police interventions is not simply to immobilize the suspect (via a bullet in the back or leg, for example), but to be 'rid of him'. They point out that the military police do not target only those they consider highly suspect or dangerous, but often innocent civilians to avenge the murders of other policemen. The lives of the poor have always been cheap, but, owing to today's drugs and arms traffic and police actions, the lives of the poor have been devalued even more (Dowdney 2003). This new violence may be the ultimate manifestation of the marginalization of the poor, the reality of marginality.

The police ombudsman or *ouvidoria*, whose job it is to follow up on citizens' complaints, reported that only sixteen of the 8,330 police officers accused of involvement in some type of crime have been fired; and that close to a fifth of Rio police officers have a formal complaint filed against them for such things as excessive violence, extortion, abuse of power, or failing to do police work. Comparison of these figures with police violence statistics from the United States generally, and within the Los Angeles and New York police departments in particular, helps show the dangers of the situation in Rio. In 2006/07, the number of deaths caused by the police in Rio alone was 1,330 people as compared with 347 in the entire United States. In 1995 in Rio de Janeiro, '9.3 percent of all killings in the city were committed by the police – more than doubling the casualties caused by the reputedly brutal LAPD (Los Angeles Police Department) and more than quadrupling the casualties of the NYPD (New York Police Department)' (Cano 1997: 32).

Ten interacting factors of violence

Even by the end of the 1960s there was more violence in the city than in the countryside. In my first study (Perlman 1976) I reported that in the list of things that people said they most liked and disliked about living in Rio, 16 per cent said they disliked the violence. In the new study (Perlman 2009) that response was almost universal. Among the coping mechanisms for living under a state of siege is a certain physical displacement of danger. It took me a while to register this, but I noticed that in all my conversations and interviews, whomever I was speaking with said that their particular area of the community was safer, more *tranquilo* (peaceful), than 'that part over there, which was really violent and dangerous'. Still, during the time I was in the field doing the research, I was not fully aware of the dire nature of the Rio situation. I saw the death tolls from drug wars and police raids in the papers and on television, but I did not realize that Rio had the highest homicide rates of any city in the world, or that the number of adolescent boys killed or the incidence of murders by police officers were several magnitudes higher than in cities of similar size.

In my new study (ibid.) I have identified ten factors that have interacted in Rio over the past twenty years to create the epidemic of violence: 1) stigmatized territories within the city that are excluded from state protection; 2) inequality levels among the highest in the world; 3) cocaine, a high-priced illegal commodity with the alchemist's allure of turning poverty to wealth; 4) well-organized, well-connected drug gangs and networks; 5) easy access to sophisticated arms and weapons; 6) a police force that is poorly paid, under-staffed and unaccountable; 7) a weak government that does not guarantee 'the rule of law'; 8) independent militias and vigilante groups with virtual impunity in the use of extrajudicial lethal violence; 9) a powerless population of over 3 million people living in poverty; and 10) a sensationalist mass media empire fomenting such fear of criminality as to foster acceptance of police brutality.

Stigmatized territories excluded from state protection Since their inception, *favelas* have been considered a 'no man's land'. They are deemed to be outside the state's mandate to protect life and limb, or to ensure the personal security of citizens. It took almost a hundred years for *favelas* to appear on city maps – during which time the number of inhabitants grew to a third of the total city population. After the coup of 1964 established a military dictatorship, police saw the *favelas* as enemy territory, harbouring communists and criminals. There were many unheeded complaints of police brutality, but both the mayor of the city of Rio de Janeiro and the governor of the state were appointed, not elected, during that time and there was no recourse.[7] The topography of the *favelas* makes them ideal hiding places. The natural environment is often hilly and steep with only narrow passages crawling up to the topmost parts of the settlement and plenty of trees and rocks for cover. The built environment takes advantage of the topography by using every inch of space, building houses on stilts, behind other houses, on top, alongside, under and over. It is easy to get lost in the maze, and that is a second factor making *favelas* an ideal place to hide. The ultimate advantage from a strategic point of view is that most *favelas* are on hillsides looking down upon anyone approaching, which makes them easily defendable.

The first independently elected state governor after the return to democracy in 1985 was Leonel Brizola, who had been in exile during the military rule. Evidently he made a deal with the police according to which they were not to enter the *favelas*. It is not clear whether he intended to protect the *favela* residents from the police brutality that had been going on during the dictatorship or whether he yielded to the pressures of the middle and upper classes to concentrate police protection in the wealthy areas of the city. In any case, that decision deprived *favelas* of state protection. The absence of police in the *favelas* made them attractive locations for the illicit activities of the drug gangs. These two events were very close in timing. The removal of police responsibility for safety and security in the *favelas*, which happened around 1985, coincided with the rise in the drug traffic. Within five years, the traffickers had become sufficiently well organized and well armed to take control of many *favelas* and had begun to challenge the hegemony of the state in these areas. The level of violence and the high volume of money involved in the drugs trade changed the meaning of the keep-out arrangement. By 1990, the military police were entering the *favelas* en masse, not to protect the residents but to kill the local drug lords and to confiscate drugs and arms. Gradually, between 1985 and 1990, the *favelas* became fair game for police surveillance and coordinated raids.

Extreme inequality Inequality levels in Rio are among the highest anywhere. Several years ago, the United Nations Development Programme developed a quality-of-life index called the Human Development Index (HDI), which covers education, life expectancy and healthcare as well as per capita income. The index, ranging from a low of zero to a high of 1, can be used to compare countries, cities, neighbourhoods or any size of community. The Complexo de Alemão, where Nova Brasilia is located, scores lower than Gabon and much lower than Cape Verde; while South Zone neighbourhoods such as Gavea and Lagoa have living standards comparable to Scandinavian countries.[8] But rather then being continents apart, having different histories, cultures, languages and expectations, residents of Nova Brasilia and Gavea coexist within an hour's bus ride in the same city and pay the same price for food, electricity, public transit and other basics. This makes the sense of relative deprivation much more acute for *favela* youth. Their aspirations are set by the consumption standards they constantly see on television and are reinforced every time they enter the wealthy South Zone.

To make matters worse, legal jobs are hard to come by, even for those who complete secondary education, so many kids drop out after the mandatory attendance age of fourteen or even before. They have nothing to do. Their desire for money, status, belonging and an identity of import makes the lure of the drug traffic almost irresistible. Gang members often mention the freedom of having cash to spend as one of the pay-offs. They don't become rich overnight, but they might earn in a single week the equivalent of what they could earn over several months at a minimum-wage job – and they do not incur the cost of transportation and bringing or buying lunch. Their role models have such prestige items as motorcycles, gold chains and rings, designer shirts and shoes, and unending supplies of gifts for the most desirable girls in the community.

Cocaine routes to markets In the mid-1980s, coinciding with the end of the dictatorship and the rise in globalization, Rio de Janeiro became the main South American distributor for cocaine and marijuana to Europe (via North Africa) and the United States (via Miami and New York). It was with the diversion of the cocaine trade through Rio that the explosive mixture of cash and crime began to devastate life in the *favelas* (Leeds 1996; Dowdney 2003). Brazil became involved as a repackaging and distribution hub when the US 'War on Drugs' closed down Colombia's borders, creating the need for new routes for distribution. More recently, the jungles of Brazil at the borders with Paraguay, Bolivia, Colombia and Peru have become the site of processing laboratories for the manufacture of cocaine from the raw coca brought across the borders.

The increased volume of cargo trade due to trade liberalization and globalization makes it even easier to hide material in air or ship freight for import and export. Rio is an ideal port as well as distribution centre. Cargo ships sailing from Rio are checked for drugs and found clean. They then pull out of the harbour and small fishing vessels come out at night and load the precious freight. The same thing happens when boats arrive in Rio. The ships stop and offload the drugs on to islands just beyond the bay – again by fishing boat – and the ships come in for official inspection squeaky clean. When the shipments enter the city, they come in bulk and require a hiding place for repackaging and distribution. Rio's *favelas* are ideal for this. They have sales points called *bocas de fumo* ('mouths of smoke', a name given to them in the era when marijuana dominated), where the rich 'playboys' can come to buy. Their lack of police protection and particular topography, discussed above, make them particularly useful.

Drug gangs competing for territorial control The first organized drug gang was born in the prison on Ilha Grande, in Rio State, during the time I was first living in Rio's *favelas* in 1969. The military regime made the mistake of placing political prisoners together with bank robbers, most of who were poor and came from *favelas*. The leftist activists, students and intellectuals taught them Marxist-Leninist principles and interpreted their crimes as acts of defiance against an unjust capitalist system. The activists learned about poverty, powerlessness and the importance of being well financed if they planned to be agents of change. The government, realizing its error, compounded it by separating the inmates from Ilha Grande and sending them to different prisons around the country – thereby enabling them to spread the word. When they got out of prison, they organized a collective called the Red Phalanx and later the Red Command (Comando Vermelho, CV), Rio's first powerful drug gang. Many went back to their *favelas* and found a source of capital from the illegal gambling racket called the *jogo de bicho* (animal game), which enabled them to enter the lucrative cocaine trade (Leeds 1996: 52–5). Most *favelas* already had sales points (the *bocas de fumo*) for locally grown marijuana. These became the focal points for the cocaine sales by the Comandos, who set up shop inside the *favelas*, often recruiting locals as aides de camp (see Dowdney 2003: 27, 30, 31, 33, 36–7, 39).

In only a few years conflicts over the spoils within the CV led to two break-off groups which became bitter rivals – the Terceiro Comando (TC, Third Command) and Amigos dos Amigos (ADA, Friends of Friends). This is how the drug wars began. Now the traffic is so well organized that a kingpin such as Fernandinho Beira-Mar, the local hero from the Beira-Mar *favela* in Caxias, can continue to run complex coordinated operations from within a maximum-security prison.

Sophisticated weapons traffic If the drug gangs had only fists, knives and broken beer bottles for their wars, the death toll would be but a small fraction of its present scale. Today's drug gangs have access to highly sophisticated weaponry such as AK-47s, M16s, AR-15s, IMBEL MD 2s, FN FALs, H&K G3s, bazookas, grenade launchers, and even anti-aircraft missile launchers. These weapons are more advanced than those of the regular military police, which is why there is so much confiscation and resale or reuse by the police – and they make killing on a mass scale easy. The drug dealers are better financed than the police and have better weapons. In fact, the police often confiscate the weapons in one *favela* and then keep some and sell the rest to a gang in another *favela*. Most of these weapons are manufactured in the USA, Russia and Europe. Some are swapped at the border of Paraguay for drugs so that no cash is required, or sold by rebel armies such as the FARC in Colombia. It is a big business akin to the drug traffic. The criminal firearms market in the city of Rio (in 2000) was calculated to be worth US$88,392,299 (Rivero 2000: 147). Firearms are responsible for the vast majority of deaths in Rio.[9]

Corrupt police force The police in Rio de Janeiro have a long history of corruption and of functioning outside of formal sanctions, accountability and transparency. Most members of the police come from low-income families, many from *favelas*. For them, getting a job in the military police is a great leap forward and puts them under pressure to 'perform well' so that they can continue to support their families. Yet their salaries are hardly sufficient for a decent life. On average, they earn about US$440 to $500 dollars per month, between $5,250 and $6,000 dollars a year. The majority of police recruits are young men experiencing power and demanding respect for the first time. Once they get the rush of power that wielding a lethal weapon gives them, they are sorely tempted to abuse that power. There are no sanctions or deterrents within the force. They can kill indiscriminately and use torture with impunity. And they make no distinction between *favela* residents and drug dealers – all are targets in their efforts to 'restore law and order'. Yet, with all this leeway, Rio's police solve only 3 per cent of the murders reported.[10] As a large number of murders of poor people remain unreported, this paltry figure makes the police look better than they really are. It does not help that only 20 per cent of the state police are deployed in the city of Rio, where 40 per cent of the murders are committed.

The absence of the state The absence of the state is essential to the mix as it leaves a power vacuum, ideal for the cat-and-mouse game that the traffickers and the police are playing. It also means turning a blind eye to convenient payments of drug money to members of the judiciary, political candidates and office-holders at every level.

Twenty-three years have passed since the return to democracy in Brazil. That is three years longer than the duration of the military dictatorship. People who attained voting age in 1985 are now over forty and many have children of voting age themselves. Yet Brazil remains an 'incomplete democracy' with a weak government and a population divided between full citizens and pseudo-citizens. A full discussion of the popular disappointment with democracy is beyond the scope of this chapter, but it warrants mention as an ingredient that helps the stewpot of violence reach boiling point.[11]

Militias and vigilantes have free rein As the drug factions fought each other over the spoils of the trade and bargained with the police over their take, newly formed militias started taking law and order into their own hands. The militias are not part of a network like the dealers, nor part of the government like the police. They are autonomous, self-appointed vigilante groups composed of retired and 'off-duty' policemen and firemen who take control of the communities through their brand of violence. They create drug-free *favelas* by shooting users or sellers, executing those known to be involved in the traffic and demanding complete control over all aspects of life in return for 'protection'. Without anything to sell, the militias supplement their salaries through extortion, charging the residents a series of fees for everyday necessities, such as the delivery of cooking-gas canisters (with a mark-up as well), cable television and access to the Internet. They have a monopoly on all vehicles, vans and motorbikes that go up into the *favela* and charge a fee for each trip.

Until 2004/05, there was only one *favela* – Rio das Pedras in the West Zone – controlled by a militia. But by 2008 they controlled over a hundred communities. No government action has been taken to impede the activities of the militias or hold them accountable for unwarranted deaths. In fact, in some circles there is talk of supporting them, and perhaps eventually legalizing them. The rationale is that the state cannot occupy 800 *favelas*, but the militias can.

These lucrative businesses – along with the drop in the street price for cocaine – have induced some to leave the drug trade and go into the extortion racket instead. This puts them on a second collision course with the militia. At the time of writing, the militias appear to control the broadband Internet and are running the underground Internet Service Providers. The police estimate that at least 70 per cent of *favela* residents pay for pirated TV and monopolized Internet. With such vast profits at stake, the violence continues to escalate and innocent people continue to be killed. Both dealers and militias enjoy immunity from prosecution in their use of extrajudicial lethal violence, and government gets a cut one way or another.

Poor people are powerless The degree of lethal violence in Rio is possible only because a third of the population is disenfranchised and considered worthless. If they were well organized, the poor would have the numbers to constitute a potent voting bloc and mount a convincing consumer boycott. But the firearms are in the hands of the traffickers, the militia and the police. The poor, whether in *favelas*, *conjuntosor* or apartment blocks, *loteamentos* or invasion neighbourhoods, or simply low-income neighbourhoods, are pawns in a much larger game, unable to turn to 'the authorities' for protection, and intimidated into quiet compliance. Their fear is comparable to the fear of communism that the Brazilian dictatorship encouraged in *favela* residents in the 1960s and 1970s. Now this fear is directed at murderous drug addicts.

Sensationalist mass media In no small part, the public acceptance of un-justified (illegitimate) police violence within an otherwise civilized city is facilitated by the media-induced frenzy of fear. Not a day passes when Roberto Marinho's media empire Rede Globo does not add to the panic over safety and security, whipping up public sentiment against the *bandidos* who are often conflated with law-abiding, hard-working *favela* residents. In this way the coverage reinforces the stigmatization and criminalization of poverty and deepens pre-existing stereotypes of *favela* residents, which in turn makes it even more difficult for them to get jobs. No one wants to let *favelados* into their home or shop or office – it's 'just too dangerous'. The cycle is self-reinforcing, since the fewer jobs there are the more temptation there is to become involved with the traffic. In short, aside from selling well, the constant messages of violence fan public hysteria, increasing acceptance of militaristic solutions to public safety/security; they turn drug lords into youth role models and antiheroes; they reduce tourism – one of the few remaining sources of revenue for the city of Rio; and they legitimize the escalation of violence on all sides.

The vicious cycle of violence and its consequences

The above-mentioned ten elements reinforce each other and create a self-perpetuating, vicious cycle. The profits from the drug traffic enable the competing factions to acquire ever more sophisticated weapons to use in their wars over the 'contested space' of the *bocas de fumo*, the selling points of drugs. The police confiscate these weapons for their own use, killing residents and dealers indiscriminately. The police justify this violence as necessary to get rid of the traffickers. Instead, the violence provokes the gangs to make dramatic demonstrations of their control over the city and the impotence of the government.

If the state is absent in the *favelas* and impotent in the city at large, the question of rights in the city becomes even more pressing. Putting drug lords in prison in no way hinders their ability to command their vast operations. They easily bribe the (underpaid) prison guards for use of cellphones even in the 'maximum-security prisons' and they have total control over who lives and who dies. In this way, the marginalized poor are trapped in a five-way vector of violence. They are caught between 1) the drug gangs who are fighting for territorial control; 2) the police who kill them with impunity; 3) the government, which is absent or complicitous; 4) the militias who control them through extortion and death threats; and 5) the media, which sell their product by terrifying the audience and reinforcing the divide between 'us' and 'them'. This cycle is constantly re-created, completing the *marginalization and victimization of the poor* (the criminalization of poverty itself) and the militarization of the police

It is unconscionable that, while millions of dollars from the Rio drug and arms traffic are enriching criminal networks extending beyond Brazilian borders and 'greasing the skids' of all branches of the Brazilian government, thousands of people in the *favelas* are being killed as 'collateral damage' and millions are being tithed because they live under the control of traffickers and militias more dictatorial towards them than the dictatorship had been. Unlike the ethnic and religious wars going on around the world today, the killings in the *favelas* amount to a war on the poor – the exact opposite of the US war on poverty.

Loss for individuals and families At stake for the people living in the 'war zones' (any poor community) is not only the loss of life, but the loss of peace, freedom and personhood. Take first the loss of life. Among all those I interviewed, in all three generations, one in five had lost a family member to homicide. And that was in 2001, so I can only assume that it would be more now. This result reflects not only the situation in *favelas*. Murder rates were nearly as high in the other places in which the poor can afford to live – *conjuntos* and low-income neighbourhoods on the urban fringe. And these rather high death rates affected the original interviewees in my study, their children and their grandchildren in almost identical numbers.

People have nowhere to turn for help. The notion that the traffic constitutes a 'parallel power' or a 'parallel state' that provides services to the community in lieu of the government is misguided (Arias 2006: 1; Arias and Davis Rodrigues 2006; Dowdney 2003: 70–72). It is true that it is a ruling faction that fills a vacuum created by the state's absence, but the traffic takes no responsibility for the general welfare of the population. Early on, when the traffic called itself *o movimento* ('the movement'), there was a certain Robin Hood mystique to the

63

community having its own force against the police. The term 'parallel power' was sometimes used to glorify the image of the dealers as the protectors of the community. But mostly the term is used by politicians and the media in justifying the extrajudicial use of lethal force that characterizes the 'war on the poor'. This hardly qualifies the traffic as a community service provider. In fact, community residents feel trapped between the dealers and the police. In the eyes of the residents, neither the dealers nor the police help them very much, and both do more harm than good. In the new study (Perlman 2009), among over 1,200 people interviewed by random sample the response was even more emphatic:[12] 81 per cent reported that the police, the traffickers or both commit violence harmful to the community and another 7 per cent said they did not know, which probably meant that they were afraid to answer the questions. Almost half answered 'both' and, among the respondents who picked only one, twice as many said the police were the most violent.

This generates the third consequence, the loss of peace of mind, of tranquillity, of the privacy of one's home. In *favelas* and *conjuntos* people are living under constant stress, unable to sleep through the night, listening to the sound of gunshots. This 'siege' atmosphere takes its toll on both the mental and the physical heath of the residents. Stress-related diseases such as hypertension have become endemic. People age early, they lose their health. Almost all the women I spoke to also expressed anxiety and dread at the loss of privacy – even within their own homes. They said that when the police barge into homes under the pretext of searching for *bandidos*, they pull everything apart, tear up the furniture, rip bedspreads off the beds and break kitchenware. When they fail to find anything, they leave the wreckage behind and storm out disgruntled. The things they destroy have taken a lifetime of care and savings, and, like the sense of security, cannot easily be put back together. The other side of the coin is that if a trafficker wants to hide in your home in a *favela* or *conjunto*, you will be shot if you do not accept.

With the added stigma of conflating *favelados* and *bandidos* has come the loss of work opportunities. Employers are reluctant to hire anyone who lives in a *favela*, whether as a domestic who will have a set of keys to their home or a sales clerk with access to the cash register. Then there is the devastating loss in home value. Regardless of whether the urban poor own or rent their home, it is their single greatest asset and their greatest lifetime investment. *Favelas* and *conjuntos* have thriving real estate markets despite being 'informal' or, in the case of *conjuntos*, in limbo between formal and informal neighbourhoods. But as violence has increased, their value has dropped, often to the point at which leaving means walking away with nothing.

The loss of liberty and freedom to move about at will is less tangible, but no less devastating. As a rule, the traffic has 'soldiers' with loaded rifles stationed at the entrance to each *favela*, and anyone not recognized as a resident is stopped and asked what they want. In order to keep police vehicles out and protect their turf, they construct roadblocks that can be removed when they want to let someone pass. They also control who leaves after dark. Ironically, drug traffic has turned *favelas* into places where you need permission to enter – just like the gated ghettos of the rich.

Loss for the community In addition to the consequences for individuals and households mentioned above, the violence has dire repercussions for the community as a whole, for community life, for conviviality. The loss of public space – or, to be more precise, its expropriation and control by the traffic – means there is no place for sitting and watching the parade of life go by, for playing soccer, for recreation, for leisure.

The loss of independent residents' associations meant the loss of voice, the loss of the only institution that represented the interests of the *favelas*. Since their inception over forty years ago, they had always had open elections for president and the other offices. Now most of the former presidents have been assassinated or forced out of the communities (escorted by the police as they and their families carried what they could of their possessions). In 1999/2000, about half of the *favelas* in Rio still had independent residents' associations with popularly elected presidents. One by one, as the years progressed, the elected presidents were eliminated, and, by 2005, almost all of the residents' associations were controlled by the traffic. The one exception was Rio das Pedras, which was controlled by militias. The people have thus lost the small degree of bargaining power they had during the dictatorship.

The fear of getting killed in the crossfire or hit by a stray bullet has kept much-needed urban services and programmes out of the poor communities. This loss of service providers, teachers, nurses, social workers, day-care workers, NGO programmes and even home deliveries and ordinary taxi services has deprived residents – especially youth – of what they most need to overcome the challenges they face just by living in a *favela*. It is hard to get qualified people to work in an 'area of risk', and even when there is a police station right inside the community, no security is provided as the police literally barricade themselves inside the station and do not emerge until they go home for the day. To my horror, I found that it can take children years to complete primary school because many teachers show up only two or three days a week. A recent decision was made to pass all children on to the next grade whether or not they passed the year – just one more indication that the lives of these youngsters are expendable and their prospects have been written off.

Loss of social capital and civil society One of the most deleterious consequences of what I have called *'o mundo de medo'* (the world of fear) is the erosion of social capital, one of the few assets for getting out of poverty, or at least for attaining relative improvement in the conditions in which one lives one's life. The violence and its twin offshoots – fear and distrust – not only prevent the use of public space, but also diminish socializing among friends and relatives, reduce membership in community organizations, weaken trust among neighbours and erode community unity. The flow of information about jobs, programmes and all manner of opportunities that was spread through informal community networks has dried up, and the coping mechanisms based on *mutirao* (mutual aid) are barely intact.

The erosion of social capital and internal solidarity represents a marked decline in the quality of life for community residents. When I first went to live in the *favelas*, the community spirit and solidarity were among the great pleasures of *favela* life. In stark contrast to the well-to-do areas where no one knew their neighbours, in the *favelas* most people knew each other by name and took care of each other in times of crisis. The mutual support networks were part of the survival mechanisms that the poor could count on to reduce the vulnerability of living on the edge.

The fear of getting caught in the crossfire or on the wrong side of a friendship in a drug war, however, has resulted in people going out less and keeping to themselves more. Each measure of community unity, trust, socializing and participation declined dramatically. This cannot be attributed solely to the drug, police and militia violence in *favelas*, since the erosion of social capital over the past decades has been documented in many places. Conversely, there is no doubt that *favela* life would be more convivial and social cohesion more robust had the drug traffic been located elsewhere.

It would be misleading to give the impression that there were no drugs and no violence in the *favelas* in the 1960s and 1970s. The main 'drugs' then were beer, *cachaça* (sugar-cane rum) and marijuana. The instruments of violence were fists, knives or broken beer bottles. The cocaine and weapons that are now ubiquitous were not readily available then.

And there was a generalized idea of respect. Respect is a recurring theme in the narratives of the people I interviewed. The quotations below offer a small sample of the oft-repeated comparisons the *favela* residents in all of the study communities make of the past and the present in terms of the traffickers' relation to them and other residents.

> The gang members and drug dealers were generally boys from the community – they grew up here, they knew who we are – they respected the old-timers, the workers. They did not threaten them; in fact they protected them.
>
> In the last ten or twelve years drug dealing has become more and more like a big business. Nowadays we don't know many of the *bandidos*; they come here from other places; they don't care if you are innocent or hard working, or young or old, or if you sacrificed to build this community.

Parallel with the decline in respect and the increasing anonymity of the traffickers is the increasing leniency of the law. The other major change is a growing trend towards consumption of drugs inside the *favelas*. When the drugs first entered, repackaging and selling them for the *asfalto* (the middle class and well-to-do neighbourhoods) was a way of earning money, and people in the community were in no financial position to consume cocaine themselves. But lately, many of the younger gang members are being paid in drugs instead of cash and are becoming addicted at an increasingly early age.

The people whose lives are lost – and those whose quality of life is lost – in Rio's *favelas* are small players in a high-stakes global game. They are expendable and easily replaced. Those who enjoy the profits are safe in their luxury penthouses in Rio, Europe or the United States.

Notes

1 An earlier version of this chapter appeared in Perlman (2009), a reworking of Perlman (1976).

2 www.nationmaster.com, Rio de Janeiro, accessed on 30 November 2008.

3 See Perlman (2004). For more on the relationship between inequality and violence, see Cano et al. (2004).

4 The highest rate is among twenty-to-twenty-four-year-olds – at 303 per 100,000 (ibid.).

5 www.nationmaster.com, Rio de Janeiro, accessed on 30 November 2008.

6 During incursive operations, the military police have been allowed to carry a 'second gun', a weapon of their own in addition to their official one. This allows them to plant their personal gun on an unarmed victim they have killed and claim that the victim was shooting at them. That is only one of many little tricks they use to hide the real number of innocent people killed.

7 In 1975 the separate state of Guanabara and the city-state of Rio de Janeiro merged.

8 The Alemão complex HDI is 0.587, lower than that for Gabon at 0.637 or that of Cape Verde at 0.722. In some European countries, the index is almost double that of Rio's *favelas*: Norway (0.927); Belgium (0.923) and Sweden (0.923). Brazil as a whole stands 69th in the ranking of the world's 177 nations in terms of HDI, with an index of 0.792 (see www.nationmaster.com, Rio de Janeiro, accessed on 30 November 2008).

9 In 2001, 83 per cent of the victims

were assassinated by firearms (Cano et al. 2004).

10 See www.nationmaster.com, Rio de Janeiro, accessed on 30 November 2008.

11 I borrow this phrase from the brilliant book by James Holston (*Insurgent Citizenship*, 2008). See also Holston and Caldeira (1998).

12 Selected in Catacumba (represented by Quitungo and Guapore), Nova Brasilia, Vila Ideal and the other *favelas* and *loteamentos* in Caxias, Metropolitan Rio.

4 | Coping with urban violence: state and community responses to crime and insecurity in Guayaquil, Ecuador

CAROLINE MOSER[1]

In many cities in Africa, Asia and particularly Latin America, the level of daily violence has reached such critical levels that it not only threatens the well-being of urban dwellers, but also the economic productivity and development of cities themselves (Moser 2004). Therefore, along with the challenges of exclusion, poverty and inequality increasingly associated with the growing size of the urban population, there are also the manifold problems linked to the safety and security of urban residents. Addressing such concerns is undoubtedly an important priority for the state (at national and local level) and citizens alike. What happens, however, when the state, at either national or local level, fails to address the problem of insecurity? Are neighbourhood communities forced to respond on their own, and in such contexts do informal norms of legality and illegality relating to violent crime always coincide with those of the state? This chapter seeks to address these questions drawing on a case study from Indio Guayas, a poor marginal neighbourhood in Guayaquil, Ecuador, while at the same time highlighting the complexity of the problem of urban violence at the local level.

As Koonings and Kruijt (2007) have argued, cities throughout Latin America increasingly contain territorial space where formal governance is either absent or ineffective. In such spaces the uncivil logic of coercion takes over, and such zones become synonymous with violence and insecurity. The case study of Indio Guayas, where drug dealers, criminals and domestic abusers live side by side with 'peace-abiding' citizens, addresses a number of common assumptions. Are such areas zones of anomie or do local community responses take over? If so, how effective are they? The chapter is intended to contribute to the debate about informal responses in two ways. First, are the poor living in peripheral urban areas passive recipients of 'low-intensity warfare' that they are powerless to confront, or active agents who make decisions and act proactively in charting their 'encounters with violence' (Moser and McIlwaine 2004)? Second, are their responses to illegal and violent activities homogeneous, or do a diversity of judgements made by different social actors relate to their particular interests, as well as their power to confront violence on their own terms?

This case study challenges a dualist spatial distinction within cities, as between more prosperous areas and the low-income 'slums' experiencing 'the reality of marginality' (Perlman 2007), and demonstrates that low-income communities themselves fall within a continuum in terms of levels of integration into the city, and, associated with this, differentiation in terms of agency and associated power to confront or respond to violence on their own terms. Nevertheless, it is important to recognize that this chapter provides evidence from one city. In comparative terms a broad range of issues, including transnational migration, spatial location in terms of drug production/drug distribution countries as much as city-level political, economic and social factors, may affect the norms of legitimacy and illegitimacy that determine well-being. Nevertheless, such an analysis cautions against simplistic perceptions of exclusion, fear and passivity, and shows how communities confront, collude and judge violent crimes. In a context where formal systems of policing and the judiciary are ineffective, and distrust of police solutions is widespread, this illustrates the way internal forms of power and control are contested as local citizens identify and confront violence on a daily basis.

Background issues[2]

The background to this case study is a research project that has focused on household asset accumulation strategies over the past twenty-six years using anthropological and sociological research methodology in a poor urban community in Guayaquil, Ecuador, called Indio Guayas. Its history has been contextualized within the broader macroeconomic and political structural context during different phases of Ecuador and Guayaquil's history. First was the 1975–85 democratization process, during which Ecuador emerged from military rule and established new democratic parties. This resulted in the municipal reforms that gave mangrove land to the poor in Guayaquil (Moser 1982) and in the community-driven processes for the acquisition of infrastructure. The second period, from 1985 to 1995, was marked by macroeconomic structural adjustment policies associated with a decline in state social sector provision and the increasing presence of international anti-poverty-focused agencies such as Plan International and UNICEF (Moser 1997). The third period, from 1995 to 2005, was one of globalization and dollarization associated with financial crisis, increased penetration of private social sector delivery systems, and rapid expansion of international migration as an alternative 'safety net' for many households.

Indio Guayas, named after its community committee, is an eleven-block neighbourhood area within the barrio of Cisne Dos, located on the south-west edge of the city. This area, about seven kilometres from the central business district, was originally, in the early 1970s, a mangrove swamp at the far end of the parish, running up to one of the estuaries of the River Guayas. In those years, when the first 'homeowners' arrived in the area, the swamp area was sold off by professional squatters as 10- by 30-metre plots to settlers anxious to escape high rents in the inner city.[3] The young population survived living in bamboo houses on the water and lacked not only land but all basic services such as electricity, running water and plumbing, as well as social services such as health and education.

Over the past thirty years the Indio Guayas community committee has mobilized and contested national and local government authorities, as well as political parties and international agencies, and acquired basic services. The success of this process demonstrated that this was a community characterized by high levels of community social capital, capable of mobilization and con-testation when required (Moser and Felton 2007a). By 2004 Indio Guayas was a stable urban settlement with physical and social infrastructure, and, owing to the city's rapid expansion, was no longer on the periphery. Children of the original settlers had formed families of their own, either in the community or in other parts of Guayaquil, or had migrated abroad, many to Barcelona, Spain. Community social capital had declined as the contestation role of the local community committee became less of a priority; in contrast household social capital, the trust and cohesion within nuclear and extended households, increased as families became increasingly dependent on multiple income earners and intra-household strategies to balance childcare and domestic tasks with productive work (ibid.).

Violence and insecurity in Indio Guayas contextualized in the broader urban environment

Where does Indio Guayas, and indeed Guayaquil and urban Ecuador, 'fit' in terms of its levels of violence and crime? At the national level Ecuador rates as an 'intermediate' country in terms of violence, as measured in terms of num-bers of homicides, with 13 annually per 100,000 inhabitants (Loor et al. n.d.: 2). This increased, however, from 6.4 in 1980 to 10.3 in 1990 and 15.3 in 2000, as compared with world rates of 5.5, 6.4 and 8.9 respectively (Villavicencio 2004). Although the highest levels are in the Colombian border area, nevertheless 75 per cent of the total number of 'deaths by external causes' (homicides, suicides and road accidents) occur in urban centres, mainly Quito and Guayaquil.

While the latter has the largest level of homicides caused by firearms, the former has higher levels of general violence (Andrade 2006b: 16–17).

Guayaquil, with a population of 2,158,976, according to the 2001 census, is the largest city in the country and the country's most important port. Despite a severe lack of systematic or reliable data on organized armed violence in Guayaquil, it is apparent that in the last two decades 'social violence(s)' has grown, transformed and diversified, with the large rise in organized crime of particular importance (Villavicencio 2001). The homicide rate in Guayaquil varied between 12 and 19 per 100,000 inhabitants throughout the 1990s, and reached 20 in 2001, making the city similar in terms of violence levels to Miami, Mexico and Lima, but still far behind cities like Rio de Janeiro or Bogotá (Loor et al. n.d.: 3).

According to Andrade (1994: 142–3), in 1986 and the first three months of 1987 there was a total of 33,000 crimes in the two provinces, which represented a 10 per cent increase from 1985. In this period, in Guayaquil, twenty-seven crimes were committed daily, and in Quito, eighteen. Also, more than half of all rapes and homicides were concentrated in Guayaquil. Throughout 1987 and 1988 levels of crime kept rising, and by 1990 around four cars were stolen by organized gangs in Guayaquil daily.

At the national level prison population data show that throughout the 1980s, especially in the first half, the majority of crimes were 'crimes against property' and 'crimes against people' (ibid.: 141–2). By 1990, however, data on the prison population showed that a majority of the crimes were drug-related: 35.3 per cent, compared with 18.46 per cent in 1982. This percentage was even higher in the case of women: 72 per cent of the national female prison population had committed drug-related crimes, which is seen as evidence of the growing participation of women in criminal activities, albeit in very specialized roles (ibid.: 142–3).

Villavicencio (2001, 2004), a researcher from Guayaquil, differentiates between three types of urban social violence in Guayaquil. First is organized crime, which includes activities related to narco-trafficking, money launder-ing, smuggling, bank robberies and assaults on other types of businesses, stolen cars, house robberies, road assaults, 'coyoterismo' (illegal trafficking of people), kidnappings, and public and private corruption; second, common street crime, which involves mainly gangs, small drug vendors, neighbourhood violence, domestic violence, suicides, assaults on urban public transport, and others; and third, other types of social violence(s), such as traffic accidents, labour-related accidents and malnutrition (food insecurity).[4]

Violence in Guayaquil mostly affects the poor. Fiscalía (Public Prosecutor) data on the province of Guayas for 2003 suggest that more than half were related to crimes against property and people, mostly a reflection of day-to-day violence in poor neighbourhoods. Gender and inter-generational conflict and violence are also a big problem, but reliable data are even harder to find. Violence against women started to achieve visibility in Ecuador by the end of the 1980s, mainly through the efforts of women's organizations, although the problem is still generally dealt with by 'blaming the victim' and remains a 'silenced' issue (Andrade 1994: 135–7).

Of increasing importance is the phenomenon of youth gangs. A recent typology differentiates among three types of youth groups (Loor et al. n.d.: 6–7; Andrade 1994: 157) as follows:

- *Bandas*: armed groups formed by young people (between the ages of eighteen and thirty), led by adults and organized mainly to commit crimes (mostly drug-related). Each *banda* has around thirty to forty members.
- *Pandillas*: mostly composed of young men between the ages of eleven and eighteen with an informal hierarchical structure, and organized around common interests (music, dancing and sport). These exist in specific geographical neighbourhoods, have no leader or rules, with some members having access to weapons and drugs. Recently, they have started identifying themselves by specific hand signs and the use of particular colours. There are an estimated one thousand operating in Guayaquil, with around twenty to forty members each. Some of the most well known are: 'Los Contras', 'A Muerte', 'Los Intocables' and 'Los Rusos'.
- *Naciones*: they emerged in the 1990s, as a reaction to official repression against *pandillas*. They are better organized, with a hierarchical, pyramid-like leadership structure, and a wider geographical base with branches in different sectors of the city and country. Their objective is to dominate a territory and obtain the recognition of other groupings. There are some fifty of them, each with a hundred to a thousand members between the ages of twelve and twenty-four. The larger ones include: Latin King, Ñetas, Masters, Rebel People, Hierro, Big Clan, New People and Némesis. They use cultural-artistic strategies to attract new members and publicize their operations.

Three of Guayaquil's twelve urban marginal areas have been identified as the most dangerous given their concentration of *pandillas*, *naciones* and *bandas*, namely El Guasmo, in the south-east, Isla Trinitaria, in the south-west, and Bastión Popular, in the north. All three areas adjoin Cisne Dos; yet community members in Indio Guayas refer interchangeably to *bandas* and

73

pandillas without categorizing them specifically and make no reference to *naciones*. In Indio Guayas the critical characteristic is whether or not young men are *sano* (healthy) or are involved in drug consumption (see below).

Andrade (2006b) identifies a 'circularity' of *pandilla* violence which occurs and is resolved inside popular and marginal neighbourhoods. The most common type of violence is the elimination or intimidation of the members of other *pandillas* from popular sectors, or other equally deprived people from the area. Historically he identifies the origin of these groups as occurring in 1970, associated with conflicts surrounding the land invasions and the emergence of new marginal neighbourhoods (Loor et al. n.d.). This was not the case in Indio Guayas, however (Moser 1982). Where *pandillas* arose in response to invasions they initially organized around neighbourhoods or schools. By the mid-1980s youth gangs were recognized as one of the main contributors to criminality; in 1987 the police reported that 1,000 groups were operating in the poorest neighbourhood, at first limited to the 'red areas' around the port, but then extending into middle-class areas. By 1989, there were between 1,200 and 1,500 *pandillas* in the city. The most recent data estimate that there are around 1,050 informal groups linked to organized armed violence, with between 40,000 and 65,000 young people involved (Loor et al. n.d.: 7; Andrade 2005).

The causes of gang violence in Guayaquil can be identified in terms of a number of interrelated structural factors causing some groups to become increasingly violent. These include the growth of the drug trade, increased availability of small arms and above all a sense of growing alienation and exclusion. As Woolcock (2007: 5) comments,

> ... inequality can serve to undermine any hope by those at the bottom of the income ladder that 'hard work', and 'playing the rules', rather than criminal or subversive activity can yield them (and/or their children) a life of basic dignity (let alone economic advancement).

Also important is the increase in poverty and inequality in Guayaquil, especially after the economic crisis of 1999 and the associated dollarization of the economy. In 2000 estimates showed that three-quarters of households were considered poor, of which a third were female-headed, with unemployment increasing (Villavicencio 2003). Along with economic exclusion has also come a growing spatial segregation of the city, promoted by urban renovation plans, between 'modernized' sectors and the so-called 'hidden areas', the illegal settlements and marginal neighbourhood, polarizing the space where youth live (Andrade 2006a). Rehabilitation of the city centre of Guayaquil is identified as a development miracle by planners and politicians, changing the city's image internationally. This plan also resulted, however, in exclusion of thousands of hawkers who were now banned from their traditional occupation of walking the city streets, selling everything from TV antennae to sweets. The economic inequality gap between aspirations and reality means that conflict occurs not only between groups but also within them (Tilly 1998). Guayaquil, now part of the global economy and full of consumer goods (TVs, DVDs, refrigerators and washing machines), has witnessed a change in social norms such that crime and robbery among neighbours and within the community occurs in ways that never happened a generation ago.

The state's response to drugs and violence in Guayaquil

The main response of the state to increased levels of crime, violence and gang activity has been one of 'repression'. Anti-drugs policies in Ecuador, for instance, have been based mainly on equating drugs with evil, and privileging repressive measures, i.e. reinforcing a 'policing-punitive' approach, especially since the creation of a new judicial framework in 1990 (Andrade 1990: 65). These policies have been applied to small dealers, and even users, with the construction of common criminals as 'social enemies' and evil people (Villavicencio 2001). There has been a lack of efficiency and efficacy of the police and judicial apparatus, however, as well as the corruption and the lack of legitimacy affecting such institutions. The prison system, for instance, which serves more to corrupt and further harden criminals, rather than rehabilitate them, is just one example of the state's inability to address the problem (Villavicencio 2001, 2004).

Anti-drugs policies have also been an excuse to justify wider repressive measures used against the popular sectors, given the association between *pandillas* and illegal drug consumption. The response of both national and local authorities to the *pandillas* has again been one of repression, with a special police unit created in 1986 to deal with the 'war on drugs' (Andrade 1990: 91). For instance, the More Security Plan (based on the experiences of Giuliani in New York) was launched by the municipal authorities in 1990, to control the spread of crime in the city (Andrade 1994: 142). The repressive apparatus was further strengthened in 2004, under a new plan to increase the number of police officers, their equipment and the spread of security cameras. Despite all the resources and effort poured in, however, results would appear to have been poor (Andrade 2006a: 16–21).

Finally, urban renewal and renovation plans in Guayaquil have also been associated with repressive policies since they have polarized urban space, increasing the marginalization of certain sectors of the population, and their delimitation to specific spaces (those non-renovated), and an increase in the privatization of public spaces (Andrade 2005, 2006a)

Increasing levels of violence and insecurity in Indio Guayas

Turning to the situation in Indio Guayas between 1978 and 2004, the longitudinal study shows that it has been a relative success story in terms of asset accumulation and poverty reduction (Moser and Felton 2007a). But along with the overall increased prosperity has come growing insecurity. In twenty-six years Indio Guayas has changed from a marginal squatter settlement without services and infrastructure, but with little youth violence or street gangs, to a consolidated, well-serviced neighbourhood, with second-generation families with children completing high-school education. With better services and education (but not necessarily jobs) has come increased aspirations and unfulfilled capacity to earn a decent living and acquire consumer durables. Associated with this has been a slow but invidious acceleration in the levels of daily violence, and along with this increased fears about personal insecurity involving property as well as personal safety from assault. Crime and violence in Indio Guayas are not new; it is the nature of their manifestations which has changed. At the same time, along with a deterioration in the security situation, there has been a consistent lack of state presence or involvement to support local communities in addressing the situation.

Households in Indio Guayas have always experienced burglary. During the 1970s, when the majority of houses had easy access through split-bamboo walls, it was the most common crime. Those houses built over water were the most vulnerable, easily accessible and not visible when approached at night by canoe; burglars generally came in from outside the community. During the 1980s, households responded individually by reconstructing walls and changing from bamboo to cement blocks to improve security. In addition, residents also invested in precautions such as bars on windows and steel doors, indicating a growing preoccupation with crime and petty theft.

In a 1992 survey in Indio Guayas, women identified personal insecurity as the second-most pressing community problem after inadequate water supplies (Moser 1997). Almost one-third of women interviewed had had their home burgled during a six-month period in 1992. Of most concern, however, was personal assault in public places, particularly on local buses. During the same period, half the respondents had been on a bus when a robbery occurred, of which one in five had been personally robbed. Almost one-third of women had been accosted on the street. The danger in this area was exacerbated by

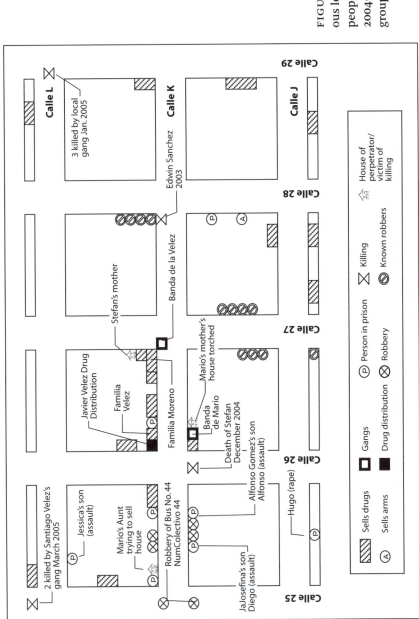

FIGURE 4.1 Map of danger-
ous locations, events and
people during December
2004–March 2005 (focus
group of three local women)[5]

the fact that local gangs repeatedly vandalized the existing street lighting. In 1992 the problem of *pandillas* was identified as increasingly serious. Working in small groups, young men, armed with knives or machetes and occasionally even handguns, moved through local buses threatening passengers and robbing them of jewellery, watches and money. Consequently, women began to curb their mobility, fearing transport was not safe, especially at night. This was particularly problematic for younger women, attending night school to improve their educational level and chances of securing a job. Because of security concerns, many either dropped out or did not enrol at all. This had the greatest impact on poorer households, whose children for a variety of reasons were more likely to attend night school.

By 2004 the situation had deteriorated even further, with daily life dominated by the banality and complexity of everyday violence, particularly as a consequence of increased access to cheap drugs, higher levels of drug consumption and associated crime to pay for the habit. The sheer complexity of crime and violence where perpetrators and victims live side by side, as well as those involved in a range of income-generating activities associated with robbery and drugs, is illustrated by Figure 4.1, a perception mapping undertaken by four women who live in the Calle K. While their spatial knowledge of murders extends well beyond their immediate vicinity, their knowledge of individuals involved in lesser crimes in the street close to their homes is far wider.

As Figure 4.1 shows, in a two-block area of the same street, comprising some one hundred households, widespread violence manifests itself in some of the following ways:

- six gang- or drug-related killings;
- a minimum of fifteen known robbers ;
- three young men currently in prison for robbery;
- one of the biggest drug distribution leaders residing six houses from where I live;
- a minimum of fifteen known small shops sell drugs – mainly cocaine paste – along with other household items.

Not shown in the diagram, but also critically important, were such phenomena as an uncountable number of teenagers cycling around selling or distributing further drugs at a dollar a go, folded into home-made school-paper envelopes; police cars cruising past with such frequency they were not even noticed. Pay-offs of robbers picked up on suspicion of an offence were part of everyday life, as were armed young men robbing women getting off the bus laden with shopping. Finally gender-based violence was widespread, although inter-generational changes in attitudes meant that tolerance levels with respect to domestic and gender-based violence were lower among some younger women than among their mothers.

Example of a violent incident in Indio Guayas and the community's response

Embedded in Figure 4.1 is an example of a very violent killing that occurred in December 2004, which illustrates the contrasting nature of local community and state responses. The tragic event was the shooting dead of Stefan, a known criminal and drug taker, by Mario, a healthy (*sano*) young man studying at the university. Mario was a member of a group of young men who often gathered outside their houses on the local street in the evenings, drinking beer and playing street football. In contrast, Stefan was the leader of a criminal gang that broke into houses and stole from local neighbours. He had constantly taunted Mario, threatening to kill him. One night Mario's friends had been drinking for several hours when Stefan arrived, took out his gun and, threatening Mario, said, 'I'm gonna kill you right now.' Mario grabbed Stefan's gun and shot him, and Stefan fell down dead in the street. Ricardo, Mario's brother, rushed out to help him flee from the neighbourhood. Then Stefan's gang arrived and tried to burn down the house of Mario and Ricardo's parents.

The police came, and their immediate response was to arrest Ricardo, who was innocent of everything that had happened. The local neighbours quickly formed a support group to stop the police taking him away. Everyone waited for an attorney to arrive, while local neighbours all contributed their savings to raise a fund of US$150. This ensured that when the attorney arrived he was able to bribe the police officers not to take Ricardo away as they knew he would be killed in prison. One neighbour then offered his truck so Mario's mother could quickly move their household possessions before they got burnt. When the gang members returned to steal everything from Mario's family home, the community leader, Susanna, and her neighbours tried to stop them gaining access. But the gang still managed to destroy the house, leaving it without a roof or doors and with smashed windows.

As the president of the local committee Susanna commanded enormous respect in the neighbourhood. Her leadership role over a thirty-year period had been key to setting up the entire social and physical infrastructure in the area. She also felt a deep love for and proprietorial ownership of the community and considered that it should be respected by younger men like those in Stefan's gang. Like her neighbours, she supported Mario, the perpetrator, rather than

Stefan, the victim. This reflected a widely felt community consensus that the killing was justified since Mario had been taunted beyond measure.

For the community members the tragedy was that the future career and happiness of a young *sano* university student would be permanently marked by this event, along with the lives of his family. In addition, his mother, Clara, was a local teacher, as well as secretary of the community committee. Loyalty to her meant she had safe passage out of the area. Equally Susanna was able to justify to Stefan's grandmother, Inez, also a community leader and a very close political colleague over the past twenty years (with the friendship formalized as co-godparents or *comadres*), that her grandson deserved his fate – as a criminal and particularly a drug dealer.

Residents had little faith in the capacity of officials to control the increase in crime and violence. Although a number of policemen lived in the area, it did not have a police station, and the community effectively policed itself. As a result, local community leaders played a prominent role in law enforcement and solving community disputes. Finally, the entire justice system was mistrusted. Judges were perceived as taking bribes, with those with greater financial resources better able to win legal cases. Getting out of jail was a matter of bribes with revenge killings often taking place once prisoners were released.

Concluding comments

This tragic event highlights a number of important violence-related issues. First, the ubiquitous presence of gangs in the community, but associated with this the distinction between gangs of young *sano* men that hang out on street corners playing football and drinking as a recreational activity, and other gangs that were involved in criminal thieving and drug-selling activities. Second, the instantaneous response from close neighbours to help a local family in need. Third, the unquestionable reaction to the police – bribing them rather than allowing a young man who was innocent to go to jail. Fourth, and undoubtedly most important, the informal assessment by the majority of community members as to who was guilty, and who was innocent.

Despite the significant erosion of community social capital associated with the acquisition of physical and social infrastructure and the withdrawal of community-based services (see Moser and Felton 2007a), Susanna and the Indio Guayas committee still wielded power in the community. Local barrio community leaders generally felt increasingly unable to deal with the new drug dealer elites and the gun-related violence. Yet with both perpetrators and victims in the same communities, ultimately Susanna and others recognized that they had to try to deal with the problem with practical solutions, particularly relating to keeping young men in school, as well as ensuring that they were directed to appropriate training opportunities.

This chapter shows that the all-pervasive crime in the poor areas of Latin American cities is often simply the tip of the iceberg. Underneath is far greater anxiety and fear associated with gratuitous murder, as well as rape. In the case of Indio Guayas, once Mario's killing of Stefan had occurred, it became the epicentre of an ominous dread that overtook all the neighbours living in the same street. As the case study also shows, however, it is important to recognize that not all young people are victims of violence; neither are they all perpetrators of violence. Different types of youth violence therefore call for different types of social justice.

At the same time, community perceptions of justice may differ from those of the state or other institutions. In the eyes of local people in Indio Guayas, Mario, the leader of a *sano* gang of kids seeking education and better opportunities, was the victim. He was taunted and harassed to the point where, after a steady night's drinking, he shot Stefan, a known leader of a drug-dealing gang. Such a disjuncture in perceptions of urban violence poses important challenges for policy-makers and planners, making it important not to de-contextualize youth as social actors, but to recognize that their identity and agency are embedded in the reality they experience.

Notes

1 My thanks to Katy Lankester for creating Figure 4.1 from the original community drawing, to Anastasia Bermudez for assistance with the background material, to Xavier Andrade and Gaitan Villavicencio for so generously sharing their documentation on violence in Guayaquil, to Cathy McIlwaine for her support and, as always, to Peter Sollis for his insights and solidarity. I would also like to acknowledge Kees Koonings and Dirk Kruijt for their patience on deadline delays.

2 See Moser and Felton (2007a, 2007b) for a discussion of the asset accumulation framework. See Moser (1996, 1997, 1998) for more detailed descriptions of the community and research results at earlier stages of the research project. The issues raised in this chapter contributed to the detailed documentation of asset accumulation and poverty reduction in the Indio Guayas community between 1978 and 2004 (see Moser 2009).

3 Despite minor differences between households in terms of family size and marital status, these neighbours were surprisingly similar in age, life cycle, household structure and professions. The men were craftsmen – tailors or builders – and the women were domestic servants, washerwomen or dressmakers. Both men and women were also involved in informal sector retail selling.

4 See Moser and McIlwaine (2004) for a categorization that distinguishes between social, economic, political and institutional violence.

5 The names of all community members have been changed to ensure anonymity.

5 | Middle Eastern megacities: social exclusion, popular movements and the quiet encroachment of the urban poor[1]

ASEF BAYAT

Urban 'activism' in the Middle East

This chapter examines the relationship between social activism and social development in Middle Eastern cities. It focuses on the myriad strategies that the region's urban grass roots pursue to defend their rights and improve their lives in this neoliberal age. By the end of the 1990s, more people in the region were living in the cities than in rural areas, with a large number of them subsisting in poverty. The proportion of the urban population in Middle Eastern countries in 1996 was as follows: Bahrain, 79 per cent; Egypt, 44 per cent; Iraq, 73 per cent; Jordan, 70 per cent; Kuwait, 96 per cent; Lebanon, 86 per cent; Morocco, 47 per cent; Qatar, 91 per cent; Saudi Arabia, 80 per cent; Syria, 51 per cent; Tunisia, 56 per cent; Iran, 60 per cent; and Turkey, 67 per cent. Because of this rapid process of urbanization, cities increasingly have become sites of conflict and struggle, and national struggles are increasingly assuming urban expression.

Prior to the advent of the political-economic restructuring of the 1980s, most Middle Eastern countries were largely dominated by either nationalist-populist regimes (such as Egypt, Syria, Iraq, Libya, Sudan, Turkey) or pro-Western rentier states (Iran, Arab Gulf states). Financed by oil or remittances, these largely authoritarian states pursued state-led development strategies, attaining remarkable (21 per cent average annual) growth rates.[2] Income from oil offered the rentier states the possibility of providing social services to many of their citizens, and the ideologically driven populist states dispensed significant benefits in education, health, employment, housing and the like (Biblawi 1990). Such provision of social welfare was necessary to build popularity among the urban workers and middle strata at a time when these states were struggling against both the colonial powers and old internal ruling classes. The state acted as the moving force of economic and social development on behalf of the populace.

The advent of 'liberalization' and marketization through the International Monetary Fund (IMF)-sponsored Economic Reform and Structural Adjustment programmes (ERSA) has provoked important socio-economic changes.

A large number of public sector workers and rural labourers, as well as educated, once well-to-do members of the middle class (government employees and college students), have been pushed into the ranks of the urban poor in labour and housing markets. In the meantime, states have gradually been retreating from the social responsibilities that characterized their early populist development. Many social provisions have been withdrawn, and the low-income groups largely have to rely on themselves to survive. In Egypt, for instance, as early as 1993 the United States Agency for International Development signalled the 'deteriorating social conditions in Egypt' (USAID/Cairo/EAS 1993: 2). Although certain social indicators such as life expectancy and infant mortality have improved, unemployment, poverty and income gaps reportedly increased in the 1990s (Westley 1998; Amin 1998; Assad and Roshdi 1998).[3] Similar changes are taking place in Jordan, resulting from a series of events such as the second Gulf War, which deepened the crisis there (Majdalani 1999a). Compared with other countries in the region, the direction of economic liberalization in Iran has been slow, owing partly to labour resistance and partly to the struggle among political factions. Although the Syrian economy remains predominantly under state control, the private sector is being allowed to expand gradually (Hinnebusch 1996).

The inability of populist states to incorporate or suppress new social forces such as lower-middle and middle classes that they have helped to generate has led to the growth of civil society institutions. When states are unable to meet the needs of these classes, they resort to (and encourage the establishment of) civil associations to fulfil them (Ibrahim 1998). Recent surveys on civil society in the Middle East suggest that, despite the authoritarian nature of many states, human rights activists, artists, writers, religious figures and professional groups have brought pressure to bear on the governments for accountability and openness (Norton 1995).

These overall economic and social changes raise some crucial questions. How do the urban grass roots in the Middle East react to their changing social and economic realities? And if they indeed confront their changing circumstances, what is the logic behind the shift in the nature of demands, sites of protests and patterns of activism in the region? To what extent is 'pressure from below' required for meaningful policy change and institutional reform conducive to social development for defending people's livelihoods and rights in the cities of the Middle East?

As a generic term, 'activism' refers to any kind of human activity – individual or collective, institutional or informal – that aims to engender change in people's lives. As an antithesis of passivity, 'activism' includes many types of activities, ranging from survival strategies and resistance to more sustained forms of collective action and social movements (Bayat 2000). My focus on the issue of activism is a reaction partly to the virtual absence of the people from the economic development discourse, notably ERSA, and partly to the dearth of scholarly work on urban social movements and social development in the Middle East compared with Latin America and South Asia.

I discuss six types of activism expressed in urban mass protests, trade unionism, community activism, social Islamism, non-governmental organizations (NGOs) and quiet encroachment. I argue that past collective or mass urban protests and labour unionism failed to improve the living conditions of a large number of people. Community activism has been feeble. And social Islam and NGOs address only some of the problems. Middle Eastern societies thus foster quiet encroachment as a viable strategy that gives the urban grass roots some power over their own lives and influence over state policy. Quiet encroachment is characterized by direct actions of individuals and families to acquire the basic necessities of their lives (land for shelter, urban collective consumption, informal jobs, business opportunities) in a quiet and unassuming, illegal fashion. These prolonged and largely atomized struggles bring about significant social changes for urban grassroots actors.

Urban mass protests

The urban riots of the 1980s were an early expression of discontent with some aspects of neoliberal policies in the Middle East, as various countries tried to reduce their deficits through austerity policies, such as cuts in consumer subsidies. Although it is difficult to determine the precise profile of the participants, the urban middle and lower classes were among the main actors. In August 1983, the Moroccan government reduced consumer subsidies by 20 per cent. Riots broke out in northern Morocco and other regions. Similar riots occurred in Tunis in 1984 (eighty-nine killed) and in Khartoum in 1982 and 1985 (number of dead unknown). In the summer of 1987, Lebanese involved in the civil war got together to stage a massive demonstration in Beirut against the drop in the value of the Lebanese pound. Algeria was struck by cost-of-living riots in the autumn of 1988, and Jordan experienced similar violence in 1989 (Richards and Waterbury 1990: 268).[4] Despite the acceleration of neoliberal policies, urban mass protests ebbed noticeably during the 1990s. Several factors played a part. Alarmed by the earlier unrest, governments imposed tighter controls while delaying or implementing unpopular policies only gradually. Aside from internationally sponsored safety nets, such as the Social Fund for Development in Egypt and Jordan, additional outlets were offered by the growth of welfare NGOs and social Islam.

The experience of the Islamic Revolution and the war with Iraq distinguished Iran from its regional counterparts. While many regimes in the Middle East were shedding their populism during the 1980s and 1990s, Iran began to experience populist rhetoric and policies only after the revolution. The Islamic regime's rhetoric in favour of the downtrodden (*mustaz'afīn*) contributed to the mobilization of the grass roots. The war suppressed internal dissent; once it ended, a new opportunity for collective activities, such as urban mass protests, arose. Thus, unlike in the relatively quiet 1980s, six major protests took place in Tehran and other Iranian cities in the early 1990s. Riots in Tehran in August 1991 and in Shiraz and Arak in 1992 were carried out by squatters because of demolition of their shelters or forced evictions. Even more dramatic unrest took place in the city of Mashad in 1992 and Tehran's Islamshahr community in 1995. In Mashad, the protests were triggered by the municipality's rejection of demands by city squatters to legalize their communities. This massive unrest, on which the army failed to clamp down, left more than one hundred buildings and stores destroyed, three hundred people arrested and more than a dozen people dead. The three-day riots in Islamshahr, a large informal community in South Tehran, in April 1995 had to do with the post-war economic austerity – notably, increases in bus fares and the price of fuel – under President Hashemi Rafsanjani.

Urban protests in the Middle East have had mixed results. Following immediate repression, governments in many cases have had to revoke unpopular measures. At times, they have made tactical concessions, such as increasing wages; this, however, affects only wage earners at the expense of the self-employed poor and the unemployed (Walton and Seddon 1994: 204–15). Where the protests are local or small-scale, the governments usually have managed to end them by force. When, however, social protests have gained national support by embracing diverse issues and actors (such as students and the middle classes making economic as well as political claims), they often provoke significant changes, including political reform (as in Algeria, Jordan, Tunisia and Turkey in the late 1980s).

Despite their drama and, at times, their remarkable impact, urban mass protests are usually spontaneous, ad hoc and consequently uncommon; they often involve violence and a risk of repression. Urban riots are a response to the absence of effective institutionalized mechanisms of conflict resolution. The social groups without institutionally based power to disrupt (such as the unemployed, who cannot strike) and those who enjoy such power but find it

85

inadequate (workers, students) are likely to follow leaders in initiating mass protests. This is not to say, as some have claimed, that Middle Eastern masses essentially lack a 'truly collective life', resorting instead to 'mob action'.[5] For in favourable conditions, they also engage in modern forms of collective action – notably, trade unionism.

Trade unionism

Trade unionism represents an older and sustained institution through which urban working people have defended their rights or exerted pressure on economic elites and governments to bring about social change. Trade unions have the potential to respond rapidly and systematically to unjust labour practices, distributive issues and political matters. At the same time, they are most affected by the current neoliberal economic policies, which often result in new labour discipline and redundancies. Originally, trade unions in the Middle East emerged in the context of European colonial domination. Their struggles, therefore, involved both class and nationalist dimensions – usually a tense strategic position. At independence, most trade union organizations were integrated into the state structure or the ruling parties, resulting in the current situation, in which unitary, compulsory unions make up the majority of labour organizations. This type of union, in which public sector workers constitute the core members, operates in countries with populist pasts (such as Algeria, Egypt, Iraq, Libya and Syria) as well as in Kuwait and Yemen. The Arab Gulf states, using mostly foreign workers, impose tough discipline and disallow labour organizations in exchange for relatively high pay. Surveillance, however, has not prevented occasional outbreaks of labour unrest (*Al-Ahali*, 3 November 1999: 3). Only Jordan, Lebanon, Morocco and Turkey have pluralist unions that are relatively independent from the state or ruling parties.

Union structure affects workers' ability to maintain their gains or advance them. Independent unions, more than corporatist ones, are likely to defend workers' rights. In the experience of the region, however, workers tend to use the existing, corporatist organizations to further their own interests, as is shown in the state-controlled Workers Syndicates before the Iranian Revolution and Workers' Shuras and the Union of Unemployed Workers after (Bayat 1987, 1997b). This applies also to the corporatist trade unions in Egypt established by Nasser following the liberal era (1928–52), when labour unions enjoyed a period of relative independence (Beinin and Lockman 1988). Currently, organized public sector workers, more than any other group, feel the immediate consequences of economic adjustment. Thus, trade unions are concerned with and often struggle against cuts in consumer subsidies, price rises, reductions in wages and allowances, layoffs, and government interference in union affairs (Land Centre for Human Rights 1998). The Egyptian press, citing official statements, reported in early 1999 the occurrence of more than five strikes and sit-ins per week. These actions resulted largely from reductions in allowances and perquisites and the introduction of fines (*Al-Wafd*, 5 February 1999: 1). In Iran, the 1990s saw a rapid increase in worker strikes (Walton and Seddon 1994: 10). According to one account, strikes by workers trying to catch up with inflation were so common that the authorities hardly noticed them (*Middle Eastern Digest*, 21 February 1991). New labour laws, redrafted to accord with the neoliberal era and economic realities, have been hotly contested, because they often strip workers of several traditional rights – notably, job security, especially in Egypt and Iran (Posusny 1997: 5).

Notwithstanding its social and political impact (Walton and Seddon 1994), organized labour in the Middle East has continued to comprise only a small portion of the total urban workforce. The vast majority have been self-employed, with a large fraction of wage earners working in small workshops in which paternalistic labour relations prevail. Although tension between bosses and employees is not uncommon in these establishments, labourers are more likely to remain loyal to their bosses than to ally with their colleagues in the shop next door. On the whole, between one-third and a half of the workforce in the cities (Egypt, 43 per cent; Iran, 35 per cent; Turkey, 36 per cent; Yemen Arab Republic, 70 per cent) are active in the informal sector, and thus remain unorganized and beyond the provisions of labour law (Richards and Waterbury 1990: 140). The economic restructuring of the 1980s has further undermined organized labour, as the public sector, the core of trade unionism, is shrinking because of closures, downsizing and early retirements. Numerous reports point to the declining capacity of the region's labour movements to mobilize. Organized labour in Egypt, Lebanon, Morocco, Tunisia and Iran is described as 'disjointed', 'defensive', 'decapitated' and 'de-proletarianized'.[6] Labour is becoming more informal and fragmented, with less or no protection, and dispersed across vast arrays of activities and spaces among the unemployed, casual workers and domestic labour, in the small workshops, and on street corners.[7]

Community activism

For the urban grass roots, then, urban community or neighbourhood may offer a sense of common identity and a ground for collective action instead of the workplace. In the neighbourhoods, most face the same difficulties in ensuring secure housing, paying rent and acquiring access to urban amenities, schools, clinics, cultural centres and the like. Community-based collective struggles for such 'collective consumption' through institutional settings are what in a sense characterizes urban social movements (Castells 1977; Kruijt and Koonings, Chapter 1, this volume). This kind of community activism, often contentious, should be distinguished from the notion of 'community development'. The latter has had a double effect of both maintaining the status quo and engendering social change.[8] Yet community development may also open space to cultivate resistance against the elites and foster social change. This is often the case when the grass roots initiate development on their own or are mobilized by local leaders, NGOs, religious groups or politicians (as in Brazil or in India). How do the Middle Eastern cities fare in terms of such community activism?

In recent years, a number of community mobilizations have taken place in Middle Eastern cities that bear some resemblance to urban social movements. At certain periods – notably when states become more vulnerable – even more enduring and large-scale mobilization develops. The collapse of the state during the Lebanese civil war caused community mobilization in the Muslim south, where its institutions continue to this day. Thousands from the south moved to the southern suburb (*dahiya*) of Beirut, building illegal settlements that currently make up 40 per cent of the homes in the area. Following the Iraqi invasion of Kuwait in August 1990, networks of volunteer and associational groups played a vital role not only in supporting civil disobedience, but also in filling the vacuum created by loss of municipal services (Ghabra 1991). The Palestinian Popular Organizations acted as the main organs of social provisioning and development in the Occupied Territories both during the First Intifada and after (Hiltermann 1991). Immediately after the Iranian Revolution of 1979, many poor families took over hundreds of vacant homes and half-finished apartment blocks, refurbishing them as their own properties and establishing apartment councils to manage them collectively. In the meantime, land takeovers and illegal construction accelerated. With the help of local and outside mobilizers, squatters got together and demanded electricity and running water; when they were refused or encountered delays, they acquired them illegally. They established roads, opened clinics and stores, constructed mosques and libraries, and organized refuse collection. They further set up associations and community networks and participated in local consumer cooperatives. A new and a more autonomous way of living, functioning and organizing community was in the making.

When compared with some Latin American countries, however, these experiences seem acutely uncommon. They tend to happen in extraordinary social and political circumstances – in revolutionary conditions or in times of crisis and war, when the state is undermined or totally absent, as in Palestine. Thus, few such activities become a pattern for sustained social mobilization and institutionalization in normal situations. Once the exceptional conditions come to an end, the experiments begin to wither away or get distorted. In Iran, community activism did not get a chance to consolidate itself. Lack of experience, the rivalry of outside mobilizers and political groups, and especially the hostility of the government seriously undermined the experiment. Instead, Mosque Associations were established not only to offer the locals assistance in distributing basic necessities such as food during the war with Iraq; they served also to control political discontent in the neighbourhoods. They resembled the 3,000 Community Development Associations (CDAs) that currently operate throughout Egypt.[9] Although CDAs contribute to the poor's social well-being, their mobilizing impact is minimal. As a field researcher working in a popular quarter of Cairo stated: 'Even in the highly politicized Sayyeda Zeinab, organized social action that involves the area's inhabitants seems minimal. The residents' role is usually limited to that of beneficiaries of whatever services ... are available' (El-Karanshawy 1998).

Needless to say, urban communities are more than small villages subject to individualism, anonymity and competition. Nevertheless, they contain numerous forms of networks and institutions. In the modern city of Tehran, neighbourly relations, according to a recent study, still prevail; members participate in assisting one another, pay visits, consult, and take part in weddings and funerals (Sarvestani 1997). In Egyptian cities, Migrant Associations have institutionalized some of these functions; funeral activities and maintaining cemeteries for the people from 'home villages' are their main activity.[10] Influential individuals may take advantage of the state-controlled neighbourhood councils (*majālis al-mahalliyyah, shūrā-yi mahallāt*). But the informal credit systems (such as the *jama'iyat* in Egypt and *sanduq-i qarz al-hasanih* in Iran) serve as perhaps the most important form of community network in urban centres. Social networks that extend beyond kinship and ethnicity remain largely casual, unstructured and paternalistic. The weakness of civic or non-kinship cooperation at the community level only reinforces traditional hierarchical and paternalistic relations with people depending on local leaders (*kibār*, sheikhs, Friday prayer leaders), problem-solvers and even local bullies (*lāts* or *baltajiyya*) rather than on broad-based social activism. In such social conditions, the modern institutions such as political party branches, local NGOs or police are susceptible to clientism (Hopkins et al. 1998).

Why is community activism addressing issues of collective consumption, relatively uncommon in the Middle East? One reason has to do with the legacy of populism, which continues to influence the political behaviour of the ordinary people in most Middle Eastern countries. Populist regimes established a social contract between the lower and middle classes and the state, whereby the state agreed to provide the basic necessities in exchange for their support, social peace and consequently demobilization, or just a controlled mobilization. This legacy has also contributed to the tendency among many ordinary people to seek individualistic solutions to their problems (Bayat 1996). More often than not, families of different social strata tend to compete when resources are scarce. This occurs even more often in the new and heterogeneous communities in Cairo and Tehran than in the old city quarters, where the relative homogeneity of inhabitants and the longevity of residence have produced a spatial identity. The coexistence of identifiable strata in a community – such as old-timers and newcomers, those with and without security of tenure, and different ethnic groups – often sharpens the existing competition, leading to conflicts.[11] Consequently, with solidarity intangible among the people, recourse to the mighty state – this provider and punisher – becomes an alternative way of achieving their goals. Many of them know, however, that the bureaucracy is unable or unwilling to respond formally to the growing demands of the urban poor, and they tend to seek informal, individualistic and even opportunistic ways to cultivate *wasta* or *parti* (connection) or bribe the officials. In much of the Middle East patronage seems to work more through individual channels and rarely leads to group activities. Favours are granted to individuals or families (in obtaining security of tenure or jobs, for instance) who then can bargain with their patron in exchange for his support rather than groups.

In brief, community activism in the form of urban social movements seems to be largely a Latin American model rooted in the socio-political conditions of that region (although it can be found in South Africa and, to a lesser extent, in India). The likes of local soup kitchens, neighbourhood associations, church groups and street trade unionism are hardly common features in the Middle East. The prevalence of authoritarian states and the legacy of populism, together with the strength of family and kinship ties in this region, render primary solidarities more pertinent than secondary associations and social movements.

Islamist movements and social development

Some observers view the current Islamist movements in the region as the Middle Eastern model of urban social movements. In this vision, Islamism – in particular, 'social Islam' – articulates the concerns and struggles of the under-privileged urban Middle Easterners.[12] The Islamist movements contribute to social welfare first by directly providing services such as healthcare, education and financial aid; at the same time, they offer involvement in community development and a social network, most of which are carried out through local, non-governmental, mosques. Second, the Islamist movements tend to foster social competition wherein other religious and secular organizations are compelled to become involved in community work. Finally, the governments, in order to outmanoeuvre the Islamists and regain legitimacy, are often forced to implement social policies in favour of the poor.

Although Islamic social welfare has a long history in the Middle East, it has multiplied and taken on new forms in recent decades. During the recent growth of Islamism in Turkey in the 1980s, 'mosques and their attendant religious associations represented direct channels of neighborhood organization and recruitment' (Margulies and Yildizoglu 1996: 149). The Islamist RP continued in the 1990s to focus on grassroots community issues – 'garbage, potholes and mud'. Many RP mayoral candidates even distributed in-kind incentives to secure support (Akinci 1999: 77–9). Similarly, the Islamic Salvation Front (FIS), a coalition of different Islamist parties in Algeria, prevailed in municipal elections in June 1990 in a very similar fashion. When the National Liberation Front allowed a multiparty system in 1989, FIS activists began to work within the existing Charity Associations (mosque-centred networks) that had been established in the 1980s by religious activists. Supported by the Charity Associations, the FIS took its political ideas into the neighbourhoods (Verges 1996: 292–305).

In a quite different context, Hezbollah filled the vacuum created by the absence of the state in southern Lebanon to construct the infrastructure for social development. During the 1980s, Hezbollah began gradually to address social problems faced by the Shiite community. It developed plans to offer medical care, hospital treatment, electricity and water trucking. It also paved roads, built housing, managed sewage systems, set up gas stations, and operated schools, nurseries, hospitals and sports centres (Kfoury 1996). It provided 130,000 scholarships, aid for 135,000 needy families, and interest-free loans. Repairing war-damaged houses and attending to daily needs of the population in areas of Shiite concentration were priority areas of intervention (Majdalani 1999b: 13).

Egypt's social Islam has become perhaps the most pervasive phenomenon in the region. The Islamic associations, often centred in *ahli* mosques (built and controlled by the people rather than the state), grew extensively, in part because the government's development programmes had fallen into crisis in the past two decades. They accounted for one-third of all Egyptian private voluntary organizations (PVOs) in the late 1980s, and at least 50 per cent of all welfare associations (or 6,327) in the late 1990s,[13] offering charity and health services to millions (Qandil 1998). One typical association, the Ansar al-Muhammadiya Association in the poor community of Imbaba, built a mosque and two schools and provided day care, medical treatment and an elaborate welfare programme (Badawy 1999: 110; Sullivan 1994: 65–8). Others offered video clubs, computer-training centres and similar services to cater to the needs of such groups as the high-school graduates who are the potential recruits of the radical political Islamists. Contrary to the common perception, radical Islamists such as al-Gama'a al-Islamiyya and al-Jihad were far less involved in urban community work. As rural and urban guerrillas, they concentrated their strategy on armed attacks, targeting the state officials, police and tourism. Nevertheless, where possible, they combined their political agitation with some welfare activities, as they did in such poor quarters of Cairo as Ain al-Shams and Imbaba (Mubarak 1995).

What makes all of these activities 'Islamic' is the combination of an alternative to both the state and the private sector, the religious conviction of many of their activists, Islamic-based funding, and, finally, the provision of affordable social services. The availability of funding in the form of *zakat* (2.5 per cent of income) from Muslim businesses and activists, *swadaqāt* (various donations), *khums* (a fifth) levied on the savings of Shiite Muslims, and external aid (e.g. from Iran to Hezbollah and from Saudi Arabia to the FIS) renders these associations comparatively wealthy. In the early 1990s, the Nasser Bank, which supervises the Zakat Committees in Egypt, reported a $10 million *zakat* fund (Qandil 1998: 146). Additional advantages include the spirit of voluntarism, as well as legal favour. That is, unlike secular NGOs, which have to surmount many bureaucratic hurdles to raise funds, the religious PVOs tend to get around the law by obtaining donations and other contributions from Muslim believers in places of worship (Ibrahim 1996a; Qandil 1993a).

The urban grassroots activities of the Islamists, in the meantime, compelled other social forces to enter into the competition, hoping to share this political space. The Turkish *twariqās* (religious orders) emulated one another in community activities through mosques and their attendant associations (Margulies and Yildizoglu 1996: 149). Al-Azhar, the pillar of establishment Islam in Egypt, began to offer similar social services to the needy in competition with the Muslim Brotherhood and al-Gam'a al-Islamiyya. Similarly, secular groups – notably, secular NGOs – seem to work hard to offer their own piecemeal alternatives. An estimated five million poor benefited from the health, educational, financial and community services of Egyptian PVOs in 1990 (Ibrahim 1996a: 34). In addition, the governments were affected, as they feared losing the political initiative to the Islamists. The Egyptian government's measures to upgrade slums and squatter areas in the early 1990s clearly reflected the influence of Imbaba, the slum community in Cairo in which by 1992 militant Islamists had created, according to foreign media, 'a state within the state'.[14]

Given these activities, to what extent does Islamism represent a Middle Eastern model of urban social movements? I suggest that although Islamism, notwithstanding its variations, may be considered a form of social movement, it does not express an *urban* social movement. The identity of Islamism does not derive from its particular concern for the urban disfranchised. It has never articulated a vision of an alternative urban order around which to mobilize the community members, whom the Islamists see as deserving welfare recipients, to be guided by leaders. The members are rarely expected to participate actively in making their communities. The Islamist movements have more extensive aims than simply focusing on the disfranchised, although many activists work through the poor communities to pursue broader objectives. Not all, however, operate even in this fashion. For example, in Iran before the revolution, neither the clergy nor non-clerical Islamists, such as Ali Shariati, were particularly interested in mobilizing the poor; nor did the poor take an active part in the Islamic Revolution. The mobilization of the urban grass roots by the ruling clergy in Iran began mainly after the revolution.

The Lebanese Hezbollah, with its law-enforcement apparatus, fell some-where between a social movement and a quasi-state. Among other things, Hezbollah constructed an infrastructure of social development, but few of these services were free (Kfoury 1996: 142). Currently, the Hezbollah and Amal movements control the poor suburban municipalities of South Beirut. Their attitudes towards the local people remain paternalistic. They often select (not elect) people to municipality councils and cooperate with those NGOs which are closer to them (Harb el-Kak 1999). Alongside their mobilization of the grass roots, however, Turkey's RP and Algeria's FIS adopted exclusivist and divisive measures. The RP-dominated municipalities practised nepotism and patronage, laid off secular employees in favour of religious ones, favoured contractors who donated money to the party, and overlooked illegal real-estate construction in exchange for donations. The RP's policy of 'cultural purification' tended to divide communities (Akinci 1999).

Contrary to common perception, Islamic social-welfare organizations in

93

Egypt are not sites of Islamist political activity. They simply act as service organizations. The vast majority have no link to political Islam as such. Only a few were affiliated with the Muslim Brotherhood and a mere handful with the radical Islamists, notably al-Gama'a al-Islamiyya. The rest operate on the basis of humanitarian commitment or simple business rationale in a country where the market for 'Islamic' commodities (Islamic fashion, books, education and entertainment) has been thriving. The explicit political stance emerged in the welfare associations not in the poor areas, but in the middle-class neighbour-hoods and among professional associations of doctors, engineers and lawyers who were allied with the Muslim Brotherhood (Qandil 1993b; Wickham 1996). The spread of Islamic services and commodities is not, however, restricted to the poor neighbourhoods or exclusively to Muslims. It extends to middle-class and affluent districts and to the Christian community. The Islamic schools are not free of charge but private institutions that virtually exclude the poor. The Islamic schools are geared largely towards the well-to-do, urban middle classes. There is no evidence suggesting that the urban poor as a whole have offered an ideological allegiance to the Islamists or to the governments that have fought against the Islamists. Ideological monopolies disrupt the process of pluralist democratization and frustrate the truly participatory culture that is essential for a sustained social development. But does the vision behind non-religious NGOs offer a more viable alternative for such development?

The politics of the NGOs

The remarkable expansion of the Islamic welfare associations in the 1980s and 1990s is as much a reflection of the trend towards Islamization as of the ex-plosive growth of NGOs in the Middle East in general. There are currently some 15,000 registered NGOs in Egypt, double the number that existed in 1977. By comparison, Tunisia has 5,000 NGOs, of which 10 per cent are charity-based. Lebanon's NGOs grew from 1,586 in 1990 to more than 3,500 by 1996, in a population of 3 million; Jordan's NGOs have increased from 112 in 1980 to 800 today. The Palestinian Indigenous Ahli Organizations (IAOs) increased from 1,000 (including 800 in the Occupied Territories and some 200 in Israel) in the early 1990s to 1,800 today. With regard to Iran, some accounts put the number of NGOs as high as 15,000. This is likely to be an exaggerated figure, however. During the 1980s, in the course of the war with Iraq, many informal people's associations were set up. Yet because of the predominance of populism and Iran's 'closed-door' policy, the country's record of development NGOs is insig-nificant when compared with that of other Middle Eastern countries. Since the late 1990s, a new trend has arisen for setting up professional, women's health and environmental NGOs. The Network of Women's NGOs currently includes fifty-eight to 100 organizations, for instance. The new thinking, in the era of President Muhamad Khatami, is that the local councils should be turned into the locus of popular participation, while the NGOs, currently numbering about 2,500, should be in charge of delivering services and charity.[15]

NGOs in the region fall into four general types in terms of their rationale or the impetus behind their activities. The religiously motivated associations are organized by mosques and Islamic figures or by churches and Christian institutions. They are inspired by religious obligations or religious-political factors. Classical welfare associations, run mostly by upper-class families, have now incorporated some developmental functions, such as income generation, training and community upgrading. Professional NGOs are managed largely by upper-middle-class professionals and, at times, by development experts who are driven by their training and humanistic urge or simply by material self-interest. And, finally, there are a host of state-sponsored 'NGOs', such as the Egyptian Community Development Associations and the Iranian Foundation of Dispossessed. These groups remain, in effect, an extension of the state. Put together, these NGOs are active in diverse fields of human rights, women's issues, welfare, culture, business and development. Here I will focus on welfare and development NGOs that target disadvantaged urban groups.

Several factors have contributed to the spectacular growth of these kind of NGOs. First, as elsewhere, there was a need in the region's poorer countries (such as Egypt, Jordan and Tunisia) to fill the gap left by the states' inability and unwillingness to face the challenge of social development following the implementation of neoliberal policies. Where a state was absent or defunct, as in Lebanon and Palestine, organized self-help filled the vacuum. The second factor is the flow of foreign funding resulting from new donor policies that extend aid largely to NGOs rather than to individual states. Third, there seems to be a unique consensus along the political spectrum – among neoliberals, the World Bank, governments and liberal and radical opposition groups – in support of the NGOs. According to a prominent Arab NGO advocate, 'NGOs have replaced class struggle and socialism.'[16] Middle Eastern liberals and the left also support the NGOs for their perceived role as agents of social change from below, contributing ultimately to development and democracy. Because of their small size, efficiency and commitment to the cause of the poor, NGOs are seen as true vehicles for grassroots participation in development. Consequently, they serve as a bulwark against the creeping spread of Islamic fundamentalism by offering an alternative outlet to the Islamist agendas.

How effective are the development and welfare NGOs in facing the challenge of social development in the urban Middle East? Most studies confirm that the sector is 'a vital component of the nations' social safety net and important provider of valued social services'.[17] In Iraq, Lebanon, Palestine and Sudan, where the states have been absent, defunct or in deep crisis, NGOs play a vital role in survival, emergency aid and relief. In addition, given the growing privatization and high costs of healthcare and education, the poorest segments of society would hardly be able to afford their increasing costs without these associations. In a sense, NGOs assist the declining public sector on which millions of citizens still rely. In my research in Cairo, for example, NGOs' premises often served a community function and could be used free of charge or for a nominal fee as day-care centres; medical clinics; family-planning services; recreational and vocational training classes in sewing, doll-making, electrical appliance repair; and the like. NGOs' headquarters often served a social function, as well, allowing local poor families, mostly women, to gather in public and learn social skills, such as how to talk in public or behave 'properly'.

Paternalistic NGOs perceive their beneficiaries more as recipients of assistance than as participants in development. It is not the place of beneficiaries to question the adequacy and quality of services or the accountability of the NGOs, for this would be interpreted as interfering in NGOs' affairs. It is not the target groups but the NGO leaders and donors who define the needs and priorities of a given NGO. A common problem among Middle Eastern NGOs is project duplication, which results not only from inadequate coordination, but also from ignoring the specific concerns of the beneficiaries. Competition and factionalism among NGOs, and the variations in donors' (often intermediary NGOs) policies prevent coordination of development strategies and create the problem of duplication. Indeed, local associations are often subjected to clientelistic relations with the intermediary NGOs, which extend funds to the former.

The professional NGOs, which grew exponentially in the 1990s, seem to have overcome some of the administrative and attitudinal shortcomings of the more traditional welfare associations. They attempt to practise participatory methods both internally and in relation to their clients, placing the emphasis on professionalism, education and efficiency. A number of women's, human rights and advocacy NGOs reflect this trend today (Schaefer Davis 1995). Certain features of professional organizations, however – hierarchy of authority, fixed procedures, rigidity and the division of labour – tend to diminish the spirit of participation. Rima Hammami has shown in the case of Palestine that local activism and mass organizations before the peace process were mostly mobilizational – that is, the activities were initiated, decided on and carried out with the involvement of the grass roots. After the Palestinian National Authority (PNA) was set up, however, the conditions of foreign funding turned these groups into organizations of the professional elite, with particular discourses of efficiency and expertise. This new arrangement tends to create distance between NGOs and the grassroots (Hammami 1995). Thus, what NGO activism means in reality is the activism of NGO leaders, not that of the millions of targeted people. These NGOs serve their employees more than the political beneficiaries.

In addition to the internal problems (paternalism and administrative inadequacy), government surveillance poses a real obstacle to autonomous operation of NGOs. In general, as with the grassroots associations, states in the region express a contradictory position towards NGOs: they lend them support as long as the NGOs reduce the burden of social-service provision and poverty alleviation. Yet the governments also fear losing political space, because there is the possibility of NGOs turning oppositional. In a way, this implies that in practice the state favours certain NGOs (depending on what they do) and is leery of others. For instance, associations that are patronized by well-connected high officials are treated better than are critical human rights and women's rights organizations.[18] It is, therefore, crucial not to approach the NGO sector as a homogenous entity. Unlike those of trade unions and cooperatives, the beneficiaries of NGOs are not its members and therefore cannot hold it accountable for inadequacy. The same relationship, in turn, persists between local NGOs and donor agencies; as a result, the NGOs are accountable not to their beneficiaries but to their donors.[19]

In the cities of the Middle East, the existing forms of activism in the communities, trade unions, social Islam and the NGOs do contribute to the well-being of the excluded groups. They fall short, however, of activating and directing a great number of people in sustained mobilization for social development. The socio-political characteristics of the urban Middle East instead tend to generate a particular form of activism – a grassroots non-movement that, I think, has far-reaching implications for social change. I have called this the 'quiet encroachment of the ordinary'.

Quiet encroachment

The notion of 'quiet encroachment' describes the silent, protracted and pervasive advancement of ordinary people on the propertied and powerful in a quest for survival and improvement of their lives.[20] They are characterized by quiet, largely atomized and prolonged mobilization with episodic collective action – open and fleeting struggles without clear leadership, ideology

97

or structured organization. Although the quiet encroachment is basically a non-movement, it is distinct from survival strategies or 'everyday resistance' in that, first, the struggles and gains of the urban grass roots are at the cost not of fellow poor people or themselves but of the state, the rich and the general public. In order to light their shelters, the urban poor tap electricity not from their neighbours, but from the municipal power poles; to raise their living standard, they do not prevent their children from attending school so that they can work but, rather, reduce the time they spend at their formal jobs to have more time for their secondary work in the informal sector. In addition, these struggles should be seen not as necessarily defensive merely in the realm of resistance but as cumulatively encroaching, meaning that the actors tend to expand their space by winning new positions to move on. This kind of quiet activism challenges many fundamental state prerogatives, including the meaning of 'order', control of public space, and the meaning of 'urban'. But the most immediate consequence is the redistribution of social goods in the form of the (unlawful and direct) acquisition of collective consumption (land, shelter, piped water, electricity), public space (street pavement, intersections, street parking places) and opportunities (favourable business conditions, locations and labels).

Post-revolution Iran experienced an unprecedented colonization, mostly by the poor, of public and private land, apartments, hotels, street pavements and public utilities. Between 1980 and 1992, despite the government's opposition, the land area of Tehran expanded from 200 square kilometres to 600 square kilometres; well over one hundred mostly informal communities were created in and around greater Tehran. In a more dramatic fashion, millions of rural migrants and the urban poor in Egypt have quietly claimed cemeteries, rooftops and state and public lands on the outskirts of the city, creating largely autonomous communities. Greater Cairo contains more than 111 'ashwā'iyyāt, or spontaneous settlements housing more than 6 million people who have subdivided agricultural lands and put up shelters unlawfully. Some 84 per cent of all housing units from 1970 and 1981 were informally built. The capital for construction comes mainly from the *jam'iyyāt*, informal credit systems located in neighbourhoods. Many rent the homes unlawfully to other poor families. The prospective tenant provides the 'key money', which he borrows from a *jama'iyya*, to a plot holder, who then uses it to build but rents it to the provider of the key money. The plot holder becomes a homeowner, and the new tenant finds a place to live. Both break the law that allows only one year's advance on rent.[21]

Once settled, the poor tend to force the authorities to extend living amenities, or collective consumption, to their neighbourhoods by otherwise tapping them illegally. Many poor in Tehran, Cairo, Istanbul, Tunis and other cities use illegal running water and electricity by connecting their homes to electricity poles, extending water pipes to their domiciles, or sharing or manipulating utility meters. This informal and often uncharged use of collective services leaves governments little choice but selectively to integrate the informal settlements, hoping to commit the residents to paying for services they have thus far used illegally. Securing property and community tax is another consideration. Although the poor welcome the extension of provisions, they often cannot afford to pay the bills. Therefore, it is not uncommon to see reinformalization springing up from the fringes of the new formalized communities (as in Tehran's Islamshahr and Cairo's Izbat al-Hajjana). In the domain of work, 'street subsistence workers' quietly take over public thoroughfares to conduct their business on the vast parallel economy. The streets in the commercial districts of Middle Eastern cities are colonized by street vendors who encroach on favourable business opportunities that shopkeepers have created. Cairo reportedly has 600,000 street vendors, and Tehran, until recently, had some 150,000. Informality means not only that the actors generally escape the costs of formality (tax regulation, for instance) but that they also benefit from the theft of imported goods, brands and intellectual property. Thousands of poor in Cairo, Istanbul and Tehran subsist on tips from parking cars in the streets that they control and organize in such a way as to create maximum parking space. They have turned many streets into virtual parking lots, which they privately control by creating working gangs with elaborate internal organization.

Governments usually send mixed signals about quiet encroachment. On the one hand, they see the people helping themselves by building their own shelters, getting their own services, creating their own jobs. On the other hand, they realize that these activities are carried out largely at the cost of the state, the propertied and the public. Equally important, the poor tend to out-administer the authorities by establishing a different public order, acting independently and often tarnishing the image of modernity the nation seeks to portray. Yet encroachment is tolerated in practice as long as it appears limited. But once it goes too far, governments often react. Post-revolutionary Iran, for instance, saw many bloody confrontations between the security forces and encroachers. Daily police harassment is a common practice in many Middle Eastern cities. Nevertheless, the frequent offensives against squatters and street vendors often fail to bring a result. The actors either resort to on-the-spot resistance (as in Iran) or, more commonly, resume their activities quietly following each tactical retreat (as in Egypt).

Quiet encroachment, therefore, is not a politics of collective demand-making, a politics of protest. Rather, it is a mix of individual and collective direct action. Yet, in the long run, the encroachment strategy generates a reality on the ground with which states often find no option but to come to terms. In the end, the poor manage to bring about significant changes in their own lives, the urban structure and social policy. It is precisely this centrality of the agency, of the urban grass roots, which distinguishes quiet encroachment from any incremental social change that may result from urbanization in general. Although this kind of activism represents a lifelong, sustained and self-generating advance, it is largely unlawful and constantly involves risk of harassment, insecurity and repression. As fluid and unstructured forms of activism, encroachment has the advantage of flexibility and versatility, but it falls short of developing legal, financial, organizational and even moral support. Yet the poor's encroachment on the propertied and powerful, the public and the state is surely not unlimited. The grass roots might be able to secure many necessary provisions, jobs and urban services – and these are certainly crucial. But how can they attain schools, public parks, health insurance and security at home and work, which are linked to the larger structures and processes? One should perhaps begin by recognizing both the potential and the limitations of grassroots activism, as well as state involvement in redistribution matters on a large scale.

Conclusions

Early reaction by the urban grass roots to aspects of ERSA policies during the 1980s included developing coping strategies and mounting urban riots. These strategies, however, seem to have given way to more institutionalized methods of dealing with austerity. The safety nets provided by social Islam and NGOs (coupled with state repression) contributed to this shift in method. With political Islam undermined (institutionalized, co-opted or curbed) by the end of the 1990s, social Islam, 'NGOization' and quiet encroachment, despite their flaws, appear to have become the dominant forms of activism that now contribute to improving some aspects of people's lives in Middle Eastern countries. Although quiet encroachment has a longer history, the spread of Islamism and NGOs gained new momentum in the 1980s and especially in the 1990s, the period in which neoliberal economic policies began to be implemented. The growth of these types of activism (along with the new social movements associated with women and human rights) coincides with the relative decline in traditional class-based movements such as trade unionism. The growth of urban informality means that struggles for wages and conditions, the typical focus of traditional trade unionism, are losing ground in favour of broader concerns for jobs, informal work conditions and affordable cost of living. Rapid urbanization, however, increases the demand for urban collective consumption – shelter, decent housing, electricity, piped water, transportation, healthcare and education. This desire for citizenship, expressed in community membership and developmental rights, is one that traditional trade unionism is unable to address.

By the close of the 1990s, some Middle Eastern governments were cautiously recognizing the activities of some civil-society organizations, especially the social-development NGOs. New NGO laws in Egypt and Palestine, public expression of more positive attitudes in Jordan, and the support given by reformist President Khatami to popular participation in Iran demonstrate some change of attitude. Yet these measures fall short of empowering civil-society organizations from above and encouraging social development from below. It is, therefore, mainly to the strategy of quiet encroachment that the urban grass roots in the Middle East resort in order to fulfil their growing needs.

Thus emerges a salient feature of grassroots activism in the region: it is characterized less by demand-making movements than by direct actions, be they individual, informal or institutional. Hence, largely because of the inefficient and authoritarian nature of states, people are less inclined to get together to demand housing than to acquire that housing directly. Similarly, Mosque Associations, instead of mobilizing people to demand welfare from the state, attempt to supply the services directly. Otherwise, people exert collective pressure when their already acquired gains are threatened. In this process, the intervention of advocacy NGOs (such as those for human rights, women or democracy) to publicize the cause of the grass roots often contributes significantly to their struggles.

These claim-making acts, collective or individual, have both practical and policy implications. Through direct actions, the grass roots and their middle-class supporters make themselves heard; they create realities on the ground with which the authorities sooner or later must come to terms.[22] In short, pressure from below in the experience of the Middle East is highly relevant to social development. Given the gradual retreat of states from their responsibilities in offering social welfare, the urban poor in the Middle East would have been in a far worse condition had grassroots actions been totally absent. Yet grassroots activities do have limitations in terms of their own internal constraints, their capacity to win concessions adequately, and in relation to the constraints directed from the states. It is a mistake to leave the entire task of social development to initiatives from below; a bigger mistake is to give up on the states – in particular, on their crucial role in large-scale distribution. Yet imagining policy change and the concrete improvement of people's lives without their pressure or direct action seems no more than an unwarranted illusion.

Notes

1 A previous version of this chapter was published as 'Activism and social development in the Middle East', *International Journal of Middle East Studies*, vol. 34 (2002), pp. 1–28.

2 The average gross national product growth rates for selected Middle Eastern countries during the 1970–79 period were as follows: Egypt, 7.6 per cent; Iran, 22.2 per cent; Saudi Arabia, 37.2 per cent; Turkey, 15.1 per cent; Kuwait, 22.6 per cent; Syria, 15.4 per cent; Iraq, 28.8 per cent; Jordan, 19.6 per cent (International Monetary Fund 1996).

3 For a more recent evaluation of Egypt's development process, see Adams (2000).

4 For a more thorough analysis, see Walton and Seddon (1994).

5 See, for instance, Lapidus (1967: 107).

6 For these, I have relied on papers presented at the Workshop on Changing Labour and Restructuring Unionism, First Mediterranean Social and Political Meeting, Florence, 22–26 March 2000. See the papers by Catusse (2000); Kawthar (2000); Rekik (2000); and Clement (2000). On Egypt, see also Farag (2000: 7) and Gamile (2000).

7 For Egypt, see various reports, including Farag (2000: 7). In Iran, the conservative parliament ratified a law in early 2000 that excludes workshops with fewer than five workers from the provisions of the Labour Law in order to increase productivity and investment.

8 See *Community Development Journal*, special issue, 32(3) (1997), esp. Popple and Shaw (1997).

9 For a good analysis of the CDAs, see Mahfouz (1992).

10 In 1990, there were 823 such associations, 80 per cent of them concentrated in the greater Cairo area (Tanada 1996).

11 For a report on Kafr Seif, see Abdel Taher (1986); and for Khak-e Safid, see Khosrowkhavar (1992).

12 See, for instance, Kepel (1986); Ayubi (1991); J. Ismail (2000); and Lubeck and Britts (2001).

13 The latter figure as given by the current minister of social affairs, Mervat Tallawi (*Aqidati*, 28 October 1997: 17).

14 Not surprisingly, Western Munira of Imbaba, the stronghold of the Islamists, has been allocated more funding for its development than any other district in North Giza, to the east of Cairo. Between 1992/93 and 1995/96, some 372.5 million Egyptian pounds were spent on constructing, upgrading and burnishing this area (*Al-Ahram Weekly*, 24–30 October 1996: 12).

15 See the interview with Saiid Hajjarian, a leader of Tehran City Council and an adviser to President Khatami, in *Middle East Report* 212 (1999). For the data on NGOs, see Qandil (1998: 139); Majdalani (1999c: 14); Majdalani (1999a: 2); Nakhleh (1991); *Cairo Times* (2–15 September 1999: 21); Ebtekar (1998: 10). Namazi (2000) provides useful early data.

16 This statement was made in the Regional Follow-Up Conference of Arab NGOs, held in Cairo, 17–19 May 1997.

17 Among many reports expressing such views, see, for instance, LaTowsky (1994).

18 Interview with Hasan el-Banna, an official specializing in NGOs in the Ministry of Social Affairs, 1996.

19 For more detail, see Lindberg et al. (1995: 57–8).

20 For these theoretical segments, I draw on Bayat (1997a: ch. 1).

21 For a more detailed description, see Wikan (1997).

22 Thus, on 1 May 1993, a year after the Imbaba incident in Egypt, President Mubarak authorized 'an immediate implementation of a national program in upgrading the most important services and facilities in haphazardly built areas in all governorates'. A national five-year-plan campaign was announced covering the period from 1993 to 1998, costing 3.8 billion Egyptian pounds. By 1996, 127 of 527 targeted zones had been 'fully upgraded' (*Al-Ahram Weekly*, 17–23 October 1996: 12).

TWO | **Political and policy dimensions of urban exclusion and violence**

6 | Urban governance and the paradox of conflict

JO BEALL

Cities, in particular megacities that incorporate both urban problems and political and mobilizational creative potential on an enlarged scale, are sites of cooperation and contestation; between government and citizens, workers and employers, service providers and users, producers and consumers, known communities and distant strangers. Conflict is an inevitable dynamic of urbanization and a necessary catalyst for social change. Yet it can be an ambiguous process with variable outcomes. A question that preoccupies urban scholars is whether cities and urbanism and the cooperation and contestation they generate fuel vigorous democratic politics. Put another way, does the size, density and proximity of people in living cities and the greater complexity and interdependence of urban institutions give rise to socio-spatial forces that stimulate or impede collective action in a way that is specific to urban agglomerations? This chapter explores the factors that render conflict in cities creative or destructive. In doing so it considers the increasing prevalence of urban violence and its consequences for urban governance.

The creative potential of cities

Lewis Wirth famously defined a city as a 'relatively large, dense and permanent settlement of socially heterogeneous individuals' whose proximity gave rise to a distinctly urban way of life (Wirth 1938). The economist Alfred Marshall also argued that the proximity of economic agents could improve the performance of a firm or industry, allowing access to a wider and more diverse pool of labour and other inputs and facilitating learning and diffusion (Marshall 1920: 267–7). The late Jane Jacobs argued that the diversity found in cities fuels economic innovation, to the advantage of both urban and national economies. For her cities were 'unique in their abilities to shape and reshape the economies of other settlements, including those far removed from them geographically' (Jacobs 1984: 32). Except in the case of badly run or dysfunctional cities where the negative externalities of urbanization prevail, contemporary economists generally see the benefits of agglomeration as outweighing the costs, owing to economies of scale and reduced transaction costs (Henderson 2003; Venables 2005).

Sociologists and anthropologists are more equivocal about the benefits of highly concentrated and socially differentiated populations owing to: 'the economic and ecological interdependencies and the creative – as well as occasionally destructive – synergisms that arise from the purposeful clustering and collective cohabitation of people in space' (Soja 2000: 12). Hence the broader social sciences celebrate the forging of urban identities through processes of hybridization and creolization but they are also circumspect about the favourable prospects of cosmopolitanism and focus on the challenges posed by difference (Tajbakhsh 2002; Vertovec and Cohen 2002). Mostar in Bosnia-Herzegovina provides a stark example of both the potential and challenges posed by a multicultural cosmopolitan city. For centuries Muslims, Catholic Croats and Orthodox Serbs lived successfully together, with the seventeenth-century Turkish bridge linking these communities becoming a symbol of this harmony. Surviving both the First and Second World Wars, its very symbolism led to this ancient bridge being blown up in 1993 during the bitter civil war that saw the end of the former Yugoslavia. For equally symbolic reasons it was reconstructed after the war as a matter of priority, opening in 2004 amid lavish celebrations and international attention.

Urbanism is seen as particularly important for politics, making cities 'privileged places for democratic innovation' (Borja and Castells 1997: 246–51). Borrowing from social psychology the term *propinquity* – meaning physical or psychological proximity among people – political geographers have applied it to the constructive political effects on urban social actors that result from being near to one another and to decision-making processes (Amin and Thrift 2002). Cities have been identified with the formation of citizenship. Holston and Appadurai have argued, for example, that the proximity and visibility of inequality in cities can lead to more intense struggles for citizenship:

> The mobilizations of those excluded from the circle of citizens, their rallies against the hypocrisies of ideology of universal equality and respect, have expanded democracies everywhere: they generate new kinds of citizens, new sources of law, and new participation in the decisions that bind. (Holston and Appadurai 1993: 1)

Over a much longer time horizon Tim Dyson has demonstrated a historically positive relationship between urbanization and democratization across the world. While not necessarily claiming causality, he suggests that urbanization focuses attention on the distribution of political power in society that helped bring about modern democracy (Dyson 2001: 17).

A critical issue, then, is to understand the circumstances under which the density, diversity and complexity that characterize cities lead to creative rather than destructive engagement. Useful as a starting point is John Walton's identification of factors that influence the nature of collective action in cities. He argued that patterns of activism and passivity are often cyclical, with different forms of collective action occurring and succeeding depending on the 'distinct constellations of economic, political and cultural causes' and the particular 'mobilized energies of the moment' (Walton 1998: 477). He identifies three types of collective action. The first is *labour action*, where the struggle is over income and conditions of employment. This embraces conventional trade union activities, where workers engage in strikes, demonstrations and other forms of protest against policies with adverse implications for jobs and wages, such as privatization. His point is that traditional trade unionism works best under conditions of full or near-full employment, but during periods of economic decline, labour action tends to recede in favour of a second area of struggle that he calls *collective consumption action.* Here consumers of collective or public goods such as land, housing, urban services, healthcare and transportation are mobilized, often at a community level, with the aim of reducing the cost of consumption in lieu of increasing returns on labour. He suggests that labour action usually takes place in middle-income countries or those with a strong tradition of industry and trade unions rather than in the very poorest countries, where it is relatively rare and where collective consumption action is more common (ibid.).

The third area Walton identifies is *political and human rights action*, which involves mobilization around issues of social justice, security, freedom from repression, as well as representation and democratization: 'expressed in marches, demonstrations, vigils, hunger strikes and similar acts of conscience' (ibid.: 463). Drawing on analyses of democratization movements in countries across eastern Europe, Africa and Latin America from the 1970s onwards, Walton suggests that 'the locus of all these movements is almost invariably in urban areas and structures of civil society' (ibid.: 477). Drawing on the experience of urban social movements in Brazil, Lucy Earle suggests that the distinction Walton makes between these categories of action is too tightly drawn and that there is considerable crossover between different types of collective action (Earle 2009). In similar vein Elizabeth Wood points to political trade unionism in South Africa and how during the transition from apartheid to a non-racial democracy, it transcended shop-floor concerns and participated in alliances with the national democratic movement and umbrella associations of community-based organizations engaged in struggles one might aptly label collective consumption action (Wood 2000).

Walton's typology is a useful heuristic device even if his categorization is difficult to maintain among actually existing urban social movements everywhere. Also helpful is his critique of the unhelpfully polarized debate between those who see urban politics as characterized by progressive 'activism' and those who focus on 'clientelism' and emphasize patronage and political passivity. It is certainly the case that people put up with a great deal before they challenge the status quo or take up political cudgels, and a number of scholars have tried to explain such quiescence among people who suffer conditions of incredible hardship and misery (see, for example, Gilbert 1994; Scheper-Hughes 1992). Why is this the case when cities are supposed to provide ideal conditions for social organization and political encounter? Explanations for widespread inertia range from the ideas that 'the poor are fundamentally satisfied with urban life' or are 'too busy making ends meet to protest' to the view that inertia often disguises low-grade action. Walton says of the urban poor that they can 'become astute petitioners in the "demand-making" process' (Walton 1998: 461).

This argument is supported by the evidence marshalled by Diana Mitlin in relation to political systems where neighbourhood-level block voting or 'vote banks' are prevalent: 'Vote bank politics can facilitate access to land and services, protect poor groups from demolition by richer ones, resolve local disputes over property boundaries, and help ensure the bureaucracy is responsive to local needs' (Mitlin 2004: 131). The idea that disadvantaged city dwellers autonomously and skilfully work clientelist politics to their advantage counters the view that poor people are gullibly manipulated by populist politicians and unscrupulous officials who feed them scraps in a system that ultimately benefits elites. No doubt some communities are manipulated and some politicians and leaders are corrupt, but polarized characterizations of low-income urban dwellers either as heroes of revolutionary resistance or inert dupes hopelessly dependent on patronage and favour are erroneous and ultimately unhelpful. The interesting issue is the conditions that give rise to conflict and cooperation and the conditions under which creative confrontation is able to take place. While the structural factors emphasized by Walton matter, other contingent factors are equally important.

The ambiguity of urban governance

Among the contextual factors influencing urban governance is the policy environment in which it takes place. In the contemporary period this has been influenced not only by national priorities but an international development discourse that emphazises and promotes Western-style democratization accompanied by state efficiency and multi-sector partnerships in service delivery, a discourse that has become known as the 'good governance' agenda. At its simplest, governance is the relationship between 'government' and 'citizen' (Painter 2000). As such it is hardly a controversial concept. The term became the source of confusion and controversy, however, when it was introduced into development discourse and aid conditionality during the late 1980s and early 1990s. This agenda was closely associated with the promotion of macroeconomic reforms towards market liberalization and was framed by theories of new public management (NPM). These sought to align public administration more closely to the methods and management systems of private business (Hood 1991). In cities the good governance agenda influenced what became known as the new urban management (World Bank 1991). This fundamentally redefined the role of urban government, changing its function from that of service provider to one of overseer and coordinator of urban service delivery (Batley 1996).

Towards the end of the 1990s it became clear that the assault on the state had gone too far and there was an increased focus on 'bringing the state back in' with decentralization as the primary vehicle for achieving this. The 1997 *World Development Report* acknowledged that there had been 'an over-withdrawal of the state' and that to a certain extent government could be rehabilitated by being 'reterritorialized' at the local level (World Bank 1997: 98). By breaking down government into smaller units and by entering into multi-sector partnerships with the private and community sectors it was argued that state performance would become more effective and efficient. As the terminology shifted from management to governance, and in cities from urban management to urban governance, a techno-administrative slant persisted nevertheless, with the solutions posed remaining primarily managerial (Batley and Larbi 2004). The fact that the political dimensions were ignored contributed to the hollowing out of the concept and the potential the notion of governance offered for framing the interactive relationship between government and non-governmental forces. Instrumental and technocratic approaches to decentralization failed to recognize the dynamics of local power relations and the political nature of many of the development tasks with which local government is charged.

Decentralization is closely associated with the 'good governance' agenda and was advocated by mainstream international development agencies as a way of deepening democratic political competition at the same time as containing the role of the state. A fundamental weakness of this approach was that the inefficiency and rigidity of central government and the greater effectiveness and responsiveness of local government were assumed, erroneously, to be *intrinsic* (Tendler 1997). Nevertheless, a consensus developed across a fairly wide philosophical terrain – from the World Bank to the World Social Forum – that decentralization had an explicitly democratizing function (Harriss et al. 2005). Yet there are no a priori reasons why more localized forms of governance should be more democratic (Heller 2001). Competing interests clustered around local-level resources and power bases can act as much to exclude as to include, and power exercised at the local level can be more concentrated, elitist and ruthlessly applied than at the national level (Beall 2005a). As the part of government closest to the people, the local state has the *potential* for promoting engaged and inclusive citizenship. A study by the International Union of Local Authorities (IULA), for example, found that the majority of elected women politicians at the local level first gained their political recognition and support through previous community activism (Evertzen 2001). However: 'It would be wrong to infer that poor people's greater proximity to the local state leads directly to a more active sense of citizenship, as some of the good governance literature perhaps suggests' (Corbridge et al. 2005: 113–14).

Critics on the left have expressed concern at the extent of scholarly and policy preoccupation with the importance of popular local-level organizations for democracy, seeing them as reflecting 'narrow and parochial interests, resulting in the "mischief of factions"' (Heller 2001: 138). It has also been argued that social movements and civil society organizations undermine broader and more cohesive political agendas such as those put forward by trade unions and political parties (Harriss et al. 2005; Houtzager 2003). Yet there are many for whom conventional political organization of this kind lacks salience. Vast numbers of people pursuing informal livelihoods have been failed by traditional trade unions, for instance, while political parties have consistently ignored the interests of significant constituencies. Ultimately formal political structures and processes are only as good as the opposition they confront, and social movements can and do challenge power-holders. Urban social movements are often closely related to more conventional forms of political activity such as trade unions and political parties. Obvious examples include the historic relationship between the Trades Union Congress (TUC) and the Labour Party in Britain and the Congress of South African Trade Unions (COSATU) and the African National Congress (ANC) in South Africa. Moreover, studies of collective consumption action around housing or urban services are as likely to engage as to challenge the state. Social movements can also turn into political parties. An obvious example here is the Partido dos Trabalhadores (PT) or Workers' Party in contemporary Brazil, which grew out of social-movement origins.

Furthermore, the line between what is 'social' and 'political' is often very finely drawn. Urban social movements, whether focused on labour, collective consumption or political and human rights action, or a combination of these, invariably represent the politicization of issues that were and remain of social concern as well. Feminist politics and the women's movement present clear evidence of how single-issue social movements can have wider political goals and impact and how the social conditions of citizenship are 'constitutive of its political possibilities' (Holston and Caldeira 1998: 289). Distinguishing too strictly between *social* and *political* activism can obscure how the former links into and feeds the latter. The mothers' movement in Buenos Aires, Las Madres de la Plaza de Mayo, which emerged during the 1974–83 dictatorship in Argentina, grew out of the personal distress and anger of women at the abduction of their children by the regime. They formed a regular circle around the Plaza de Mayo in central Buenos Aires and demonstrated in order to acquire information about their missing sons, daughters and grandchildren. A movement born of personal distress and social concern, the Madres effectively became the conscience of Argentinian society during this period and subsequently a reference point and 'motivator for the broader human rights movement in Rio de Janeiro' (Lind and Farmelo 1996: 14). What appeared at face value to have been a single-issue movement, Las Madres de la Plaza de Mayo developed a wider political focus in the process of their activities.

Similarly, conventional labour action through formal trade unionism has failed to engage the majority of informally employed low-paid workers without unemployment benefits and job security. Instead it has been membership-based organizations such as the Self-Employed Women's Association (SEWA) which have stepped forward to address both the social and economic needs of women working in the informal economy while also giving them a political voice (Rose 1992). Moreover, this is not a one-case scenario. Following the example set by SEWA, StreetNet International was launched in Durban, South Africa, in November 2002 as an alliance of street-vendor organizations with affiliate organizations (unions, cooperatives or associations) from countries as diverse as Bangladesh, Benin, Bolivia, Colombia, Côte d'Ivoire, Ghana, Kenya, India, Mexico, Nepal, Nigeria, Peru, the Philippines, Senegal, South Africa, South Korea, Sri Lanka, Thailand, Uganda and Zambia. StreetNet promotes the exchange of information and ideas on critical issues facing street vendors, market vendors and hawkers and on practical organizing and advocacy strategies. Far from remaining local, narrow or fragmented,

StreetNet has drawn up an International Declaration of Street Vendors that includes a commitment to creating national policies to promote and protect the rights of street vendors. A longer-term objective is to produce a code of practice to be used by municipalities across the world and to identify ways in which this can be incorporated into new laws. There are already some promising examples of local authorities engaging positively and creatively with informal economic actors. In Durban, for example, it was estimated that the annual turnover of informal transport and vending traders around the city's main public transport node was over one billion South African rand, and far in excess of the annual turnover of the city's largest shopping mall (Skinner 2007: 5). This, together with organization on the part of StreetNet's local affiliate, helped convince Durban's local authority to shift from a repressive stance towards informal trading towards greater levels of tolerance (Lund and Skinner 2004; Skinner 2007).

In contemporary Africa, Asia and Latin America, federations of the urban poor engage in *collective consumption action* designed to access housing and urban services. Sometimes, as with the União de Movimentos de Moradia (Union of Housing Movements) in São Paulo, Brazil, this is pursued through open conflict, such as during illicit building invasions, and at other times cooperative negotiation with government agencies (Earle 2009). In Thailand government itself has taken the lead. Here, Baan Mankong, a housing pro-gramme launched by the government in 2003, has provided good low-cost housing through a process in which a high degree of control is exercised by local people (Boonyabancha 2004, 2005). Elsewhere the initiative comes from poor people themselves, engaging state institutions in a wide variety of ways (Mitlin and Satterthwaite 2004). Federations of the urban poor are not apolitical but tend to advocate politics outside party politics. This means they do not fall prey to co-option but can 'negotiate and work with whoever is in power locally, regionally or nationally' (D'Cruz and Satterthwaite 2005: 55). An important rationale for favouring such an approach and for forming federations of the urban poor in the first place is that governments – including democracies – do not address their needs (ibid.: 57).

A celebrated institutionalized vehicle for channelling popular demands and collective action into the operation of local government is the system of participatory budgeting, which developed in Brazil and has spread to other parts of Latin America and indeed the world (Beall 2005b). This involves ordinary people in the planning of the annual capital budget of a city and facilitates their participation in addressing policy issues such as education, health, social services, transport and local economic development. Participatory budgeting is generally presented as successful, particularly in its original incarnation in the cities of Porto Alegre and Belo Horizonte, while critiques and caveats include questions as to whether such budgets really do reflect the priorities of the poorest city dwellers, scepticism about the proportion of local budgets that are really up for popular negotiation, and the potential for transferring the experience of participatory budgeting to political contexts that have not experienced the same level of local mobilization and dominance of leftist parties such as the PT (Workers' Party) in Brazil (Souza 2001). Initiatives such as SEWA, União de Movimentos de Moradia, Baan Mankong and participatory budgeting all suggest that far from fragmenting the political scene, social mobilization in cities can help workers and residents engage effectively and creatively in local politics and urban governance.

At their most creative, urban social movements play a highly significant role in the evolution and operation of conventional politics. In some contexts they constitute an important and necessary opposition to political parties and in others a valuable source of support. The relationship between urban social movements and the state is necessarily tense and complicated and often conflictual, even where their futures are inextricably bound together. The state response at times necessarily involves intervention and action. At other times the most important thing municipal governments can do is not limit the scope of what urban dwellers and workers do themselves to shape their own environments and livelihoods. The important point to be taken from the analysis thus far is that conflict, whether active or passive, is a necessary if not sufficient element in the urban governance mix. The following section considers the threats posed to creative contestation by urban violence and the destructive outcomes for effective and inclusive urban governance.

The destructive power of urban violence

Just as cities are predisposed to the positive effects of density and diversity in urban life, so these very same factors can give rise to negative outcomes, when urban conflict is accompanied by recourse to violence, understood as 'the intentional use of physical force or power, threatened or actual, against oneself, another person, or against a group or community' (WHO 2002 in Moser 2004: 4). Violence can result in injury, death or psychological harm. It has the social effect of generative fear and deepening deprivation, while economically it impacts negatively on individual livelihoods and economic investment and productivity more widely. Politically violence undermines creative contestation in cities. While cities can be the source of cosmopolitanism and conviviality, as urban populations grow and become more differentiated social distance is often magnified and then concretized by urban planning. The rise of no-go areas, gated communities and the privatization of security are becoming global urban phenomena (Beall et al. 2002; Blakely and Snyder 1997; Caldeira 2000; M. Davis 1990).

Conflicts rooted in divided cities where people are in conflict with neighbouring communities literally see people at war with their neighbours. The demonization of ethnic and religious minorities, commonly a feature of violent urban conflict, has been observed from Beirut to Sarajevo. Urban violence can arise between different identity groups in cities, for example long-time dwellers versus new migrants, or among different ethnic groups, as in the 'ethnic cleansing' that characterized the cities of Sarajevo and Mostar during the civil war in Bosnia-Herzegovina. The communal violence between Hindus and Muslims over recent decades in Indian cities such as Mumbai and Ahmedabad manifested itself in religious conflict, which in turn masked or stood in for other social fractures (Varshney 2003). Teresa Caldeira observed with particular reference to Latin America that today: 'the most visible forms of violence stem not from ideological conflicts over the nature of the political system but from delinquency and crime' (Caldeira 1996: 199). Some have sought to identify the origins of urban violence in economic (Fajnzylber et al. 2002), political (Bollens 2007; Graham 2004a) or social (Moser and McIlwaine 2004) causes. By contrast, Dennis Rodgers, in his study of the more prosaic forms of violence exhibited by urban gangs in Central America, sees this not as a shift from political to social violence, as is often thought to be the case, but rather as ongoing conflicts that are intensified by contingent circumstance and manifest in new settings, notably urban slums (Rodgers 2009).

Urban violence also results from the state attacking its citizens. When cities are systematically and violently targeted through pernicious urban planning this has been identified as a form of urban violence described as 'urbicide' (Berman 1987). In developing countries this can be seen in evictions, involuntary relocations and the deliberate destruction of the urban infrastructure for political purposes (M. Davis 2004). The term 'urbicide' has also been applied to the deliberate destruction of the urban fabric in order to deprive people of its benefits, such as in Israeli attacks on the West Bank and Gaza and the prevention of Palestinians from forming enduring urban centres (Graham 2004b). Indeed, Palestinian urbanism has been described as a cancer on the body of the Israeli state (Weizman 2004). The vigorous destruction of urban settlements, whether by the government of Ariel Sharon during the bulldozing of Jenin in April 2002, or that of Robert Mugabe during Operation Murambatsvina in June 2005, constitutes if not urbicide then a pernicious form of state terrorism exercised on an urban scale. In Harare, Operation Murambatsvina saw unprecedented violence unleashed by the state against citizens of Zimbabwe's capital city. Within a six-week period an estimated 700,000 people lost their homes and livelihoods, with up to 2.4 million people affected overall. Overnight, self-help housing and informal structures were declared illegitimate as bulldozers and demolition squads led an assault that resulted in injury and even death: 'Families were forced to destroy their own homes by hand under threat of beatings, fines or imprisonment' and were then forcibly removed to rural areas or peri-urban holding camps (Tibaijuka 2005: 40). Literally meaning 'drive out the rubbish' (or more euphemistically 'restore order'), Murambatsvina was directed at the eradication of certain kinds of urban citizens, notably street vendors and others in the informal economy, as well as generating fear among the largely urban-based political opposition to Robert Mugabe's regime (Potts 2003).

A third form of violence affecting urban governance is when conflict generated outside the city impacts on urban life. During periods of war, for example, urban centres are affected indirectly as refugees and the internally displaced contribute to 'the influx of villagers to towns and cities' (Tibaijuka 2000: 2). In Angola, for example, the capital city of Luanda grew in size fivefold during that country's civil war, while Mogadishu provides a particularly stark example of the dramatic effect that war can have on the demography of a city: between the end of January and the middle of May 2007, 400,000 people fled Mogadishu and a further 300,000 were displaced within the city (*Independent*, 15 May 2007). Moreover, contemporary wars are increasingly being fought on urban terrains (Beall 2006). Baghdad, Basra, Kabul and Kandahar are all closely associated with ongoing international warfare, while New York, Madrid, London and Nairobi are all sites that have been subject to attacks associated with the so-called global 'war on terror' (Graham 2004a).

In the past, cities have been avoided by the military if at all possible. In part this is because what is euphemistically called 'collateral damage' (noncombatant casualties) is difficult to avoid. For example, in Afghanistan, despite a policy of precision attacks on elements of urban infrastructure that could support Taliban resistance, most targets chosen by the occupying forces in the capital city, Kabul, were surrounded by slums, with most civilian deaths occurring in these densely populated areas: 'Cumulatively, these numerous small death tolls meant that the US-led bombing campaign, however well-designed to minimize civilian casualties, was the most lethal in terms of bomb tonnage since the Vietnam era, resulting in the between 1,214 and 1,571 civilian casualties' (Esser 2007: 14–15).

In addition, urban warfare is the most manpower intensive and complex of all forms of military engagement. A city constitutes a difficult terrain that provides cover, concealment and sustainment while at the same time limiting observation distances, engagement ranges and mobility (Hills 2004: 236). Nevertheless, cities lend themselves to the impact of 'spectacular violence' (Goldstein 2004), and by virtue of global warfare and acts of terror we are witnessing an 'implosion of global and national conflicts into the urban world' (Appadurai 1996: 152–3). The involvement in urban warfare of very powerful forces generates high levels of endemic fear and insecurity on the part of ordinary people. Under such conditions, 'hearts and minds' activities cannot easily restore trust, let alone the effective exercise of urban governance.

Perhaps the most pernicious form of urban violence is crime and the endemic violence in cities that undermines social cohesion and the solidarity of community. This is especially the case in Latin America, which has the highest homicide rates in the world and where 'widespread fear and insecurity [are] a fact of daily life' (McIlwaine and Moser 2007: 120). Even where perceptions exceed the reality of violence, the anxiety they generate has consequences: 'Fear, just like crime, can be portrayed as having damaged the fabric of cities, to have adversely affected the quality of urban life' (Bannister and Fyfe 2001: 808). Moreover, cities are concrete manifestations of social relations and the spatial responses to crime and fear of crime, social insurrection and everyday violence are forged on to and ground into the physical fabric and design of cities, whether through the prevalence of fortress-like gated enclaves or the wide boulevards of Baron Haussmann's nineteenth-century Paris, designed to facilitate not social mobility and interaction but military control of the city (Lemanski 2004). While private security arrangements and gated communities are generally confined to wealthy elites, there are also examples of low-income settlements being turned into defensible spaces with similarly negative consequences for urban governance (Beall et al. 2002). Crime and endemic violence not only cost residents and local authorities but they also represent significant economic costs, putting off potential investors as well as skilled and educated workers, who in a competitive global economy can take their resources and talent elsewhere (UN-Habitat 2007).

Conclusion

Historically cities have exhibited the capacity for economic and political innovation and social transformation in ways that relate in no small measure to the kinetic energy deriving from the density, diversity and institutional complexity to be found in urban centres. These same characteristics also present challenges to effective urban governance given the negative externalities or adverse effects of large and fast-growing urban agglomerations. By the same token, the proximity of people in cities to sites of power, together with the visibility of social differentiation and political exclusion, can serve both as a stimulus to and a brake on the kind of urban governance that encourages inclusivity and state responsiveness (Beall and Fox 2009). The creative tension that provides the bedrock of effective and inclusive urban governance is fundamentally undermined by the fear and insecurity generated by crime and endemic urban violence or acts of war increasingly being perpetrated in and on cities. When states are weak or unable to exercise legitimate force, and when they turn on groups of their own citizens, cities become ever more fortified and militarized spaces with urban planning and governance strategies more and more geared towards separation and control rather than inclusivity and conviviality. Under such conditions the prospect of cities being conducive spaces for democratic innovation and progressive governance becomes increasingly circumscribed.

The paradox of conflict

7 | Shoot the citizen, save the customer: participatory budgeting and bare citizenship in Porto Alegre, Brazil

SÉRGIO BAIERLE

Bare citizenship as a neoliberal dystopia

One of the more surprising current trends is the increasing importance given to the subject of poverty in the discourse of many governments and multilateral agencies. Yet if we look at government budgeting efficiency, the importance given to poverty alleviation appears much less pronounced. In Brazil, for example, debt servicing has been about 10 per cent of GDP (gross domestic product) every fiscal year for the last ten years. The portion of labour income reflected in GDP has dropped more than 1 per cent since the 1990s.[1] Meanwhile, the best-known social welfare programme of the current administration, the poverty-reducing programme Bolsa Família, has already reached 11 million families, reducing the percentage of the population in extreme poverty from 28.2 per cent in 2003 to 19.3 per cent in 2006, overshooting the UN's Millennium Development Goals for Brazil. The cost of Bolsa Família in 2007, however, was only 0.3 per cent of total GDP. At the same time, workers' rights are being systematically dismantled and the universalist policies of social security are becoming precarious to the point of being unsustainable, especially with regard to health.

The official discourse about 'social responsibility' and 'popular entrepreneurship' has increased exponentially. Along with a product, consumers buy a social project. Banks try to attract new clients by showing the social importance of the bank's philanthropy. Media conglomerates create websites to assist private donors in finding the best social programmes where their charity can be applied. It is indeed strange to see advisers to the major business federations 'worried' about the high amount of taxes paid by taxi drivers, for example. Another example is their promotion of 'days without taxes', where some products are sold with a discount equal to the amount in taxes usually paid (sponsored by the businesses). 'We end hunger with strong agriculture' is the slogan of Brazilian landowners. 'Doing more with less' is the motto of the current state government of Rio Grande do Sul, national champion in tax exemptions (40 per cent of potential tax income is not collected). The state has also just saved a little more money in education, putting different grades in the same classroom in order to avoid hiring any more teachers and doubling the number of students in each classroom of public middle schools (25 + 25 = 50).

Porto Alegre's municipal government, on the other hand, has preferred to adapt an old positivist slogan – to modernize by preserving – only reversing the phrase 'Preserving conquests, building changes'. After the defeat of the Workers' Party in the 2004 municipal elections (ending sixteen years in which a exemplary model of urban participatory governance was built), Participatory Budgeting (PB) was not abandoned; it was taken over by the new administration of mayor José Fogaça in the name of solidarity. In other words, popular participation is trapped by the 'philanthropization' of poverty. Not only have municipal investments dropped to about 5 per cent of the budget, in comparison to the historical average of 8 per cent, but the parcel of works and services requested by the PB was reduced to one-fifth of this percentage. All of this has taken place alongside increasing outsourcing of health and education, as well as increasing dependency on private philanthropy to support programmes such as community day-care centres and online education centres. The decision about where and how public works are to be done has escaped popular control in PB forums, and has started to depend on the sympathy of private donors. What PB used to have as a positive in its history – the conflict between the reclamation of rights and the precarious situation of their exercise – is reconstructed as bare citizenship, which means participative self-exclusion.[2] The utopia of a city that turns social conflicts political – in the sense of broadening the sphere of rights – nowadays tends to be substituted by a dystopia[3] – the dictatorship of common sense.

The former Secretary for Political Coordination and Local Governance of Porto Alegre in the Fogaça administration (2004–) used to say that PB made good governance viable in Porto Alegre by providing an extensive supply of accumulated social capital, preparing the terrain for a commitment of co-responsibility to obtain sustainable local development and minimize the occurrence of local problems, acting in a preventive and educational way towards the maintenance services of the city government, creating a culture of balanced entities and stimulating the active participation of the manager-citizen (Busatto 2005). The manager-citizen is precisely the key person in this process; a person able to contribute, along with the government, to managing poverty in the city in a sustainable manner, which in practice means tying poverty to the local management of capitalism. This neoliberal dystopia (the 'flat world') is articulated by the concept of good governance. It is not the objective of this text to explore the origin of this concept (Santos

1998), but it is necessary, for the argument we intend to develop, to examine the political context of its emergence in Brazil.

Urban governance, citizenship and participatory budgeting

The majority of studies about the participatory budgeting (PB) experiences are still marked by a predominantly descriptive character. These experiences did not generate a political theory of their own. They were framed in pre-existent casts involving communicative action, public spaces, co-management, social contract, institutional design, decentralization, governance, social capital, and social and fiscal responsibility. Apart from the leading role assigned to the state and/or society in the studies about participatory budgeting, there is a strong emphasis on terms such as civil society and citizenship that may reach the point of turning these concepts into myths. Instead of class struggles and social movements, what tends to stand out is the civic activism of citizens as constitutive of new rights and of a new state–society relationship. It is curious that strong political traditions in the context of Latin America, such as populism and local political leadership, are mentioned mainly only as a background against which the new citizen should emerge.

It is this mythic citizenship which explains the difficulty many participative democracy defenders have in explaining the current context of popular participation in contexts more to the left, as in the case in Venezuela and Bolivia, or in contexts more conservative or centrist, as in the case of Colombia, Mexico, Chile and Brazil. As a tool for a popular revolution or as an instrument of a republican administration, or even as a micro-political technique of social control, participative experiences are characterized less by the imagined empowerment of the citizen and more by the political guidelines of each government, entailing the impossible generic concept of citizenship as an autonomous variable.

This abstract citizen – the manager-citizen of the current government of Porto Alegre, the revolutionary-citizen of Caracas or the republican-citizen of Medellín – does not exist. What do exist are huge urban peripheries characterized by economic informality and informal land occupation, as well as by precarious access to infrastructure and basic services. The identity and organizational bases of these peripheries have been through a complicated transformation involving class, ethnic group and gender, as we will see next in the case of Porto Alegre's PB. If, in the past, the urban popular struggles were capable of producing great protests, even with the patronage system that has traditionally characterized state–society relations in Latin American history, nowadays there is an apparent contradiction. It seems that as more institutional spaces are opened for participation it becomes more difficult to turn daily organization political. The social and political basis on which the current participative opportunities have been operating – which seemed in the beginning to be able to overcome this vicious circle – requires further research. Instead of the citizenship of the popular classes working as a historical agent, there is a tendency to produce a bare citizenship, a 'sustainable' poverty self-administrated by the poor. In Caracas, for example, at the beginning of the new millennium, after years of work by 'technical water boards' (*mesas técnicas de agua*) in the urban periphery, it was possible to improve the frequency of the potable water supply from one day every twenty-eight days to one day every twenty days. There remains a lack of service, but it becomes 'sustainable'. In Manchester, through the participative urban renovation programmes proposed by former prime minister Blair, a whole set of workers' houses on the eastern side of the city, next to the gym, were demolished and new houses were built by contractors in their place. The former residents had to pay for the new houses having already paid for the old houses in decades past.[4]

In Porto Alegre, one of the street vendors' associations agreed to conduct a 'dialogue', proposed by the city government, to assist 'entrepreneurship' and 'revitalization' of the city centre. The latter would entail the expulsion of the street vendors from the city centre to enable the construction of a mall through a public–private partnership, in which the displaced street vendors would receive only 800 of the available spaces (the number of street vendors was estimated at 4,000), and would have to pay a monthly rent of about fifty dollars per square metre.[5] The street vendors remaining excluded from the mall project would be evicted from the downtown area. Other similar 'Sophie's choices' in Porto Alegre hit the residents of poor neighbourhoods in areas of interest to big corporations. Examples include the construction of more access roads to the local Catholic University (Pontifícia Universidade Católica) and the construction of a shopping mall, the Barra Shopping Sul, which is predicted to be the biggest shopping 'bunker' in Latin America. The mayor personally gave assurances that nobody would be removed 'by force'. He didn't need to, since those people have been living there for more than twenty years and legally have the right to stay there. Nevertheless, in an 'exceptional situation' there are always reasons why the state can ignore an individual's rights. The neighbourhood in which the shopping mall would be built lacks sanitation and suffers from constant flooding. The government has already presented a project, with funding already approved, that would solve the urbanization problems of the neighbourhood but would also remove a significant number of families. The choice is easy: the community accepts this removal or the necessary socio-environmental infrastructure improvements will not be undertaken. Is this participative democracy? Will those who succeed in staying prove that they have more 'social capital' than those removed?

Bare citizenship, in this way, reveals itself as a process in which class solidarity is substituted by 'solidarity generosity', in which despair sets the deprived population against itself.

From the Third Wave to the Third Way: the emergence of decentralization and participatory governance in Brazil (1989–2007)

The constitution of a mythic vision of citizenship does not operate in abstract. It expresses a strategic political option and it also is rooted in popular beliefs about democracy and social rights. After the (negotiated) end of military rule in the mid-1980s, the new 1988 constitution brought promises of a more active civil society role in public management, which was materializing during the 1990s, above all through the creation of councils specializing in health, social assistance, housing, education, urban planning and other areas. This participation model had already brought in and of itself, *avant la lettre*, the birth of the idea of good governance, because it was about bringing together the users of governmental services, governmental entities, private managers, workers' organizations, professional associations, universities and others in working meetings to define political guidelines for the administration of each area. The fundamental difference with regard to good governance was the fact that, in the model contained in the constitution of 1988, basically only public resources are discussed, so much so that the constitution itself also ensured that the federal government, states and municipalities were obliged to spend determined percentages of their budgets in education and health areas. In other words, even accepting the delivering of services by the private sector, there was the principle that the rights of citizens can only be guaranteed through their legal inscription by the state in a social contract.

Nowadays in Brazil there are more than 30,000 sector-specific councils among more than 50,000 existing municipalities. The 1990s can be characterized as an institutionalizing period for Brazilian social movements. The development of spaces for participation around social policies generated a tremendous mobilization effort. From the national forums developed at the time of the creation of national and state constitutions and municipal charters, large national conferences have arisen. The basic strategy in creating a council, a fund and cooperative management, or even organizing the communal management of supplies and social services, seemed to be able to democratize public policies by itself. In this context, democratization is understood as democratization of access, management and content of the government services involved. In reality, what we realize now is that these participative processes stopped halfway, limited to the integration of state and societies, being able neither to effectively change the bureaucratic structure of the state nor supersede the limitations of liberal democracy, failing, for example, to change the economic model under which the policies took place. In a certain way, all this institutional fervour operated in the context of a form of political schizophrenia. While social policies as a whole were being decentralized to the municipal level during the 1990s, the formulation of economic policy stayed strongly centralized in Brasília. The 1988 constitution helped free the budgets of the municipalities to an extent, enlarging the municipalities' share of taxes collected from 11 per cent in 1985 to 15 per cent in 1990. But this did not happen at the expense of the federal government, which preserved its share of about 60 per cent (see Table 7.1).

TABLE 7.1 Distribution of total available tax revenue in Brazil, after transfers

Year	Federal	States	Muncipalities	Total
1960	59.5	34.1	6.4	100
1970	60.8	29.2	10.0	100
1980	68.1	23.3	8.6	100
1990	57.1	28.0	14.9	100
2000	59.9	25.1	15.0	100
2004	60.6	24.6	14.8	100

Source: Bordin (2005)

As a result, since the decentralization of social policies was achieved through negotiation, offering a larger share of resources to the municipalities while giving them more responsibility for the administration of policies and allowing the creation of local-sector councils, a large majority of municipalities joined in the wave of participatory policies less out of conviction and more out of opportunism. In the first place, the establishment of participative spaces could bring political bonuses to local governments. As time passed, however, the pressure for a raise in expenditures in social areas tended to increase, in terms of equipment and human resources, at the same time as the state of 'permanent exception' generated by the discourse surrounding the economic crisis during the administration of Fernando Henrique Cardoso (inflation control, public debt, international crisis, etc.) made the federal government freeze cash transfers to the municipalities or create tricks to justify a larger retention of fiscal resources (tax receipt disassociation, a euphemism used to create new taxes by calling them provisional contributions and in this way allowing the federal government to appropriate them completely, denying resources to state and local government; establishment of 'Robin Hood' funds based on the resources of the municipalities; fiscal exemptions that affected only the states and municipalities; limits to municipal and state debt levels through the Fiscal Responsibility Law, etc.). This situation as a whole tended to make the sector councils more and more like window dressing and less effective, since a double trap, both fiscal and bureaucratic, essentially captured them. Another limit, however, more related to the internal dynamics of the social movements themselves, ended up entering the picture: the transformation of a great number of these movements into the Third Sector: NGOs providing public services.

Today, most of the activities of the sector councils are dedicated to proposing and negotiating contracts for the NGOs, neighbourhood associations, private foundations and advisers, so that the entity in question may deliver services. When the neighbourhood associations are transformed into part of the Third Sector, for example, there is the creation of a popular myth of empowerment that, in fact, is an expression of a real loss in power. While the effective inclusion of the popular classes does not go much beyond informal and symbolic participation in the realm of mass consumption (which, at its core, consists of street vendors and dollar stores), the popular movements tend to lack direction and their leaders become resocialized under the new banner of entrepreneurship. The work of social mobilization is reduced to the management of poverty and is replaced by the negotiation of bureaucratic projects. Neighbours are transformed into clients, in particular children, elders and those in situations of extreme vulnerability, not by chance those who most lack the autonomy to react.

The battle over participatory budgeting in Porto Alegre

Even though 177 cities have adopted different variations of participatory budgeting in Brazil since 1989 (Wampler 2007), Porto Alegre's experience has become the main national and international reference point regarding the subject, especially after the city hosted the World Social Forum on four occasions (in 2001, 2002, 2003 and 2005). Between 2000 and 2004, 43 per cent of the Brazilian population living in cities with more than 100,000 people were living in cities with PB (Marchetti 2005), despite only a small number of the 5,561 cities fitting this criterion having adopted the idea. In Porto Alegre's experience, PB appeared as a combination of process and structure. It was not a previously defined design but a progressive construction, involving at least three phases.

PB as class struggle (1989–92) The first phase of PB in Porto Alegre has some similarities with what is happening now in Venezuela, keeping in mind the difference in scale: popular enthusiasm, starry-eyed optimism, boldness and confrontation with the dominant classes. In spite of the limits given by the 1988 constitution, there was still some expectancy of a radicalization of the democratic transition process in the local governments, above all in the big urban centres. This outcome was consistent with the strategy of the social movements that had been taken over by the Workers' Party (Partido dos Trabalhadores – PT) since the end of the 1970s: undertaking grassroots work, consolidating strength incrementally, taking advantage of the political moment to develop what was then called a pincer movement: one side in the organization of the popular classes, the other in institutionality. The first years of the PT's administration in Porto Alegre were marked by multiple tensions, inside and outside the party. At first there was the lockout of the concessionary companies that operated the public transportation system, which, when faced with pressure for fare adjustment, tried to keep their traditional control over the government through intimidation. The decision of the administration to intervene in the operations of the companies started an open conflict with the business sectors of the city and provoked fear of a rupture in the existing institutional structure, even though the government's proposal was not to put the sector under state control but rather only to more effectively regulate the industry.

On the other hand, there was also a fiscal crisis that was dealt with through raising local taxes, running contrary to the general trend of reducing expenditures that was common in Brazil at the time. This solution involved tax reform, which was difficult to pass in the local parliament, in which the opposition held a majority. Olivio Dutra, from the PT, had been elected mayor by little more than one-third of the voters. Although the party had achieved strong penetration of the civil servants' unions and unions involving workers with university-level education, penetration in the popular sectors was still very new. This was true above all in the residents' associations, where the populist thinking from the 1950s still prevailed. The need for social mobilization to coerce the city council members made the administration share power, which was expressed through the formation of PB. The key element in the formation of a participative agreement between government and working-class com-

127

munities was the adoption of the principle of direct participation. In other words, it would not be the government which would determine who could or could not participate, and the presidents of neighbourhood associations would not have a representative monopoly in the deliberative spaces being developed. This meant in actuality a negotiation, since the government implicitly did not directly confront the difficult subject of 'political community oligarchies' (*caciquismo*) in the neighbourhood associations. The beginnings of doubts surrounding *caciquismo* in these entities, however, already existed in the community movements themselves, through the work of the Catholic Base Communities or through the effort of organizing neighbourhood unions or popular councils in several regions of the city, which involved not only the residents but also professionals who worked in those regions (teachers, health professionals, social workers, etc.). There was a pluralist dynamic from the point of view of the popular classes, as a perspective of social transformation, through the organization of a popular leftist space in the country, above all in the big urban centres.

Except in the civil servants' union, in Porto Alegre not even the metal-workers or the construction workers demonstrated much coercive power beyond wage-related disputes. Not by chance, when organizing the Municipal Organic Law, passed in 1990, the support of trade unions such as the artisans and architects was fundamental. In a similar way, the community movements were characterized by a policy that placed the state, not capitalism, as a guarantor of rights. 'The government should come here to the shanty town to see what people need and provide it' was a popular community activist slogan in the Cruzeiro Region of Porto Alegre in the early 1990s.

Even though there was a mix of different organizational structures, we can distinguish four models of shanty-town organization existing at the time: (a) traditional *caciquismo*, in which the leader holds a monopoly over discourse and mediates with government administrations and society in a personal manner, in the name of 'his/her' community (authoritarian/paternalist ties); (b) collective communion, adopted by Catholic Base Communities and operating on the basis of emotional catharsis and the consequent affective identity of the group (religious-affective ties); (c) the model of partisan cells, where an assembly is organized, discourse is designed to serve an agenda, minutes are taken and people are responsible for particular tasks (discursive-civic tie); and (d) the social organization management model, whether or not related to religious groups, where the mother superior or the technical director establishes the criteria of access to space and services (technical-hierarchical tie).

A specific example will help an understanding of the boundaries of the class struggle they were trying to initiate at the time. Convinced that it must contribute somehow to the strengthening of the movements, but without the chore of confronting the democracy issue in neighbourhood associations, the local government tried from the beginning to encourage the creation of popular councils (here the socialist inspiration becomes clear) in those regions of the city where they had not yet been created. They selected the Islands Region, where fishermen and garbage pickers were the predominant residents. In only a little time a contradiction became clear. The popular council of the Islands was formed more by agents of the government than by the local communities themselves, acting more like a popular state council. This was precisely the kind of nationalization of civil society that, at least in its discourse, the PT criticized, for example in dealing with trade unions. 'The CLT is the worker's AI5,' Lula used to say in the 1980s.[6] Nowadays this position has changed, since the PT has ended up becoming stronger inside this inherited structure, reproducing it.

The strategic alternative for the popular state councils was their reconstruction as public spaces, the so-called Regional PB Forums, not a space of popular power any more but an expression of 'multiple subjects', formed by community activists, government agents, civil servants, NGO advisers and others. The popular councils did not cease to exist, but they started to lose relevance as a locus for citizen participation, with participation dropping from close to 9 per cent in 1995 to only 3.7 per cent of the population in 2002. Even among delegates and council members, participation in councils failed to reach 20 per cent in the PB meetings of 2002. On the other hand, participation in neighbourhood associations in 2002 covered 48 per cent of the participants in general and about 70 per cent in the case of delegates and council members.

PB as a plebeian public space and its crisis (1993–2004) It is in this phase that the other three basic principles of PB are defined, besides (1) direct participation: (2) self-regulation based on public parameters of social justice; (3) discussion of the whole budget, including revenues and expenditures, current and capital; and (4) social control of the fulfilment of requests, along with creation of work commissions in regions of the city to follow up on the works and services promised and also to hold the government accountable. This combination of principles pointed towards a marriage of democracy and republicanism, in an effort to not be frozen at this institutional phase (to remain a permanent revolution) and at the same time to consolidate public parameters through a social contract built from the bottom up. In this sense, PB presented a double dualism of power, as identified by Santos (2002): between 'organized citizenship and City Hall', solved through the notion of public space and cooperative administration; and between 'City Council and PB', confronting an official legal process with an extra-official one (since PB is allowed by law but is not institutionalized by any specific ruling). Since the 'political contract' established by PB does not extend to the City Council, even though the powers of the City Council were not confiscated by PB, there was a constant tension between PB and the City Council, especially when the vote for the annual budget was held. Since the PT never held a majority in the City Council, it would have been very hard to get the administration's proposals and those in PB's interest approved without traditional patronage concessions to the members of the City Council. The popular pressure exerted by PB obliged the City Council to play a contradictory role, both republican (i.e. not based on the private and corporate interests of the city council members) and democratic (i.e. recognizing the interests of 'organized citizenship'). This did not prevent the City Council members from either denouncing 'contraband' proposals from the executive branch disguised as PB or questioning broader fiscal issues.

For the critics of the PT, the fact that PB was not institutionalized in a specific law expressed the 'non-democratic' nature of the party (failing to make the distinction here between republic and democracy). For the advocates of self-regulation, without being framed within a specific law, PB would preserve its democratic institutional feature (its revolutionary side). In this sense, this resource of popular mobilization repeats, perhaps in a new way, the historical pattern of Vargas's populism, in which a social commitment to development used the pressure of the masses to restrain the conservative oligarchy. What is new here is the idea of a popular subject, of a plebeian citizenship, brought about by PB, different in concept from the state control over society of Vargas's time. In any case, if any *raison d'être* must be attributed to the PB 'republicans', it resides in historical impotence, now repeated, in terms of confronting the conservative structures that restrict democracy in the country. We did not break with the trade unionism linked to the state; we did not break with the *caciquismo* of the neighbourhood associations; we accepted a transition from the military regime guided by the large corporations preserving the power of the military to moderate from the rafters. In the end, moving from political realism to political realism, we arrived at a dual society: middle and upper classes in a legalistic society and integrated in the growth brought by globalization, and the lower classes in a society of informalization and exclusion (even if now in a participative way), where the popular classes are not outright criminalized.

Let us now see how this thesis of a plebeian public space has, in practice, generated its antithesis. The consolidation of the Regional PB Forums and the consequent creation of the Regional PB Coordinator mark the transition of PB from a mobilization and pressure process into the sphere of cooperative administration. Through the Regional Administrative Centres and the Regional PB Coordinator, the institutional mediations began to be undertaken by government agents chosen for these particular jobs. The inequality of resources between the popular councils and the PB forums would lead to an overlap of roles, with the result that the meetings of the popular councils in some regions were coordinated by government agents. The consequence from an organizational point of view was that the social movements progressively lost autonomy, since the construction of identities started to happen directly in the 'public spaces', in conjunction with the government. By the end of the 1990s, passionate disputes within the different factions of the PT over the strategic control of the Regional PB Coordinator and the Regional Administrative Coordinator's duties were already obvious in most regions of the city. This situation also narrowed the agenda of the social movements in terms of possible municipal policies.

The need for a follow-up on the community's demands ensured what Soares (2001) described as the lightning conductor of the internal dispute between different parts of the PT – in other words, the effective presence of the popular communities in participative spaces. Worried about the weak presence of the middle, business and even trade union sectors in the PB (in 1995 only 4 per cent of the participants of the assemblies belonged to trade unions), the municipal government created thematic meetings, along with increasing participative arenas, adding sector conferences and congresses, culminating with citywide congresses. These processes worked as an excellent system for selecting the new political elite. In 2002, about 60 per cent of the delegates and members of the citywide Participatory Budget Council supported the PT and other parties of the Popular Front and only 2.4 per cent (delegates) and 6.5 per cent (council members) demonstrated support for parties of the opposition. This golden era of PB in Porto Alegre, characterized by a strong capacity to draw public investment and an institutional process in several areas that indicated a change to the previous focus on demands for infrastructure, allowing hopes for the integration of PB as an urban planning nucleus based on a 'plebeian' social base, started to show signs of crisis in 2000, exactly when PB was being internationally recognized by both sides of the political spectrum, from Chávez to Blair and the World Bank. Even though the most evident symptoms of crisis were fiscal and economic in nature, the process was more complex:

- difficulty in maintaining the growth of government revenue above total economic growth; reduction of state and federal monetary transfers, because of the relative loss of Porto Alegre's position in terms of national GDP and the fiscal exemption and fiscal adjustment policies of those entities;
- the temptation to use international loans to undertake large infrastructure works (i.e. the ring road, urbanization of slums at the entrance to the city and basic sanitation programmes);
- political resistance to fiscal restraint, leading to successive deficits between 2002 and 2004, in spite of a progressive delay in works and services related to PB;
- an increase in disputes within the government and the community leadership apparatus, fracturing the cohesion and coherence of the government's actions;
- limitation of the quantity of participative arenas at the level of socio-political interaction, without a subsequent transformation of the public machine; and
- the abandonment of the idea of a national PB by Lula's government in favour of neo-corporate arrangements.

PB as Third Sector and its 'genetic' mutation into the World Bank's participative governance model (after 2005) The defeat of the PT in the municipal elections of 2004 was not a defeat of PB itself, but above all an expression of the difficulty the party had in providing solutions to the city's middle class and in continuing the previous levels of investment in the shanty towns. The configuration of the PT as a new political class showed the increasing detachment between militants and the party's base, in the trade unions, community organizations and social movements in general. While trade unionism was reverting to a strictly wage-agreement corporatist model, while the community leaders became professional through the partnerships that outsourced public services, while the NGOs were transformed from popular training centres into government advisers, while militant PB supporters sought job openings in the government largely from a perspective of personal advancement, while the 'lightning conductor' with the 'plebeians' was being ripped out, their almost-citizenship was reduced to bare citizenship.

So the big question is not why the PT lost the elections in 2004 in spite of

PB, but rather how it was possible that this party stayed in power for sixteen years with such a fragile social base. If Lula's ascension to the Brazilian presidency marks the end of a popular-democratic project and its reconversion into the administrative confines of government, the arrival of the conservative modernizing front led by the Socialist Popular Party (PPS) in the municipal government of Porto Alegre marks the consolidation of a new power bloc in the state of Rio Grande do Sul (of which Porto Alegre is the capital), further sanctioned in 2006 by the victory of the electoral front led by the Brazilian Social Democracy Party (PSDB) leading to control of the state government.

The names and origins of these parties should not confuse us. Both arrived in power with an almost identical project whose strings are pulled by big business in partnership with the media and the advisers of organizations created specifically to contribute to restructuring the interests of our state's bourgeoisie. The novelty in the governmental management of these sectors at the beginning of the 1990s lies, on one hand, in their synthesis with national business centres and, on the other, in their conversion into the discourse of the 'Third Way', in which they simulate concessions to social issues when actually the idea is to turn poverty into something functional to capital, as we have seen.

In the state of Rio Grande do Sul, and in the city of Porto Alegre as well, a state of exception was established. The same state that loses 6.5 billion reais (around US$4 billion) through fiscal exemptions every year is proud of showing a realistic budget for the following year in which, of the 12 per cent that the constitution mandates must go towards health-related needs, they will allocate only 6 per cent because it is 'honest', and they do not want to lie about something they cannot accomplish. In Porto Alegre, the three years of deficit left by the PT were an excuse for a generalized cut in expenses and the opening of public–private partnerships. Since the city does not have more resources, they hand resources to the private sector. So, the projects for the gateway to the city, the elevated shopping centres for street vendors[7] (*camelodromo aereo*) and public squares are given to the private sector; the biggest municipal theatre is outsourced in exchange for repairs to the roof; the partnerships for day-care centres and other programmes are linked to resources coming from private donors and/or the federal government. In the name of attracting investment, a fiscal exemption strategy has been initiated in the city and urban laws made flexible in order to adapt to the operating needs and voracity of the large contractors.

Even though the administration was afraid of what could happen in the field of the PB, it was relatively easy to maintain the declining trend of the budget share of works and services originating from the PB, as well as reconverting the identity of most PB delegates and council members. In 2005, the PT itself agreed with the establishment of a state of exception by endorsing the Pact for Rio Grande, a fiscal adjustment proposal with compensations in social policies proposed by the business federations.

It does not seem possible, therefore, to maintain the participative affirmation model of the 1990s, where the basic question answered by PB was how to transform excluded populations into active citizens.[8] In that model, the natural avenue for participation seemed to be the broadening of the public sphere by incorporating new rights. This idea of a citizenship able to widen the space of politics to include the popular classes was deconstructed by a dual movement, internal and external to the political field that was promoting the model. In this sense, what Fogaça's administration (the current administration of Porto Alegre) unveiled was the fact that this external movement had already existed for some time at the national level (São Paulo, Vitoria, Curitiba, for example, already guided by poverty philanthropization since the end of the 1990s). In other words, the 'novelty' brought by the new administration was the attempt to reproduce in Porto Alegre the governance model already adopted in other cities by the PSDB (of which PPS seems to be a Siamese twin). It also started to become evident that, internal to the participative model, there was already a progressive backsliding in which participation becomes less political in favour of a technical solution: social programmes to manage poverty and their respective outsourcing of community contracts. In other words, PB as a way of listening to what people in the popular communities has to say, as a social process, as development of a broader social movement, tends to disappear.

Nowadays the government shows up very seldom at the regional forum meetings. When representatives do show up, it is not to listen but rather to communicate their decisions. And if they do not attend the meetings, they arrive by surprise at the house of a community leader to persuade him to demand what the government wants (low-cost services instead of structural works). PB is not ending; it is being reduced to a government policy. As Mayor Fogaça says, 'PB today is an institution of the city', the same as museums and statues or the *Brique da Redenção*.[9] It is part of the city's folklore. Moments of effective confrontations with the new government in the 2005–07 period were rare: (a) a demonstration of garbage-truck drivers against changes in the city's rubbish collection; (b) a civil servants' strike against a salary reduction; (c) local demonstrations in some regions against unstable or non-functioning services (health clinics, garbage collection, road maintenance, delayed works);

(d) a protest concert against the outsourcing of the Araújo Viana Auditorium; (e) a demonstration in front of City Hall for improved definition of the housing ownership titles of the PIEC (Integrated Programme for the Entrance to the City, a handover from the former government); and (f) a protest in front of City Hall against the suspension of contracts with community entities.

The systematic disregard of the government in relation to the PB forums in terms of not showing up, ignoring the rules, not carrying out proposed projects, and offering spaces other than PB for punctual solution of services and other insults merited only the distribution of an anonymous pamphlet during the commemoration of Farroupilha Week (a revolutionary movement in 1835, symbol of regional identity) in 2006. Of course, this disregard by the administration was the target of many harsh speeches in the PB assemblies, forums and council, but there was nothing that would convert indignation into direct action. The closure of the health clinic in the Cruzeiro region resulted more from the struggle of professionals in the area than from the actions of the organized communities, who only protested when the Regional Medicine Council decided to close the clinic until certain problems were solved (rats, cockroaches, the physical condition of the building). Only then did the government start to do something. In the same way, the recent interruption of the Family Health Programme, supposedly in order to reduce costs by changing the administrating entity, found more resistance in the trade unions than in the community sectors.

It was the risk of termination of partnerships with the government which scared and intimidated community organizations the most. From the moment the government managed to activate its network of business contacts and stimulate a rise in private donations to FUNCRIANÇA (foundation for children's benefit) and to other entities directly, taking over the partnerships from the community organizations, even if partially taking the decision-making away from PB, the tensions started to be diluted. In 2007, the government announced the construction of new day-care centres that would be subject to negotiation (after requests made as far back as 2002 that had been delayed). The dispute over partnerships with those entities not subject to any agreement yet was used by sectors of the government as a form of political blackmail. If the entities decided to undertake training activities with groups not friendly to the administration, for example, they were threatened with exclusion from the programme.

It is not possible to think of more radical alternatives for local management without discussing its political construction in the social fabric of the city. Espírito Santo, one of the council members of COMATHAB (Municipal

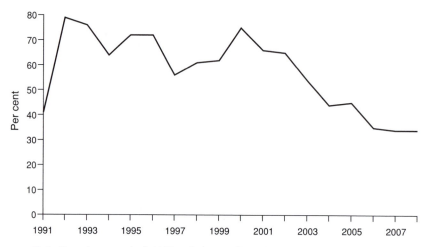

Note: the rate was calculated in relation to all previous years, including full
(= 'titular' in Portuguese) and substitute (= 'suplente' in Portuguese) membership

FIGURE 7.1 Evolution of the membership renewal rate of the
Participatory Budgeting Council

Council for Access to Land and Housing), considers that the departure of PT
from local government represented an 'anaphylactic shock' for social movements. The image is suggestive because it reveals the degree of commitment
of these movements to government spaces and the political party in power.
In other words, on the one hand, popular organizational spaces were getting
more and more mingled with government spaces. This is what we observe
in the case of shanty-town unions and popular councils, which should be
making autonomous demands but were simultaneously being diluted and/
or supervised (to the point where the same government representative was
coordinating the PB forum's meetings and the meetings in some councils).
On the other hand, these 'coordinators' (the regional coordinators of the PB
and of the regional administrative centres) are all selected by the government
and, therefore, subject to political appointment. The new government needed
only to fill the almost 700 municipal political job vacancies to have potent
conditions for neutralizing PB. This situation likewise reveals the high degree
of 'nationalization' of institutional brokers (churches, community entities
and NGOs more and more dependent on governmental money transfers).
The figures below show the reduction in the renewal of PB leaderships and
the oscillation in general participation in the assemblies (about 1 per cent
of the citizens), demonstrating that participation in the process was reduced
to a small number of professional citizens, able to fill some assemblies every
year, with the help of buses available through political-partisan patronage.

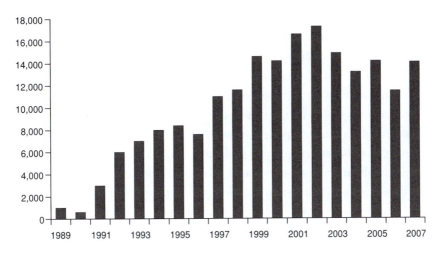

FIGURE 7.2 Evolution of public participation in participatory budgeting assemblies

It has been more and more common to find people in assemblies who do not have a clue what they are doing there. According to some PB council members of the southern region, 'A good councillor mobilizes the community and coordinates their day-care centres'; or, 'The rule at PB is to participate, to increase the number of delegates for the community'.

The 'anaphylactic shock' suffered by the local PT also contributed to this situation; it took the party more than two years to start to react to Fogaça's government in an organized manner. The most outspoken party members were transferred to the federal government and to parliamentary boards of advisers, as well as within the party apparatus. On the other hand, the community advisers became unemployed, some of them even being convinced to work for the new government (allowing them a simulacrum of a republican soul). Added to this loss of the PT's material essence was an equally corresponding loss of political identity. The neutralization of the PB by Fogaça's administration was also facilitated by the absence of a national point of reference. In other words, the neutralization of participation in Lula's administration, limited to forums and sector conferences, also helped Fogaça's administration feel authorized to consider PB a locus for popular consultation and not a space of cooperative administration of municipal public policies.

Final considerations

In this chapter we have reasoned that the deconstruction of the popular-democratic project in Brazil opened space for the re-emergence of the neoliberal project as a hegemonic act, meaning that it was based on active acquiescence. Articulated by the concept of good governance, this new version of the same concept, now in its 'inclusive' phase, is again beginning to establish 'states of exception', suspending rights in the name of their 'fiscal unsustainability'. This acquiescence, in the case of Rio Grande do Sul, generated a pact to 'save' the state endorsed in 2006 by a group of the main political and economical powers, including the PT.

Since, as a consequence, a real social unsustainability is generated, potentially capable of provoking a general crisis of legitimacy, the actions of the Third Sector and their micro-political techniques of social normalization appear to have a dual objective: (a) to promote the management of poverty as social capital; and (b) to form a 'clearing house' between the social and the market, turning social and environmental issues apolitical and reconverting them into new market sectors (recent research indicates that average salaries in the 'non-profit' sectors are currently higher than in the market sectors).

This situation indicates that the reconstruction of popular autonomy and the radicalization of its participation in participative spaces – deconstructing its existence as little more than a spectacle – having overcome the abstract logic of citizen and community and dealt with the need to reconstruct the social struggle beyond disputes over income, arrives at a questioning of the brutal alienation of a life based on a capitalism that is increasingly predatory. For an effective emancipation of the popular sectors it is necessary to first confront the corralling of citizenship through the philanthropization of poverty, something that becomes more and more necessary as the process deepens. This implies another logic, however, which presupposes the opening of a political restructuring space not yet visible in the current political spectrum.

Many people are surprised by the fact that, after almost two decades of popular 'empowerment', PB participants feel intimidated and are easily captured by a logic that excludes them, and that many community leaders, always so harsh in their critiques of public works delays, now stay silent or even justify the alleged limitations of the current administration ('if the government is not doing more it is because it cannot', because it 'inherited a difficult situation', because it 'has to resolve financing issues first', etc.). This is the same government that, between January and July 2007, had already spent more than 14 million reais (US$8.6 million) on advertising, while at least fourteen programmes of interest to the public received absolutely no funding in the same period.[10] This process is exactly the result of a citizenship rendered bare. It is natural that in this terrain so much 'generosity' blossoms.

Notes

1 For information regarding the proportion of income in Brazilian GDP, see Pochmann (2001).

2 The concept of bare citizenship is inspired by Agamben (1998). If we base ourselves in Agamben's thesis, the concept of bare citizenship is impossible, because bare life is characterized by a lack of citizenship. Our choice of this oxymoron is a provocation to neoliberalism in its 'inclusive' phase, which coincides with the Third Way project.

3 'Disutopia is the most significant project of our time. It is not the temporary absence of Utopia but the celebration of the end of social dreams. Social dreams have become a nightmare in which it is impossible to materialize our desires into a collective thought. Disutopia should not be confused with the form in which it appears: indifference. Disutopia entails an active process involving simultaneously the struggle to control diversity and the acclamation of diversity; the repression of the struggles against Disutopia and celebration of individual self-determination. The result of this is social schizophrenia. In so far as diversity, struggle and contradiction cannot be eliminated by political or philosophical voluntarism, Disutopia has to be imposed. The advocates of Disutopia spend a huge amount of time in de-construction, repentance, denial, forgetfulness, anti-critique, coupled with academic justifications and the scientific classification of the horrors of our time. Whilst the reality of capitalism is destroying planet earth, Disutopia pictures Utopia as a romantic, naïve and old-fashioned imaginary that is accused of not dealing with the real world. However, our point is that Disutopia can only be sustained by denying the real content of life, i.e. the foundations of the real world. The result of all this together is mediocrity' (Neary and Dinerstein 1998).

4 The observations about the cases of Caracas and Manchester are based on the preliminary research reports of the project Municipal Innovations, co-ordinated by Jenny Pearce (University of Bradford). The opinions expressed here about the cases are exclusively my own.

5 See www.portoalegre.rs.gov.br/noticias/ver_imprimir.asp?m1=31121 (accessed 17 September 2007). Along with the proposal regarding street vendors, there is one to remove garbage pickers from the city centre. There are estimated to be seven thousand of these people, who would have their work restricted to evening and dawn. As part of the package of participative exclusion, a project named 'City Doorways' was launched which will impede direct bus access to the centre of the city, with public transport passengers having to board new buses at transfer (read: control) stations. The 'cleansing' of downtown proposed by Fogaça's government is similar to the expulsion of the so-called 'beehive' residents by the positivist administrations that ran the city at the beginning of the twentieth century.

6 The new form of trade unionism, in which Lula started his political career, operated under the Consolidation of Labour Laws (CLT), promulgated during Vargas's administration (1943) as something similar to Institutional Act no. 5 of the Military Dictatorship (AI5), which subordinated the parliament to the ruling junta (1968). The AI5 allowed annulling mandates, suspending political rights, allowed the firing and retiring of judges and civil servants; it ended habeas corpus and increased repression.

7 As mentioned above, a public square was transferred to a private group in exchange for building the popular mall. Additional to the rent from former street vendors a car park for 800 vehicles will also be exploited privately. It is unnecessary to mention that street vendors didn't participate in the project design and were confronted by it only after the project had been decided by the government. See note 5 for information on the city's gateway project.

8 For more information, see the research of Telles (2007).

9 A handicraft market held every Sunday close to Porto Alegre's Redenção Park.

10 See *Boletim Cidade*, 6(40), September 2007. The programmes with zero funding are the following: (1) Judicial Land Regulation; (2) Flood Protection of the Cavalhada System and Urban Drainage Master Plan; (3) Urban Drainage; (4) Human Rights Training School, Peace and Citizenship, Struggle against Racial Discrimination, Reference Centre for Violence Victims; (5) Qualification and Enlargement of Illumination in Public Areas; (6) Development of SMIC Restinga Industrial Park; (7) Hortocentre; (8) Bicycle Lanes Master Plan and Development of Urban Collective Transportation; (9) Therapeutic Communities; (10) General Hospital of Restinga; (11) NASCAS – Nucleus of Assistance to Children and Adolescents; (12) Entrance to the City – PIEC, Actions of Social Policies project; (13) Guaíba Riverside, Improvement of the Tree Nurseries and Tree Planting Services, Acquisition of Equipment for Environmental Control and Stream Recovery; (14) Inclusion of the Network for Deaf and Disabled People.

8 | Crisis of the state, violence in the city

MARIANO AGUIRRE[1]

'Mini-Venices'

'Our great metropolises will soon be left as mini-Venices, little enclaves of civility in an encroaching world of unimaginable squalor and poverty,' foretold Heathcote in 2006. This alarming prediction is being confirmed by the fact that every month around five million people in the developing world become city dwellers. Migration from rural areas to urban centres, natural increase – when births outpace deaths – improved mass transport and foreign migration have generated overwhelming urban growth, and this expansion is virtually synonymous with slum formation in many regions of the world, as the latest UN-Habitat (2008) report indicates. One in three urban residents lives in slums and rapid growth is synonymous with overcrowding, poor housing, health risks and environmental degradation.

An equally pressing problem in megacities and slums, however, is citizen security. According to the above-mentioned report, high levels of inequality can lead to negative social, economic and political consequences that have a destabilizing effect on societies, and they create social and political fractures that can develop into social unrest and insecurity. In the early 1980s Harrison (1983) wrote about London's inner city as 'the most dramatic and intractable social problem', indicating that 'here are concentrated the worst housing, the highest unemployment, the greatest density of poor people, the highest crime rates and [...] the most serious threat posed to established law and order since the Second World War'.

Since Harrison wrote his essay, the problem of urban crisis has been growing in North and South, as exposed by the violence that erupted in Paris in 2005, São Paulo in 2006 and to some extent in the failed response by the US authorities to the New Orleans crisis in 2005. In 1983, the crisis of the inner city was a reflection 'of Britain'. Today, several studies and reports about megacities in crisis highlight the globalization process, and cities such as Johannesburg, Rio de Janeiro, Bogotá, Medellín, Mexico DF, Lagos, Nairobi, Kingston and Caracas have become the most dangerous in the world.

The relationship between cities and states has been so close that it is impossible to understand the development of the modern state without considering the role of cities, not only as the leading predecessors of the European state in the fifteenth century, but also as the key administrative organizers of the state. From state-cities such as Venice and Florence in the fifteenth century, through the emergence of bourgeois urban spaces like Amsterdam, to the modern globalized high-tech cities of today's Los Angeles, São Paulo or Dubai, the development of the city has played a crucial role in the formation and transformation of the modern Westphalian state system. Throughout history, the colonial and post-colonial city has played a decisive role as the administrative centre of the colonial system, pivotal to the exploitation of resources, and after independence they became the capitals of new regimes. Luanda, Maputo, Jakarta, Port-au-Prince, Algiers, Cairo, and many others around the world reveal their colonial past through run-down buildings in downtown areas that cohabit with deplorable sprawling slums contrasting starkly with enclosed and privately protected affluent areas. Post-colonial cities were the mirrors of the post-colonial states, and many of them are in deep crisis today.

A strong correlation exists between state crisis and city crisis. The relations between urban poverty, exclusion and violence can be analysed from the perspective of the crisis of post-colonial states and the role that cities, especially capitals, play in this context. Although globalization has diminished the role of the state, and consequently the role of cities as administrative centres centralizing the political, economic and social decision-making processes, both the state and cities continue to be decisive. As a matter of fact, one of the impacts of the 2008 financial crisis has been the re-evaluation of the state, particularly as an organizer of society, in terms of its capacity to establish the rules and construct international regimes with other actors.

As defined by the Crisis States Research Centre of the London School of Economics and Political Science: 'Cities are special entities that contain large concentrations of people and economic activity. They are characterized by urbanism, defined as the economic, social and political effects of density, proximity, heterogeneity and interdependence.'[2] Positive outcomes of urbanism are the provision of economies of scale in the delivery of goods, services and welfare, and the potential for innovation. But among the negative outcomes are pollution and urban violence. As this research centre underscores, there is an urgent need to analyse the relationship between cities and state transformation given the challenges of rapid urbanization, the growth of urban slums, increasing demands on the states, and the issue of weak governance in many parts of the world.

This chapter outlines the connections between crisis of the state and crisis of the city, focusing in particular on the question of violence, while addressing the following issues. First, parallels exist between states in crisis, on the one hand, that cannot fulfil basic commitments to protect and guarantee the rights of their citizens and, on the other, cities in crisis that are not able to provide security to a majority of their population. Second, central governments and city councils respond to violent urban crisis by implementing draconian security measures such as strengthening laws, particularly against youth gangs and young offenders, promoting the privatization of security, and building up enclosed areas inside the cities and raising walls.[3] Third, a corollary of this argument, most peace-building policies implemented by the international community in post-conflict situations fail to address violent urban crisis. This chapter attempts to present the broader framework of urban violence, on the assumption that the link between peace-building and urban violence is still weak in the intervention strategies used by the donor community.[4] Fourth, a comprehensive human security approach is recommended as an effective strategy to mitigate urban violence.

Fragile states and the violent city

According to different studies, between thirty and fifty states are currently coping with varying levels of fragility, which means that some or all of the modern state's basic functions are inexistent. National governments that embodied these states lack legitimacy, have lost the monopoly on the use of force and often fail to control all the national territory. They cannot uphold the constitutional order, and do not guarantee the rights of their citizens nor access to basic services. At the same time, these weak states lack the resources to resist internal crisis or external shocks ranging from *coups d'état* to natural disasters or financial fluctuations and rising commodities prices.

State weakness is the product of many factors: colonial and post-colonial structures, corrupt elites, external influences, military interventions and economic dependencies. Macroeconomic stabilization and structural adjustment programmes (namely financial liberalization, trade liberalization and privatization/deregulation), which dominated donor development policy for most of the last two decades, reduced and weakened many Southern states and, in cases such as Haiti or Sierra Leone, even led to the collapse of state structures and institutions (Thompson 2004).

A small number of states have collapsed as coherent entities in the last two decades: Somalia, Afghanistan, Liberia and Sierra Leone are examples of state failure. Some of them are in complex processes of recovery. What kind of states these fragile entities will be in the future is the subject of an important political debate between local actors and the international community, and there are contradictory signs about the structural shape that these post-colonial entities will have. States in crisis display weakness in different areas of their structure and functions, so broader definitions and indexations of these states are generally not very useful.

States that have problems in securing the monopoly on the use of force, sovereignty and the constitutional order are characterized by cities where the municipal authorities are not universal providers of goods and rights. Private security is replacing ineffective and corrupt police forces, and some urban areas are under the control of non-state armed actors. Another common factor between states in crisis and urban crisis is the fragmentation of communities. The lack of an inclusive state leads to clashes for licit and illicit resources and their control by different community groups. Thus, the crisis of the state is mirrored in its cities, giving rise to an ever-widening polarity between winners and losers, elites and the poor. Domestic actors are subsumed or co-opted by foreign actors – investors, international financial institutions, autocrats, UN agencies, NGOs, journalists and private security contractors among others. Criminal and political violence, racism and exclusion of community groups, and the culture of male violence, proliferate.

The city, particularly the megacity, is the space where many different trends of the globalization process have materialized. Urban spaces, like the state itself, are historical and political constructions. As such, current problems of urban violence taken from a historical and political perspective are the outcome of the intersection between state (and its crisis), city (as a reflection of the state) and the domestic and global economy (the way in which economic processes shape and transform the nature of the state and its relations with the world). These dimensions have always overlapped throughout history, but they are especially prevalent in the current situation of fragile states and/or fragile cities. As a priest working in Honduras observed: 'The gangs arrived with globalization and the liberalization of the global economy, while the state was unable to interpret how this maelstrom was going to profoundly affect social reality' (quoted in Mejía 2007: 27).

All external and internal policies to address violent urban crisis should be situated in the context of the post-colonial city crisis and the dynamics of globalization. In other words, there is a corresponding relationship between dual global inequalities (North/South, rich/poor, centre/periphery) and state inequalities and the projection of these factors into cities. As Dominique Vidal (2005) wrote about the violent incidents in the suburbs of Paris in 2005, the events in Clichy-sous-Bois were the confluence of three developments: 'a social crisis, a post-colonial crisis, and a crisis of political representation'.

Post-9/11 and state fragility

After 11 September 2001 the so-called fragile states became a high priority in the international security agenda. Given that Afghanistan hosted Osama bin Laden, states in crisis were seen as potential threats, a source of terrorism, expansion of pandemics, gravitational centres for illicit trafficking, and places from where migrants and refugees were waiting to enter the West. The response by the United States and other governments was to classify fragile states as one of the main sources of instability. The Bush administration pointed to them as a threat, and the European Union (EU) indicated in 2003 that the proliferation of weapons of mass destruction, terrorism and fragile states were also the main security threats to Europe.

The hegemonic narrative of the USA and its allies was that the absence of a functioning state and democratic institutions coupled with corruption and a radical version of Islam could generate safe havens for terrorism. Fragile states became targets in the global war on terror launched by the Bush administration. This approach to states in crisis was instrumental in obscuring the roots of the crisis itself, namely the alliances of the USA and European countries with corrupt elites, and the neoliberal economic models promoted by international financial institutions and Western governments that accelerated the crisis of the Southern countries in the 1980s.

In addition to the identification by the West of state crisis with terrorism and other threats, megacities of the South (and, by extension, poor immigrant neighbourhoods of Northern suburbs) were seen as sources of instability. As a result, military circles started discussing new forms of conflicts or future wars in which the slums and macro-cities of the world were increasingly included as scenarios. This tendency to approach urban violence solely from a security perspective gained ground in the USA, Europe and some Southern countries. By addressing urban violence mainly through occasional police interventions in poor neighbourhoods, where urban violence and crime originate, governments and political leaders assuage the fears of the middle classes, frightened by the perception of increasing insecurity. They fail, however, to assume political and social responsibility for the tremendous inequalities, exclusion and deprivation that are at the heart of this kind of violence (Wacquant 2007).

The characteristics of state crisis, and its impact on urban realities, should be addressed from the framework of colonial and post-colonial models of state formation, in addition to the economic models developed in previous decades, and the way in which they have shaped societies. The attendant consequences of poverty and exclusion must also be tackled. When economic and development models are seen from a historical and political perspective, unequal social structures emerge, and the relationship between inexistent or weak state structures and the needs and demands of certain sectors of society, relating to insecurity, and political and criminal violence, become more insistent.

At the same time, after half a century of independence for many countries in Africa and Asia, and almost two hundred years in Latin America, significant internal developments have taken place. Internal demands for democracy, redistribution of wealth and the fight against corruption are robust and deserve the support of the international community, not only through political rhetoric and aid but also through policies that control capital flows, the use of natural resources, and private and public investments in those countries in crisis. In other words, a simplistic view, whereby foreign actors are solely responsible, would miss the point of understanding this domestic transformation. It is precisely in this context of internal and external factors that urban poverty, violence and insecurity should be situated.

Booth considers that in the sphere of world security and peace, 'States cannot deliver world security [and thus] a different set of organising principles is needed in today's smaller and globalised world.' In other words, security cannot be provided solely by the state but must be supported by other structures and interactions in the context of a cosmopolitan system of states. 'Because states are identified in [the theory of] realism as the primary actors in world affairs – they are said to have the most agency – it is therefore assumed that they should be considered "the primary referent" in thinking about security. This does not necessarily follow.'[5] Globalization transforms states, but there is also a strong interaction between how states evolve and global processes. This is particularly important in the case of emergent regional powers such as India, Brazil and South Africa. They are no longer dependent entities but important players in their regions of influence and in the global field (for example, in trade negotiations, leading peace operations or conflict resolution and mediation). At the same time, they have common problems of informal settlements at the periphery of the cities, and occupation of land by lower-income residents in the inner city. The spatial response is the growth of 'defensive architectures and fortified enclaves' (Landman 2003: 7).

The financial crisis of 2008/09 has been decisive in disclosing the profound changes in the international system, and how the world is moving from unipolarity to multipolarity. In this respect, megacities are also mutating from post-colonial centres to multicultural spaces where national and post-national elements clash, and where affinities and tensions are reflected. As

Saskia Sassen (2001) indicates: '[...] the large western city of today concentrates diversity. Its spaces are inscribed in the dominant corporate culture but also with a multiplicity of other cultures and identities. The slippage is evident: the dominant culture can encompass only part of the city.'

Peace-building and urban violence

Over the last decade, the number of peace-building processes has increased dramatically, while armed conflict between and within states has decreased. The concept of peace-building is defined as a series of actions undertaken by national and international actors to consolidate or institutionalize peace. For some authors and practitioners, peace-building is different from state-building, but for others the processes of institutional state-building help to consolidate peaceful regimes. Post-conflict peace-building refers to efforts to create conditions in which violence will not recur, but state-building refers to the construction of legitimate governmental institutions.[6] Since the late 1980s, over twenty operations that could be labelled as 'peace-building in post-conflict scenarios' have been undertaken. It is a concept with several interpretations and practices but there is a general consensus on three essential dimensions which reinforce each other: security, political development and social and economic development. The three dimensions must be addressed simultaneously, not sequentially (see Box 8.1).

In general, the peace-building policies of many countries fail to regard urban violence as a priority problem. Implicitly, the tool known as security-sector reform and promotion of rule of law includes problems of criminality, youth gangs, vigilantism and other manifestations, but the urban violence is not directly addressed. The fact that there are fewer armed conflicts does not mean that there is less violence. In some contexts, such as Central America, for example, the level of violence is currently higher than in the 1980s during the political war. This non-political violence has a criminal base and takes place mainly in urban environments.

Human security: the people at the centre

In the last decade, the concept of security has been redefined, advancing from the traditional state-centred military focus to a more comprehensive approach where individuals play a significant role. The human security approach is useful in analysing the violent crisis of the city. The list of threats to human security is long and varied. As proposed by the United Nations Development Programme, most threats fit within seven main categories: economic, food, health, environmental, personal, community and political securities (UNDP

147

Box 8.1 Practices of peace-building in post-conflict scenarios

Security
- disarmament, demobilization and reintegration (DDR) programmes for ex-combatants;
- removal of mines;
- monitoring of small and light arms;
- security-sector reform.

Political development
- support for the political and administrative structures and authorities, including judicial reform;
- holding of elections and constitutional reform;
- reconciliation, including judicial processes and truth commissions;
- good government, democracy and human rights;
- civil society, including communications media.

Social and economic development
- repatriation and integration of refugees and the internally displaced;
- reconstruction of the essential infrastructures and public functions;
- social development: education and health;
- economic development: private sector, labour market, trade and investment.

Sources: Peace Building, a Development Perspective (2004) and *Memorandum on Post-conflict Reconstruction* (2005)

2004: 24–34). Unlike the traditional approach, which considers that the state has full responsibility for security, the concept of human security involves a much broader spectrum of actors and institutions, including people themselves.[7]

By placing people at the centre, the human security framework makes a requirement for enhancing and redirecting policies and institutions. Two key strategies are put forward: protection and empowerment. To protect people 'requires concerted efforts to develop national and international norms, processes and institutions, which must address insecurities in ways that are systematic not makeshift, comprehensive not compartmentalized, preventive not reactive' (Commission on Human Security 2003: 11). It implies a 'top-down' approach where states have the primary responsibility but international and regional organizations, civil society and non-governmental actors, and the private sector, also play a pivotal role in shielding people from threats.

Nevertheless, traditional state-centred security is being increasingly applied by local authorities and governments to respond to the expressions of violence that have emerged in cities (such as youth gangs and illicit trafficking). The human security framework, providing a comprehensive approach in which traditional security is complemented by other aspects of human development, is useful in establishing links between traditional security, development (the sustainable provision of basic needs), the environment (both rural and urban), human rights (rule of law) and gender (violence against women and girls, sexual violence, gender inequality), among other areas. The concept of human security evolved from the notion of human development: the rejection of economic growth as the main indicator of development; the rising incidence of internal conflicts; the impact of globalization in spreading transnational dangers; and the post-cold-war emphasis on human rights and humanitarian intervention (Acharya 2008: 494). From this comprehensive framework, other types of responses could be elaborated, not solely dependent on the use of force.

Human security requires a functioning state that is able and willing to provide for the welfare of the majority of its citizens. As the International Commission on Human Security argues: 'The state remains the fundamental purveyor of security. Yet it often fails to fulfil its security obligations, and at times has even become a source of threat to its own people. That is why attention must now shift from the security of the state to the security of the people, to human security' (Commission on Human Security 2003: 2). The relationship between the conceptualization of human security and urban violence emerges from the three elements of this concept: the focus on the individual/people as the referent object; its multidimensional nature; and its universal or global scope, applying to states and societies of the North as well as the South (Acharya 2008: 494).

Research and policies on urban conflict should be undertaken using a peace-building and human security approach. Issues to be addressed include economics and development (the lawful and criminal economies of the city and relations between city, regional, state and global dimensions, flows of investments and assistance, when it exists), rule of law (lack of access to justice for the poor, legalities and sub-legalities created by gangs and armed groups), resiliencies and survival strategies of different sectors of society (how the poor cope with lack of resources and how they confront violence), political

149

dimensions (how the poor organize their political representation and the role played by other internal/external actors, such as NGOs or official social workers), gender aspects (male culture and its impact on women, children and men). All these factors are crucial in peace-building processes, which generally ignore the urban component.[8] Last but not least, peace-building in this context is strongly related to state-building.

Security and poverty

Urban violence, as well as the crisis of the state, has a devastating impact on poor people. The media and populist politicians focus their attention on the impact that criminality and violence has on middle classes and higher sectors of society. But as McIlwaine and Moser (2007) have indicated in the case of Latin America, 'it is the urban poor who experience it more acutely'. Indeed, the poor themselves experience violence as victims in their everyday life, much more than the middle or upper classes. If urban violence and security problems are analysed from a human security perspective, i.e. taking into consideration a comprehensive approach to security (not only the protection of individuals as such, but also access to health, education, housing, justice and protection of human rights, among other factors), then the link between poverty and urban violence becomes evident in three fields, as described by UN-Habitat (2007: xxvii): crime and violence, insecurity of tenure and forced eviction, natural and human-made disasters. These three factors are present in the life of 'about 1 billion urban dwellers worldwide, [that] represent one part of what has been termed the geography of misery'.

Urban violence also has paradoxical aspects. Unemployment, urban growth, a high proportion of youth with little prospects, and poor welfare induce fragility and political violence. 'Many perpetrators of urban violence might be politically and economically disruptive, but they make varying contributions to asset accumulation and social protection in impoverished communities, often areas where the state has abdicated responsibility.' This means that urban violence performs core state functions, such as providing security, jobs and justice, even if arbitrary, when the state is absent. 'As such they are part of the social fabric and therefore difficult to challenge and change.'[9]

Violence adopts and would like to adopt very different forms in cities. Groups of people organize themselves around interests and identities. Viewed from above, cities are complex interconnected spaces, but exclusion is the line that divides people. Instead of addressing poverty and exclusion as the roots of violence, however, governments, from both strong and fragile states, are reacting with the use of force. In Israel and in France, there are centres for training in urban conflict, and the urban space is considered a new theatre of war (Leymarie 2009). Mike Davis also commented on the evidence that in the USA this trend is evident in military academies and in strategic think tanks that are studying and preparing the ground for fighting future wars in Southern as well as Northern cities, quoting the journal of the Army War College: 'The future of warfare, lies in the streets, sewers, high-rise buildings, and sprawl of houses that form the broken cities of the world [...] our recent military history is punctuated with city names [...] but these encounters have been but a prologue, with the real drama still to come.'[10]

In the current times of deep economic and financial crisis forcing millions of people into unemployment and greater marginalization, the responses to violence in urban spaces should be different. Police reform, anti-corruption policies, legal limits against impunity, special training for judges and officials of the judiciary system and strengthening of the rule of law are important steps. But equally important are the creation of employment, generation of opportunities for youth, and community programmes in which the police and civil society organizations can cooperate. These and other measures should be situated in the context of policies to provide education, health and housing. The international donor community must also address the crucial issue of the privatization of security that is destroying the foundations of the state.

The modern city, whether big and small, North or South, is part of a global world in which the concept of citizen should be redefined. External and domestic migrations, the presence of refugees, international crime and global issues such as the environmental crisis, international crime and epidemics reveal that the state is still a relevant actor but that a post-Westphalian order is in progress. Three particular fields are relevant and critical in this post-state order: inequality (people lacking full access to decent livelihoods owing to economic structures), lack of access to justice (because the poor cannot challenge the international forces that oppress them) and political representation (local politics cannot reach global decision-makers), as Fraser (2007) indicates in her theory of democratic justice. In the case of cities, as well as fragile states, the fight for equality, access to universal justice and political representation may bring to light new ways of social organization in a globalized world.

Notes

1 The author is grateful for the suggestions and editing contributions from Fionnuala Ni Eigeartaigh and Covadonga Morales Bertrand.

2 'Cities in fragile states', www.crisisstates.com.

3 The government of the state of Rio de Janeiro is constructing eleven walls around the *favelas* Morro de Dona Marta, Vidigal, Rocinha and others. A spokesman for the government explained that 'This is not discrimination. On the

contrary, the aim is to stop the development of slum communities and protect the environment' (*El País*, Madrid, 29 March 2009).

4 An interesting synthesis of policy approaches to violence is in Moser (2004).

5 See Booth (2007: 189–91, 195).

6 See the different interpretations in Paris and Risk (2009). See also Call and Wyeth (2008).

7 The sections on peace-building,

fragile states and human security are based on Aguirre et al. (2008).

8 Youth gangs are a particularly important expression of urban violence and state weakness. For an overall comprehension of this phenomenon, see Dowdney (2008).

9 Taken from 'Cities in fragile states'.

10 Mike Davis (2006: 203–6). See also Smulovitz (2004) for one example of response by force.

9 | Urban exclusion and the (false) assumptions of spatial policy reform in South Africa

SUSAN PARNELL AND OWEN CRANKSHAW

More than in most other parts of the world, citizens in South Africa understand that 'where' the state invests is as integral to its development agenda as 'who' or 'what' it puts its money into. Because space matters in development, no government, let alone one with spatial distortions and social problems like South Africa's, can avoid the issue of how to maximize the developmental opportunities and minimize threats posed by its locational choices. The geography of human settlement determines much of what individuals and groups can access by way of work and social support – so spatial policy is key to social inclusion and the national developmental agenda. The changing demographic and economic character of a society demands, however, that policy-makers update their responses to spatial exclusion in order to minimize the deleterious consequences of investments made on the basis of outmoded research assumptions and analysis. Inclusive spatial policy cannot make assumptions based on the way things were about what they are now or what is necessary to make them what they should be in years to come.

Because of the country's segregated past South African inequality is expressed in overlapping racial and geographical terms, making the spatial question a core issue in overcoming apartheid exclusions. Spatial policy remains one of the most politically charged challenges of transition, largely because 'blackness'/'rurality' and 'tradition' are often equated, while 'whiteness'/'urbanity' and 'modernity' are sometimes conflated in debates about the space economy. Everyone agrees that reconfiguring old spatial hierarchies and exclusions is key, but the complexity of the post-apartheid challenge makes it difficult to work out what will unlock the transformation of space and power, yet this is a key expectation of the democratic government.

Within the ruling African National Congress (ANC), which has held over two-thirds of the vote since the first non-racial elections in 1994, there is a broad spectrum of views about development, spatial planning and the role of the state. Unlike the very pubic discussion about affirmative action and black economic empowerment incentives, much of the South African debate about what to do to promote urban development and advance inclusion in the built environment has taken place within government. Thus, in this chapter we explore government's own discussions on spatial policy and assess how well the overall policy assumptions and direction accord with the evidence on the shifting nature of urban inequality and exclusion of the democratic period. We argue that, on balance, poor engagement with substantive changes in the spatial economy means that developmental policy objectives are unlikely to be realized and urban exclusion is likely to deepen under the current policy regime.

The chapter is structured to expose these dynamics. The first substantive section reveals the nature of the South African spatial impasse: there is still no clarity on how to fix the segregationist past, nor is there any idea of how to configure an alternative spatial system that serves the interests of the developmental state in the 2000s. We argue that the current debate about the spatial economy needs to move beyond, not get trapped in or, worse, reinforce, this quagmire. The next section of the chapter makes the case that it is possible to break the spatial stalemate of South African politics by re-examining current and future trends to highlight new patterns of social and economic exclusion. Here we argue that, while it is legitimate for spatial policy to have as its objective undoing the racist patterns of the past, it must simultaneously be responsive to the imperatives of the present and should seek to influence development in the future. The ideological values of the state today, the nature of economic opportunity and the location of the poor population must therefore be accommodated in evolving spatial policy and practice that is empirically grounded.

The spatial impasse of the developmental state in South Africa

The issue of how to drive reconstruction and development in South Africa is one of the most important issues facing government, but there is little conceptual consensus on how best to achieve this goal, creating a conundrum for spatial policy-makers. There is little clear guidance from academics, who disagree on the best way to overcome spatial inequality. Some favour a focus on historically deprived regions that are presented as typically African[a] and rural in character (Harrison and Todes 2002). Others point out that urban areas should get more attention in spatial targeting and that they are erroneously and simplistically depicted as wealthy and white, whereas they are in fact new sites of poverty, the economic engines of the subcontinent and the source of the purse for redistribution (Crankshaw and Parnell 1996). Using the contested South African experience of linking evidence about urbanization to the reform of spatial policy, we argue in favour of the latter position. Moreover, we suggest that addressing the current and future marginalization of urban places, rather than the historical marginalization of rural places, is an increasingly important element of a country's developmental strategy. Failure to manage the urban transition will drive increased social exclusion at both the city and the national scale.

The post-apartheid experience is fairly typical in that it reveals that giving greater policy attention and resources to issues of urban poverty is not easy, as it can conflict with the interests of the rural constituency and those of the urban elite. Unsurprisingly, many countries in the global South, where urban growth is relatively recent, struggle to give urban areas the kind of political attention that is necessary for overcoming the huge developmental challenges that they pose (Rogerson 2009). The South African example used in this chapter shows how politically difficult it is to get countries, especially those where poverty has traditionally been concentrated in rural areas, to examine the evidence of a demographic transition and thus to affirm the increasingly significant role of cites within the national development vision.

While South Africa is not alone in undergoing the struggle to define a country vision for its cities (UN-Habitat 2006), there are local dynamics, especially the apartheid legacy of race classification, that make it particularly difficult to reposition the urban developmental agenda beyond that which was expressed at the time of the first democratic elections (Pieterse 2004). The early post-apartheid vision assumed that the Reconstruction and Development Programme (RDP) would have application in both rural and urban areas (South Africa 1994). The Urban Development Framework of 1995 defined that agenda in very internally oriented terms of the racial integration of the historically segregated townships. Within the RDP framework, that was essentially a spatially blind policy; there was no expectation that cities would play any larger national role but there was also the assumption that cities could look after themselves and needed no national attention (Pieterse 2004). It is a moot point whether this assumption was ever true, but it is certainly less valid today than twenty years ago (Pillay et al. 2006; South Africa 2003a, 2008a).

Since 1994, the metropolitan centres of South Africa have expanded massively and have assumed a growing sphere of influence beyond their municipal boundaries, and so they assume increased national and continental prominence economically, politically and socially. This is especially true of the Gauteng Global City Region or Greater Johannesburg. As the city regions dominate the South African profile of population, poverty and productivity (Table 9.1), it would seem reasonable to see this reflected in national expectations about what cities could deliver or what the poor of the city required relative to their rural counterparts. In practice this is not the case and, despite increasing awareness of the importance of space in policy-making, what national direction for spatial targeting does exist is confused and contradictory.

The issue of where, geographically, the development emphasis should fall has not yet been successfully mainstreamed in post-apartheid South African policy or practice. This is despite cabinet approval of the National Spatial Development Perspective (NSDP), completed in 2003 and then approved following some revision in 2006 (South Africa 2003b). The NSDP is a policy statement that tracks the impact of urbanization over the last decades and acknowledges the importance of discouraging falsely incentivized spatial settlement patterns through unsustainable state infrastructure investments. Notwithstanding the adoption of the NSDP, the South African spatial question continues to be characterized by ambiguity, conflicting policy prescriptions and lack of coherence across the activities and incentives of departments and spheres of government (Harrison and Todes 2002; van Huyssteen et al. 2009).

TABLE 9.1 Typology of settlements showing urban dominance, 2008

	Population (% of national)	Economic activity (% of national GVA)	People under a minimum standard of living (% of national)
Gauteng city region	22	39	14
Coastal city regions	16	26	10
Cities	6	5	5
Regional service centres	14	16	15
Service towns	3	3	3
Local and niche settlements	9	2	13
Subtotal: urban as % of national	72	94	60
Clusters and dispersed rural settlements	21	2	31
Farms/rest of SA	7	4	9
Subtotal: rural as % of national	28	6	40

Source: SACN 2008

Instead of being an energizing unifier, spatial issues have emerged as a source of internal political conflict that has sapped the resources of the implementers of the developmental project of the state. More specifically it could be argued that the unintended consequence of the NSDP's inauspicious reception beyond cabinet, and the associated reluctance by cabinet to adopt a national urban development strategy, is the South African state's failure to respond adequately to enduring crime and exclusion in cities like Johannesburg, Cape Town and Durban.

What the NSDP represents is a national policy position that acknowledges that the developmental challenges of town and countryside are linked, but are not uniform. In this regard it is ahead of its time and stands apart from much of the rest of the African continent, where spatial or urban issues are largely ignored and remain totally outside of national policy formulations (Rogerson 2009). The South African NSDP is a nuanced position that acknowledges multiple forms of state spending and the different responsibilities of the spheres of government, but it has not been a popular or effective policy, and it has had to compete with contending policy positions that all espouse a commitment to greater inclusion.

The most obvious conflict is between the NSDP, sponsored by the presidency, and the Regional Industrial Development Strategy (RIDS), located in the Department of Trade and Industry (DTI) (South Africa 2008c), but it is also apparent in cabinet's inability to agree on the revised National Urban Development Framework. Although this has now been made a key action item in the Five-Year Local Government Strategic Agenda, one notes the absence of a coherent rural development framework and the stalled move, led by the national Department for Provincial and Local Government (DPLG), to have the assignment of powers and functions between the spheres of government rationalized because of the contradictions generated by intergovernmental action within localities, especially the big cities.

Agreement on the NSDP as a national spatial framework, with its carefully mediated position that addressed the imperative of redistribution while focusing on growth opportunities, should have been uncontentious given the concern within government to increase GDP so that redistribution and shared growth are advanced. The NSDP, however, with its tag line of 'investing in people not places' and its emphasis on the twenty-six nodes with growth potential, took over three years to get approval, allegedly because it was perceived as anti-rural, and by implication anti-poor.[1]

Even then its passage through cabinet was far from smooth. In some quarters it remains a contentious perspective, with more traditional views coalescing around DTI's Regional Industrial Strategy (RIDS), which weights an earlier anti-urban position on spatial prioritization put forward by the RDP Office and the Fiscal and Finance Commission. In that first wave of democratic policy-making it was felt that spatial policy should favour historically disadvantaged and marginalized places, which was commonly, if inappropriately, interpreted to mean only rural areas of predominantly African occupation. African urban townships and informal settlements were overlooked. Strangely, it was never explicitly said that rural meant the old homeland areas, and although presumably this was the implication implied by the activists pushing the policy agenda, nothing specific was introduced to deal with the apartheid legacies beyond promising greater fiscal transfers to rural areas (see Budlender 1996). It was this logic of pouring money into desolate areas where apartheid once dumped people and from which they were migrating which the NSDP challenged. The NSDP proposed an imperative of investing in areas of need and opportunity, which, notwithstanding severe resistance, now permeates at least the rhetoric of government thinking. Perhaps because Provincial Growth and Development Strategies are now required to demonstrate alignment with national policy imperatives (DPLG 2005), the NSDP is finally being embraced on the sub-national scale. On the local scale there is little acceptance of the NSDP, especially in places that are not clearly national priorities.

Following the ANC's 2008 national conference held in the town of Polakwane, uncertainty over party policy direction has resurfaced and the link between spatial policy and the debate about national priorities on growth versus poverty reduction has been reopened. In the run-up to the 2009 elections there are regular calls for a more rural focus in development spending. In this regard the DTI's RIDS is ascendant, presenting a clear articulation of an alternative view to that of the presidency and the NSDP.

There are several legitimate explanations for the resurgence of the pro-rural view in the election manifestos. Among the most important is that the depth of poverty remains most severe in the old homeland areas. But the RIDS is not a rural development strategy and it is not designed to address the fundamental development barriers of the old Bantustans, which include incomplete land reform, poor viability of commercial agriculture on denuded and arid land, the persistence of traditional tenure, the absence of legitimate or fiscally viable governance systems, declining populations due to outmigration, generations of inadequate infrastructure development, etc. The seriousness of poverty and institutional failure in rural South Africa demands a more detailed policy response and is a matter that cannot be left to traditional leaders, who dominate these spaces politically and geographically. As an alternative the NSDP is no better: it offers only high-level guidance about minimum standards and social rather than infrastructural investment to accommodate outmigration and the realities of job location in urban areas.

We have already noted that the RIDS position contradicts that of the NSDP, raising the question of what exactly government's spatial policy now is and will be after the 2009 elections. The coexistence of the divergent policies reflects at worst a systemic failure within and across government to resolve its position on the actual values that are necessary to legitimize the difficult task of making spatial choices. At best the diametrically opposed positions are confusing. In one case the Development Bank of South Africa's new Local Economic Development Fund sought to appease both positions and its resulting list of 'priority locations' covered most of the country (DBSA 2008).

The incoherence in the South African government's spatial consciousness extends to other spheres of government: most Provincial Growth and Development Strategies, other than those of the two most affluent provinces of the Western Cape and Gauteng (see WCPG 2006), have no spatial focus and do not address urban issues directly. At local level most Integrated Development Plans (IDPs) in the country are characterized by a narrow municipal concern that reveals a parochial disregard for functional city–regional dynamics (Harrison 2006). Across the spheres of government, it would not be unfair to caricature South Africa as being in a spatial logjam, unable to dislocate the imprint of the past and unclear how space relates to development aspirations in the future.

Breaking the policy impasse means, at the very least, being much clearer on how the NSDP translates into urban practice within national line departments (including the treasury) and the actions of other spheres, particularly IDP preparation (by municipalities) and settlement planning oversight (by provinces). Making this case convincingly will no doubt require a political change of heart for some, and this can be achieved only by understanding the policy contradictions better, and reviewing and updating the evidence about the challenges facing the country.

It is not clear why the NSDP failed to spawn a coherent national strategy for either rural or urban action. At the urban end it is possible that some in the ANC cabinet referred the draft NUDP for the same reasons they disliked the NSDP – they saw it as anti-rural (Turok and Parnell 2009). The NUDP, which calls for a specific government-wide approach to cities, has been stalled in the cabinet process for over three years now. Cabinet at one point, through the South African Cities Network, asked the NUDP drafters to give greater attention to urban–rural linkages and locate the urban question in the wider spatial economy. This spawned a fresh round of discussion in 2008, spearheaded by DPLG, the presidency and the Department of Housing. The NUDP revision was then presented (though not tabled) in a document setting out 'The case for a National Urban Development Perspective' at the 2008 SACN meeting in Durban. Given that the ruling ANC has entered into the 2009 election with a call for a more overt rural strategy and no mention of anything urban, it is unclear what will come of the NUDP process (ibid.).

Regardless of the fate of the NUDP, we argue in this chapter that the political case for focusing on cities as sites of exclusion needs to be refreshed. The fundamental principle of the NSDP, that there is a spatial logic to development, remains unchallenged, but the follow-on positions – first, that the rapidly expanding urban settlements as a category may need extra investment, and second, that while growing cities need greater physical investment there is also a need for social spending on poor and marginalized parts of towns – have not been fleshed out. There is the additional problem that the political leadership in government, from line departments to the national treasury, lack the will to implement cabinet's NSDP recommendations. Thus, application of the NSDP recommendation, including the idea that not all development assistance has to be infrastructural, has yet to be realized. As a result the implications of the NSDP have not been teased out in a coherent programme of urban inclusion beyond that of the social grants. In urban as in rural areas, community development plays second fiddle to housing and basic infrastructure investment, and there is no integrated vision of what a more just and inclusive city might require by way of state support.

Government is not oblivious to the geography of inequality at the subnational scale. Indeed, in 1994 the reconfiguration of the provinces and municipalities was a major attempt to redirect the resources and developmental capacity of the state and to diffuse the traditional authority conundrum (Cameron 1999). But, despite the redrawing of boundaries to remove old race-based territories, including homelands and black local authorities, the radicalized legacies of the past remain and the radicalized understanding of the structural basis of exclusion persists. Put crudely, the state has followed a logic that says 'if apartheid created unequally serviced settlements for black people then the post-apartheid agenda must be to level the playing fields by servicing all historically underserviced areas and this means rural prioritization'. In search of an idealized map of 'isothermic justice', the fact that the geography of inequality is constantly changing has been ignored. Because of the concern to right past wrongs, post-apartheid governance arrangements have been tardy in confronting the drivers of new exclusions. Paradoxically it is the African poor, especially women and children, who suffer from the outmoded 'urban versus rural', 'black versus white' understandings of the development challenge.

Patterns of exclusion – information to inform debates on spatial policy

The purpose of this section is to give a high-level overview of some of the macro-structural changes that suggest that the spatial economy of the country demands policy adjustment. We show that the urban scale is more than ever important and that the enduring use of apartheid race classification or its proxy (urban/rural) as an operational mechanism of spatial targeting is outdated. In South Africa, everyone who seeks a job moves to the city, and that means that the urban dimension of the development dilemma requires much more attention than in the past. While the old homelands clearly need focused intervention, this alone will in no way preclude exclusion.

A structural shift of special relevance to national and local spatial policy is the economy and its economic sectoral and labour market change. Over the past 120 years South Africa has moved from dependence on mining and agriculture, through a period of massive manufacturing expansion and then relative manufacturing stabilization, or in some cases decline (Figure 9.1). In the agricultural sector mechanization and the shift to capital-intensive production have fundamentally reduced the number of jobs available in rural areas. Notwithstanding population growth, employment in agriculture has been stable at just over one million workers (Table 9.2). Mining has also become more capital intensive, leading to an overall decline in primary-sector jobs (Figure 9.2). The mining sector's location changed as gold production shifted

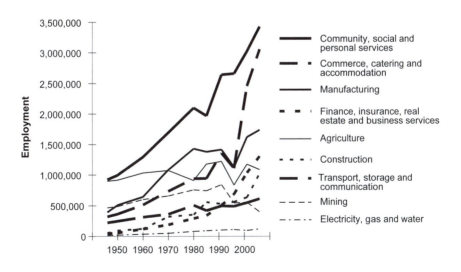

FIGURE 9.1 National employment by economic sector, 1946–2006.
Sources: CSS (1987: 211–12, 1993: 2.17–2.18); StatsSA (2007: vi)

TABLE 9.2 The changing labour force: employment by economic sector, 1946–2007

	Agriculture	Mining	Manu-facturing	Electricity, gas & water	Con-struction	Commerce, catering & accom-modation	Finance, insurance, real estate & business services	Transport, storage & communi-cation	Community, social & personal services	Total
1946	899,000	466,000	392,000	13,000	55,000	322,000	45,000	221,000	925,000	3,338,000
1950	916,300	489,000	511,000	22,000	93,000	364,000	57,000	248,000	998,000	3,698,300
1960	1,033,000	602,000	645,000	38,000	123,000	513,000	120,000	315,000	1,298,000	4,687,000
1970	1,076,000	658,000	1,086,000	51,000	322,000	737,000	191,000	361,000	1,693,000	6,175,000
1980	911,000	759,000	1,432,000	79,000	352,000	938,000	290,000	505,000	2,098,000	7,364,000
1985	1,179,590	743,065	1,379,518	92,720	556,339	941,876	339,204	418,156	1,965,040	7,615,508
1991	1,224,434	840,747	1,417,127	102,928	526,374	1,358,292	503,970	497,123	2,640,522	9,111,517
1996	832,911	543,297	1,128,109	110,196	560,124	1,109,110	687,646	487,474	2,659,594	9,255,428
2001	1,178,000	554,000	1,620,000	94,000	634,000	2,454,000	1,035,000	546,000	3,023,000	11,181,000
2006	1,088,000	398,000	1,737,000	119,000	1,024,000	3,055,000	1,309,000	611,000	3,427,000	12,800,00

Sources: CSS (1987: 211–12, 1993: 2.17–2.18); StatsSA (2007: vi)

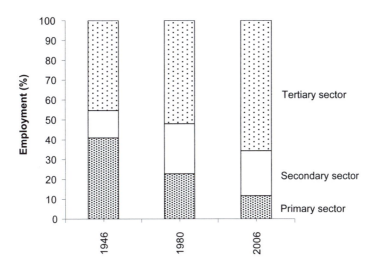

FIGURE 9.2 Changing proportion of primary, secondary and tertiary jobs in South Africa, 1946–2006. *Sources*: CSS (1987: 211–12, 1993: 2.17–2.18); StatsSA (2007: vi)

away from the Rand to the Witbank area in the 1950s and more recently to Rustenburg and Mpumalange as platinum and steel become relatively more important export commodities. The associated boom and bust of mining towns is an important element of the shifting spatial economy of the country. The dominant shift, however, is to town-based jobs.

Within the cities, the recent growth in service-sector employment has spawned both highly skilled and unskilled jobs, rupturing the spatial focus of employment (Crankshaw and Parnell 2004). On a national scale the rise of tertiary-sector work has made Gauteng an ever increasingly important contributor to GDP and fostered unprecedented urban primacy in the South African space economy (Rogerson 1996; Rogerson and Rogerson 1999). Within all of the larger cities, but especially the greater Johannesburg metropolitan region, there has been a deconcentration of employment from the old Central Business District (CBD) to the new edge-of-city nodes where the service jobs are typically concentrated (Beavon 1997). The spatial impact of the massive growth in informal employment is poorly understood, but irregular and largely unrecognized work is widely seen as providing a livelihood base for the poorest populations, who are located in informal settlements and townships. Alongside post-Fordist industrial restructuring, home-based production, casualized and informal employment have all shifted the geography of work from the CBD and old industrial areas and spread it across

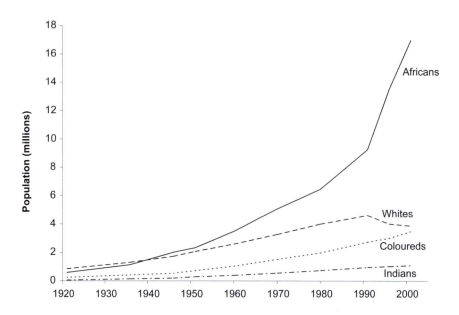

FIGURE 9.3 The urban population by race, 1921–2001. *Sources*: SA Office of Census and Statistics (1922, 1949); Bureau of Statistics (1954, 1963); Department of Statistics (1976); CSS (1985, 1986, 1992); and tables created using the Census 1996 and 2001 Community Profile Databases, supplied by Statistics South Africa

the city, in many cases taking retail and tertiary-sector employment nodes beyond traditional metropolitan boundaries. Overall, then, the ending of urban residential segregation and the post-Fordist spatial reorganization of work occurred simultaneously in South Africa (Beall et al. 2002).

Under the post-Fordist city structure economic polarization is exacerbated even while opportunities for racial integration are advanced, making the changing nature of the economy an increasingly cogent lens for urban policy-makers. Figures 9.3–9.5 give some idea of how the rapid social and demographic transformations tracked economic and political change over the last century. The most important point to emerge from this suite of graphs is that the world that we were born into and the world in which the post-apartheid imaginary of an alternative urban space was forged have changed profoundly. We live in a blacker and more urban South Africa – this is a trend that will continue and which must of necessity inform our vision of the urban future.

The rapid urbanization of the African population over the last two decades transformed the racial profile of South Africa's cities, which, until the Second

World War, mirrored the segregationists' aspirations that cities should be thought of as 'white space'. Ironically, from as early as 1948 blacks outnumbered whites in urban areas, despite apartheid ideology to the contrary. The massive growth of the existing African urban population and African migration from rural areas, even under apartheid, has combined to make cities today predominantly African places (Figure 9.3). The character of urban areas as 'black space' was already evident in 1981 when the Soweto Civic was formed and in 1995 when the Urban Development Strategy was prepared, but it has recently become an even more marked feature of the urban population (Figure 9.4). Since the 1980s there have been profound changes in settlement patterns, with the proportion of the population of South Africa living in cities doubling and the three largest metropolises steadily gaining a greater share of the overall population (see Table 9.3).[2] Almost all of these changes can be ascribed to the growth of the black urban population.[3]

TABLE 9.3 The growing significance of the three major city regions, 1921–2001 (percentage of the national population)

	Greater Durban	Greater Cape Town	Greater Jo'burg (Gauteng)	National urban population	Total national population
1921	1	4	9	25	100
1936	3	4	13	31	100
1946	3	5	15	39	100
1951	4	5	17	43	100
1960	4	6	18	47	100
1970	5	6	17	48	100
1980	6	7	20	53	100
1991	6	8	20	57	100
1996	5	7	18	54	100
2001	6	7	19	57	100

Sources: SA Office of Census and Statistics (1922, 1949); Bureau of Statistics (1954, 1963); Department of Statistics (1976); CSS (1985, 1986, 1992); and tables created using the Census 1996 and 2001 Community Profile Databases, supplied by Statistics South Africa

An equally significant demographic transformation lies in the steady overall urbanization of South African society. Like the rest of the world, the average South African is now an urban, not rural, dweller (Figure 9.4). This is a relatively recent transition, dating only from the mid-1970s, and so many

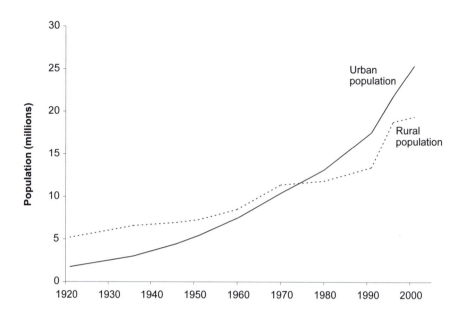

FIGURE 9.4 Total urban versus rural population, 1921–2001. *Sources*: SA Office of Census and Statistics (1922, 1949); Bureau of Statistics (1954, 1963); Department of Statistics (1976); CSS (1985, 1986, 1992); and tables created using the Census 1996 and 2001 Community Profile Databases, supplied by Statistics South Africa

urban dwellers are first-generation migrants with strong rural identities and enduring social ties to the countryside. Since the ending of apartheid almost eight million more people, almost equivalent to the population of Gauteng, have become urbanites, and this growth is set to continue, meaning that the urban population outstrips the rural population (Figure 9.5). A key question for policy-makers is whether or not the rural–urban linkages of past migrants will be retained by future generations who, unlike their elders, will be free to move permanently to town.[4]

Sticking with the numbers, an overview of census results shows that one of the most significant contributors to the predominantly urban character of the South African population is the fact that the black population is now major-ity urban (Figure 9.5). The next census will reflect that even Africans, once restricted from entering towns without passes, are already more urban than rural (Figure 9.6). These demographic trends have and will change the profile of voters, shift the place of service expectations, alter the nature of work and consumption, change cultural values and generally transform the nature of society. It is not possible to ignore demographic change when devising spatial policy, but in South Africa we are inclined to do so for fear of being seen to

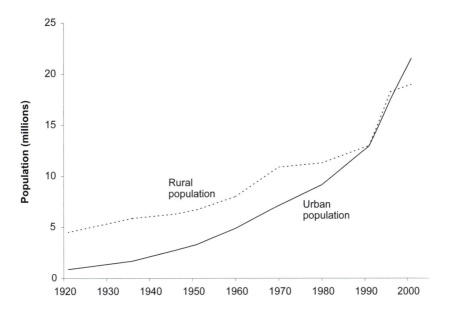

FIGURE 9.5 Urban/rural trends in the black population, 1920–2000.
Sources: SA Office of Census and Statistics (1922, 1949); Bureau of Statistics
(1954, 1963); Department of Statistics (1976); CSS (1985, 1986, 1992); and
tables created using the Census 1996 and 2001 Community Profile Databases, supplied by Statistics South Africa

be ignoring opportunities to correct past injustice and possibly because we
are unwilling to posit an alternative discourse of urbanity.

Conclusion

The de facto marginalization of the NSDP recommendations reflects both
the dominant national (not local) framing of development policy and the deep
ideological positions that favour rural traditionalism over urban modernism.
In the South African case there is a further conflation of blackness and rurality
on the one hand and whiteness and urbanity on the other. Using evidence from
policy processes and current demographic and economic trends, the chapter
has highlighted these follies, and demonstrated how the narrow adherence
to a racially framed understanding of exclusion and the marginalization of
metropolitan issues contributes to the political and intellectual impasse
that leaves South African urban residents exposed to crime, violence and
institutional exclusion.

Overall, we suggest that if real and defendable urban priorities are to be
agreed, no single scale of spatial planning can be considered in isolation.
Given the urbanizing shift of the population and the imperative of expanded

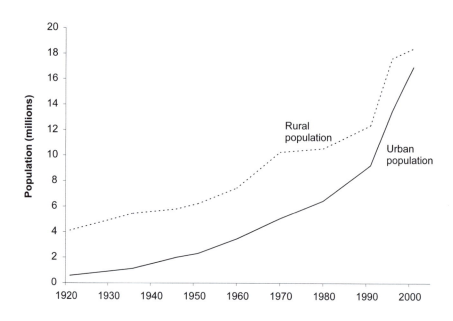

FIGURE 9.6 Urban/rural trends in the African population, 1921–2001.
Sources: SA Office of Census and Statistics (1922, 1949); Bureau of Statistics
(1954, 1963); Department of Statistics (1976); CSS (1985, 1986, 1992); and
tables created using the Census 1996 and 2001 Community Profile Databases, supplied by Statistics South Africa

economic growth, which is by its nature located primarily in urban space, it
should be uncontentious that towns and cities receive greater national priority
than before. But the spatial reorientation of the developmental agenda of the
state also needs to be contextualized and balanced by a recognition of how the
urban spatial economy, which is dominated by African people, connects to its
hinterland and how the intra-urban management of space advances different
interests within and beyond cities. Past experience suggests that there are
critical ways, such as circular migration or the persistence of traditional land
tenure, through which spatial inequality is reproduced across scales. Some
but not all of the institutional drivers of exclusion in South Africa have or
had a racial expression. As a result the logic of deracialization is a necessary
but not sufficient entry point for a transformative agenda. What we need is
a multi-scale spatial policy that not only has a clearly articulated value base,
but also a strategic understanding of the tools and instruments that could be
utilized, in cities and in rural areas, to achieve the spatial reconfiguration of
the world's most notoriously contorted and exclusionary landscape.

Notes

a Editor's note: 'African' refers to a statistical racial or ethnic category of non-mixed non-white South Africans, whereas 'black' refers to all 'non-white' South Africans.

1 This view is now widely expressed in formal and informal meetings. Similar sentiment is directed at the NUDF, which was not passed by cabinet. It remains unclear who in cabinet supported and who opposed the NUDF, or indeed on what specific grounds. Cabinet feedback to DPLG and the presidency that the urban rural linkage issue needed higher priority is one indication of the general sentiment.

2 The figures also show an absolute decline in the urban white population, but it is unclear whether this reflects emigration or census undercounting.

3 Were there accurate figures for foreign migration to South Africa it would further reinforce this picture.

4 Under apartheid in the 1960s over one million African people were forcibly moved out of town because they were no longer employed. Under Sections 10b, c and d, African people were obliged to return to Bantustans.

Conclusions: governing exclusion and violence in megacities

KEES KOONINGS AND DIRK KRUIJT

Three interlocking fields of urban exclusion have guided the analysis and interpretations throughout this book: livelihood, mobilization and participation, and violence. In Chapter 1 we argued that social and political relations in megacities are shaped in diffuse spaces in which the distinction between formal and informal, legal and illegal, order and disorder tend to disappear. The chapters in this book examined in different ways the connections between urban exclusion and violence and offered many insights into the nature and workings of these diffuse urban spaces. Here, by way of conclusion, we will try to tie these arguments together and then examine the key implications for urban politics and policies. The first question to be addressed is how the contributions in this volume deal with the fields of livelihood, mobilization and violence.

Livelihood

Although none of the authors in this volume has explicitly centred their analysis on problems of work, employment, the informal sector or household strategies, a number of chapters note the crucial importance of this field for understanding the dynamics of exclusion, mobilization and violence. Not only do recent changes in the opportunity structure for livelihood provide the context for processes of exclusion, mobilization and urban policy, obstacles to livelihood strategies are also directly linked to urban violence, especially to the emergence of drug and youth gangs.

The chapters in Part One of the book concur in observing that globalization, ensuing economic reform and structural adjustment policies, and the decline of formal employment opportunities, have contributed to growing socio-economic inequalities in Latin America and the Middle East. In these regions, as elsewhere in the world, this process has been accompanied by the declining ability of states to provide public goods and services. Gay argues in Chapter 2 that Rio de Janeiro has experienced a protracted process of decline of formal employment in industry, trade and the public sector, despite the average prosperity of the city and its role as a global tourist hub. Gay (Chapter 2) and Perlman (Chapter 3) stress the resulting extreme social inequalities as the key backdrop to the city's problems of exclusion and violence. Similar processes, but less intense, have been observed in the case of Guayaquil by Moser (Chapter 4) and Middle Eastern cities by Bayat (Chapter 5).

The master frame everywhere in the megacities of the global South has been an economic opportunity structure that has been shaped, in the past three decades, by neoliberal globalization. Although only a few cities have been admitted into the upper echelons of global power and wealth on the basis of their command and control functions in the global economy, the impact of concentration (of wealth and supporting urban infrastructure and services) and segregation (between the urban privileged and the excluded) has been widespread in megacities, and indeed in any city in the developing world. Not only in Latin America, but also in the Middle East, India, South Africa and China, nationalist-populist arrangements have not survived to provide ready-made social policies to counter the effects of socio-spatial segregation in megacities.

For livelihood this means that increasingly the poor in megacities have to rely on informal strategies to make a living. Bayat (Chapter 5) coins the concept of 'quiet encroachment' to analyse the largely unobtrusive informal strategies the urban poor use to obtain access to key resources such as wage income, housing, energy and other basic needs. This is a process quite similar to the informalization of the urban peripheries in Latin America during the 1960s to 1990s. Still, it has been demonstrated by recent research (reviewed in Chapter 1) that the informalization of livelihood strategies in large conurbations has been reaching its limits of elasticity and sustainability. But rather than adhering to the proposition (ventured by early global city research and even more forcefully by M. Davis in his *Planet of Slums*, 2006) that this is turning the slums of megacities into abandoned areas of a passive surplus population, the contributions to this volume show that this forces the urban poor to become even more inventive. The urban poor use combinations of formal and informal household strategies that allocate productive and reproductive labour (including migration of members) and neighbourhood initiatives to create reciprocity and solidarity. These strategies engage the state (formally or informally) to demand, in particular, access to the means of collective consumption. Contrary to expectations and 'Planet of Slums' imagery, these strategies can be successful in material terms over two or three generations. *Favelas* and other slums (such as Indio Guayas, studied by Moser in Chapter 4) have become more prosperous – or at least more diverse – in terms of income levels, assets and collective consumption. This means that social exclusion has become the key concept for analysing urban poverty and inequality, highlighting the hierarchical patterns of urban societies through social relations that have a material, spatial and symbolic component.

There is, however, one important direct link between exclusion from livelihood opportunities and urban violence, as discussed by Gay, Perlman and Moser (in Chapters 2, 3 and 4, respectively). The lack of occupational and income perspectives for young uneducated males in the poor neighbourhoods drives many of them into gangs (see also Cruz 2007; Jones and Rodgers forthcoming). Why resist gang life and related money and status if 'hard work' and 'playing by the rules' do not offer any prospects (Woolcock 2007: 5, cited by Moser in Chapter 4)?

Mobilization and participation

The immediate impact of the processes noted above has been the continuous vigour and reinvention of urban social movements. In Latin America, the urban movements that sprang up in the peripheries of the big cities around issues of collective consumption in the 1970s sought new relationships with the state as part of democratization processes in the 1980s and 1990s. As Perlman and Gay have shown in this volume, the active neighbourhood associations that effectively managed Rio de Janeiro's *favelas* in the 1980s raised the initial expectation of a new and decentralized model of inclusionary urban governance. A similar perspective was opened up in Porto Alegre. Baierle shows in Chapter 7 that the rise to power of the Workers' Party in the southernmost state capital of Brazil initially brought the promise of transformative urban governance, incorporating the peripheries and its urban movements and expanding the domains of subaltern citizenship. As the system of participatory budgeting was consolidated, however, it became increasingly a municipality-driven system, running out of innovative potential, funds and appeal among the urban population at large. When the Workers' Party lost office in 2004, a new coalition of pro-business and technocratic stakeholders managed to bypass the participatory system without openly doing away with it. Similarly, in South Africa, the advent of non-racial (post-apartheid) democracy did not allow for sufficient attention to the expansion of urban poverty, although the majority of the country's coloured poor, the inheritors of the brutal apartheid segregation, now live in the large cities. Parnell and Crankshaw show in Chapter 9 that the prevalent strategy to combat this legacy still favours rural areas, partly because of outdated conceptions of the nature of poverty in the country, partly because of the political/clientelistic interests of the leading political class. In the Middle East, urbanization has been an equally vigorous process, but the setting for this has been less

173

uniformly neoliberal globalization and hardly at all liberal democratization. Still, Bayat in Chapter 5 observes a similar retraction of national-popular regimes (with the partial exception of Iran), meaning that a wide variety of social movements and collective strategies has emerged to address multiple interests of the urban poor. Although mass protests, Islam-inspired social and welfare organizations and secular NGOs have been important, the brunt of social activism has been borne by 'quiet encroachment' (already mentioned above): a process of largely non-contestational *faits accomplis* created by the urban excluded to secure access to collective consumption and to have the state tolerate or eventually legalize these entitlements. Bayat calls this a 'non-movement', but at the same time he observes the long-term mobilizational impact of quiet encroachment that is directed mainly at the state and the urban well-to-do. The blurring of the more explicit and visible features of social movements, community-based and civil society organizations (CBOs and CSOs) is part and parcel of the fading of the distinctions between the formal and the informal, the institutional and the non-institutional in contemporary megacity politics.

Violence

Perhaps the single most important problem of exclusion in megacities that emerged from the chapters in this book is the spread of urban violence and its multiple, negative, if not destructive, consequences for urban social participation and empowering politics. The importance of the analyses of Gay, Perlman and Moser in Chapters 2, 3 and 4 is that they offer a unique longitudinal, transgenerational perspective on the emergence and proliferation of urban violence at various levels: individuals and households, neighbourhoods and entire cities. It is no coincidence that the case of Rio de Janeiro is central to two related chapters in the book. No other megacity has shown so dramatically the juxtaposition of separate urban forms, economically and spatially often very close and connected, but worlds apart in cultural and moral terms: the famous contrast between the *morro* (hill or *favela*) and the *asfalto* (the rich districts). Gay and Perlman show not only how social and spatial inequalities have actually increased during the past three decades, but also how new forms of urban violence created an absolute reality of exclusion that has undermined and eventually destroyed the prospects of peaceful, civic empowerment of the *favelados* and their neighbourhood associations. Organized urban violence, in the form of often heavily armed territorial gangs and militias, brings together all the syndromes of urban exclusion: lack of 'normal' livelihood opportunities, physical and infrastructural neglect of shanty towns, absence of the state and its public functions and moral and cultural disdain by the middle and upper classes towards the poor and excluded. It locks the urban excluded in a cul-de-sac. The case of Guayaquil, analysed by Moser in Chapter 4, is only relatively less extreme. The 'informal' way neighbourhood leaders dealt with the presence of a gang and a specific violent event, involving a 'decent' young man who killed a gang leader, show not only more space for grassroots civic agency than in Rio's *favelas*, which are tightly controlled by non-state armed actors; they also show a near-total lack of trust in the ability and the willingness of local authorities, especially law enforcement, to protect poor citizens and guarantee their security, just as in Rio de Janeiro and most other megacities around the world. Here we see a particularly harmful blurring of formal and informal, legal and illegal, civil and uncivil spheres. The police alternate between random violence against the shanty-town inhabitants and involvement in violent crime itself. Drug gangs defy the law and impose their own, but also maintain dyadic relations with the world of politics. Private militias, with ties to the official security forces, pretend to defend law and order in *favelas* by imposing their own regime of extortion and intolerance.

Political and policy implications

What does our analysis tell us about the policy agenda that would be required to face urban exclusion and segregation? Under what conditions will local politics open up channels of participation and empowerment to the urban excluded and their movements, who arguably are the key stakeholders for such policies? Jo Beall has cogently argued in Chapter 6 that 'urbanism' offers propitious conditions for the development of political consciousness of the subaltern classes. Cities are a fertile stage for collective action and urban movements are likely to acquire rapid visibility and potentially high impact. Since, in the context of capitalist globalization, urban municipal governments have little scope to influence directly conditions of employment and household income of the poor, urban policies that best benefit the excluded are to be sought in the domain of collective consumption, socio-spatial reintegration and the restoration of the urban public spaces for all urban citizens (this includes the key issue of public and citizen security, to be discussed below).

But how can this be done? The prevailing discourse of 'decentralization' and 'good governance' holds that sufficient political and institutional conditions for such an urban policy agenda to emerge would be formal democracy and a technically competent (and fiscally sound) urban administration.

Indeed, the experience of participatory budgeting in Porto Alegre during the 1990s underscored this idea, but this case also shows that this arrangement was internally and externally vulnerable, both politically and fiscally. In fact, participatory budgeting is a perfect example of what constitutes a key characteristic of politics, participation and empowerment in mega-cities in the global South: hybridity beyond the divide of formal/informal and institutional/non-institutional rules and practices. In those cities where the managing capabilities of institutional systems are fragile and less resilient, and service-providing NGOs that chip in for local governments are as likely to become bureaucratic, unaccountable or clientelistic, more direct and pluriform interaction between (mobilized) excluded and (often semi-formal) local power holders and brokers will essentially determine outcomes in terms of entitlements of the poor. Public policy-makers and interventions aimed at combating urban poverty and exclusion should have to take this into account. Even then, however, inclusive urban security is a necessary (but not sufficient) condition for this to be successful.

At this point we once more draw attention to the pivotal argument made by Beall in the opening chapter of Part Two of the book. She addresses the key ambiguity in present-day megacities between the potential for creative urbanism on the one hand and destructive violence on the other. Cities create collective issues on a massive scale and offer the context and the social capital for citizens to mobilize and engage the (local or national) state. But if a confluence of inequality and security voids created by public default link up with the availability of perverse alternatives, armed actors appear who play upon social, ethnic or religious divides that are equally visible and confrontational in cities. Violence employed by these extralegal or informal armed actors erodes the participatory momentum of grassroots movements and decentralized urban governance. In turn, following the attack on the welfare functions of the local and national state during the past decades, urban politicians and governments increasingly respond in a heavy-handed manner, specifically through repressive law and order, and more generally through what Beall (Chapter 6), following others, calls 'urbicide': '[...] the deliberate destruction of the urban infrastructure for political purposes'.

Our final conclusion, then, is that here we may find the key political and policy issue of exclusion in megacities: violence and insecurity. In general, as we saw, violence erodes the associational capacity of grassroots actors and distorts the channels of participation and empowerment. But more specifically, urban administrations and their political overseers prove incapable of coming up with adequate answers to this problem. Aguirre has argued in Chapter 8 that the prevalent response is repressive. This response is driven not only by political pressure generated by dominant (middle-class) constituencies, but also by the strong 'post-9/11' connection made in conventional security circles between urban exclusion and abandonment, state fragility and international terrorist violence. Although Bayat argues convincingly (Chapter 5) that violent Muslim fundamentalism is not a prevalent sentiment among the urban poor in the Middle East, megacities and shanty towns are, as noted by Aguirre in Chapter 8, increasingly seen as potential battlefields in future asymmetric warfare scenarios. Warren (2002: 615), discussing the new doctrines of MOUT (Military Operations in Urban Territories) developed by the Pentagon shortly after 9/11, states: 'It is expected that urban military action and presence will be required to deal with the aggression of "rogue" nations, individual and networked acts of terrorism, and civilian riots and disorders.' Many urban governments and (local) law enforcement agencies in megacities in developing countries consider this no longer something to be expected, but something to be faced right here and now. Gay (Chapter 2) has already drawn attention to the fact that in recent years the Brazilian army has been called on to intervene in Rio de Janeiro at critical junctions. The 'opponents' of official law enforcement strategies are most of the time depicted as 'rogue' elements: the BOPE (Batalhão de Operações Especiais) urban counter-insurgency unit of the military police of Rio de Janeiro literally refers to *elementos*, *marginais* or *bandidos* when talking about drug dealers and gang members. In practice, however, their enemies are the urban excluded at large, relegated to the status of second- or third-class citizens, or effectively non-citizens. The key priority for governing exclusion and violence in megacities therefore is to restore approaches of citizen security that incorporate rather than target the urban ex-cluded, in overwhelming majority decent, peaceful and hard-working citizens who labour daily to make the city also 'theirs'. We have shown throughout this volume that violence restricts livelihood options, undermines trust and social capital, erodes social mobilization and destroys political participation and indeed 'good governance' on all 'fronts'. To redress this vicious cycle may well be the most important focus for 'real' urban poverty alleviation efforts in the coming decades.

Bibliography

Abdel Taher, N. (1986) 'Social identity and class in a Cairo neighbourhood', *Cairo Papers in Social Science*, 9(4).

Acharya, A. (2008) 'Human security', in J. Baylis, S. Smith and P. Owens (eds), *The Globalization of World Politics*, Oxford: Oxford University Press.

Adams, R. (2000) 'Evaluating the process of development in Egypt, 1980–97', *International Journal of Middle East Studies*, 32: 255–75.

Afshar, H. (1993) *Women in the Middle East: Perceptions, Realities, and Struggles for Liberation*, New York: St Martin's Press.

Agamben, G. (1998) *Homo Sacer. Sovereign Power and Bare Life*, California: Meridian Press.

Aguirre, M., C. Churruca and S.-L. John de Sousa (2008) *Peace Building, Fragile States and Human Security*, Coimbra: Coimbra University for the Portuguese Agency of International Development and the Centre of Peace Studies.

Akinci, U. (1999) 'The Welfare Party's municipal track record: evaluating Islamist municipal activism in Turkey', *Middle East Journal*, 53(1): 75–94.

Al-Ahali (1999) 3 November.

Al-Ahram Weekly (1996) 17–23 and 24–30 October.

— (1997) 27 November–3 December.

Al-Karadawi, Y. (1985) *The Problem of Poverty, and How Can Islam Resolve It*, Beirut: Al-Risalaa (in Arabic).

Altbeker, A. (2007) *A Country at War with Itself. South Africa's Crisis of Crime*, Johannesburg and Cape Town: Jonathan Ball Publishers.

Alvito, M. (2001) *As Cores de Acari: uma Favela Carioca*, Rio de Janeiro: Editora Fundação Getúlio Vargas.

Al-Wafd (1997) 18 October.

— (1998) 3 March.

— (1999) 5 February.

Amar, P. (2003) 'Reform in Rio: reconsidering the myths of crime and violence', *NACLA Report on the Americas*, 37(2).

Amin, A. and N. Thrift (2002) *Cities, Reimagining the Urban*, Cambridge: Polity Press.

Amin, J. (1998) 'Major determinants of economic development in Egypt: 1977–1997', *Cairo Papers in Social Science*, 21(3).

Amorim, C. (1993) *Comando Vermelho: A História Secreta do Crime Organizado*, Rio de Janeiro: Record.

Andrade, X. (1990) 'Actores sociales y política antidrogas: los pequeños traficantes', in B. Bagley et al. (eds), *La Economía Política del Narcotráfico*, Quito: FLACSO.

— (1994) 'Violencia y vida cotidiana en el Ecuador', in J. Echeverría and C. A. Menéndez (eds), *La Violencia en la Región Andina: El Caso de Ecuador*, Quito: FLACSO.

— (2005) 'Jóvenes en Guayaquil: de las ciudadelas fortaleza a la limpieza del espacio público', *Nueva Sociedad*, 20.

— (2006a) 'Más ciudad, menos ciudadanía: renovación urbana y aniquilación del espacio público en Guayaquil', *Ecuador Debate*, 68.

— (2006b) 'Riesgo y activos de la ilegalidad: apuntes etnográficos desde las economías ilegales en Guayaquil', Paper presented at FLACSO, Quito: FLACSO.

Angotti, T. (2006) 'Apocalyptic anti-urbanism: Mike Davis and his planet of slums', *International Journal of Urban and Regional Research*, 30(4): 961–70.

Appadurai, A. (1996) *Modernity at Large: Cultural Dimensions of Globalization*, Minneapolis: University of Minnesota Press.

— (2002) 'Deep democracy: urban governmentality and the horizon of politics', *Environment and Urbanization*, 13(2): 23–43.

Aqidati (1997) 28 October.

Arias, E. D. (2006) *Drugs and Democracy in Rio de Janeiro. Trafficking, Social Networks, and Public Security*, Chapel Hill: University of North Carolina Press.

Arias, E. D. and C. Davis Rodrigues (2006) 'The myth of personal security: criminal gangs, dispute resolution, and identity in Rio de Janeiro's favelas', *Latin American Politics and Society*, 48(4): 53–81.

Assad, R. and M. Roshdi (1998) *Poverty and Poverty Alleviation Strategies in Egypt*, Cairo: Ford Foundation.

Avritzer, L. (2002) *Democracy and the Public Space in Latin America*, Princeton, NJ, and Oxford: Princeton University Press.

Ayubi, N. (1991) *Political Islam*, London: Routledge.

Badawy, M. A. S. (1999) *Islamic Associations in Cairo*, Unpublished MA thesis, Cairo: American University in Cairo.

Balán, J. (2002) 'Introduction', in S. Rotker (ed.), *Citizens of Fear: Urban Violence in Latin America*, New Brunswick, NJ: Rutgers University Press, pp. 1–6.

Bannister, J. and N. Fyfe (2001) 'Introduction: fear and the city', *Urban Studies*, 38(5/6): 807–13.

Batley, R. (1996) 'Public–private relationships and performance in service provision', *Urban Studies*, 33(4/5): 723–51.

Batley, R. and G. Larbi (2004) *The Changing Role of Government. The Reform of Public Services in Developing Countries*, Basingstoke and New York: Palgrave Macmillan.

Bayat, A. (1987) *Workers and Revolution in Iran*, London: Zed Books.

— (1996) 'Cairo's poor: dilemmas of survival and solidarity', *Middle East Report*, 202, Washington, DC: Middle East Research and Information Project.

— (1997a) *Street Politics*, New York: Columbia University Press.

— (1997b) 'Workless revolutionaries: the unemployed movement in revolutionary Iran', *International Review of Social History*, 42(1): 159–85.

— (1998) *Grassroots Participation in Iran: NGOs or Social Movements*, Unpublished paper, Cairo: American University in Cairo.

— (2000) 'From "dangerous classes" to "quiet rebels": politics of urban subaltern in the global South', *International Sociology*, 15(3): 533–57.

Beall, J. (2005a) 'Decentralizing government and de-centering gender: lessons from local government reform in South Africa', *Politics and Society*, 33(2): 253–76.

— (2005b) *Funding Local Governance, Small Grants for Democracy and Development*, London: IT Publications.

— (2006) 'Cities, terrorism and development', *Journal of International Development*, 18(1): 105–20.

Beall, J., O. Crankshaw and S. Parnell (2002) *Uniting a Divided City. Governance and Social Exclusion in Johannesburg*, London: Earthscan.

Beall, J. and S. Fox (2009) *Cities and Development*, London: Routledge.

Beavon, K. (1997) 'A city and a metropolitan area in transformation', in C. Rakodi (ed.), *The Urban Challenge in Africa: Growth and Management of Its Large Cities*, Tokyo: United Nations University Press, pp. 150–91.

Beinin, J. and Z. Lockman (1988) *Workers on the Nile: Nationalism, Communism, Islam and the Egyptian Working Class, 1882–1954*, Princeton, NJ: Princeton University Press.

Berman, M. (1987) 'Among the ruins', *New Internationalist*, 178: 1–3.

Biblawi, H. (1990) 'Rentier state in the Arab world', in G. Luciani (ed.), *The Arab State*, London: Routledge.

Blakely, E. and M. Snyder (1997) *Fortress America: Gated Communities in the United States*, Cambridge, MA: Brookings Institution Press.

Blat, J. C. and S. Saraiva (2000) *O Caso da Favela Natal: Polícia contra o Povo*, São Paulo: Editora Contexto.

Boletim Cidade (2007) 6(40).

Bollens, S. (2007) *Cities, Nationalism and Democratization*, London and New York: Routledge.

Boonyabancha, S. (2004) 'A decade of change: from the Urban Community Development Office to the Community Organization Development Institute in Thailand', in D. Mitlin and D. Satterthwaite (eds), *Empowering Squatter Citizen, Local Government, Civil Society and Urban Poverty Reduction*, London: Earthscan, pp. 25–53.

— (2005) 'Baan Mankong: going to scale with "slum" and squatter upgrading in Thailand', *Environment and Urbanization*, 17(1): 21–46.

Booth, K. (2007) *Theory of World Security*, Cambridge: Cambridge University Press.

Bordin, L. C. V. (2005) 'Estimativa da carga tributária Brasileira em 2004', *Estudos Econômico-Fiscais*, 11(50).

Borja, J. and M. Castells (1997) *Local and Global, Management of Cities in the Information Age*, London: Earthscan.

Brinks, D. (2002) 'Informal institutions and the rule of law: the judicial response to state killings in Buenos Aires and São Paulo in the 1990s', Paper presented at the Conference on Informal Institutions and Politics in the Developing World, Harvard University, April.

Budlender, D. (ed.) (1996) *Women's Budget*, Cape Town: IDASA.

Bureau of Statistics (1954) *Population Census, 8th May, 1951*, vol. 1: *Geographical Distribution of the Population*, Pretoria: Bureau of Statistics.

— (1963) *Population Census, 6th September, 1960*, vol. 1: *Geographical Distribution of the Population*. Pretoria: Bureau of Statistics.

Busatto, C. (2005) *Governança Solidária Local: Desencandeando o processo*, Porto Alegre: Prefeitura Municipal de Porto Alegre, Secretaria Municipal de Coordernação, Política e Governança Local, lproweb.procempa. com. br/pmpa/prefpoa/observatorio/usu_doc/gsl_desencadeando_o_processo.pdf, accessed 13 September 2007.

Cairo Times (1999) 2–15 September.

Caldeira, T. (1996) 'Building up walls: the new pattern of spatial segregation in São Paulo', *International Social Science Journal*, 147: 55–66.

— (2000) *City of Walls: Crime, Segregation and Citizenship in São Paulo*, Berkeley: University of California Press.

Caldeira, T. and J. Holston (1999) 'Democracy and violence in Brazil', *Comparative Studies in Society and History*, 41(4): 691–729.

Call, C. (2003) 'Democratization, war and state-building: constructing the rule of law in El Salvador', *Journal of Latin American Studies*, 35(4): 827–62.

Call, C. and V. Wyeth (eds) (2008) *Building States to Build Peace*, Boulder, CO: Lynne Rienner.

Cameron, R. (1999) *Democratisation of South African Local Government*, Pretoria: Van Schaik.

Cano, I. (1997) *The Use of Lethal Force by Police in Rio de Janeiro*, Rio de Janeiro: ISER.

Cano, I. et al. (2004) *O impacto da violência no Rio de Janeiro*, Rio de Janeiro: Universidade do Estado do Rio de Janeiro (UERJ), Laboratório de Analíse da Violencia.

Cason, J. (2007) 'Searching for a new formula: Brazilian political economy in reform', *Latin American Research Review*, 42(2): 212–24.

Castells, M. (1977) *The Urban Question. A Marxist Approach*, London: Edward Arnold.

— (1983) *The City and the Grassroots*, Berkeley and Los Angeles: University of California Press.

— (2006) 'Changer le ville: a rejoinder',

International Journal of Urban and Regional Research, 30(1): 219–23.

Catusse, M. (2000) 'Les metamorphoses de la question syndicale au Marco', Paper presented at the Workshop on Changing Labour and Restructuring Unionism, First Mediterranean Social and Political Meeting, Florence, 22–26 March.

Chandhoke, N. (2008) 'Some reflections on the notion of an "inclusive political pact": a perspective from Ahmedabad', Paper prepared for the Crisis States Research Centre, London: London School of Economics and Political Science.

Clarke, C. (2006) 'Politics, violence and drugs in Kingston, Jamaica', *Bulletin of Latin American Research*, 25(3): 420–41.

Clement, F. (2000) 'Changing labour and restructuring in Egypt', Paper presented at the Workshop on Changing Labour and Restructuring Unionism, First Mediterranean Social and Political Meeting, Florence, 22–26 March.

Commission on Human Security (2003) *Human Security Now*, Report of the Commission on Human Security, New York: UNCHR, www.humansecurity-chs.org/finalreport.

Corbridge, S., M. Williams, M. Srivastava and R. Véron (2005) *Seeing the State: Governance and Governmentality in India*, Cambridge: Cambridge University Press.

Crankshaw, O. and S. Parnell (1996) 'Housing provision and the need for an urbanisation policy in the new South Africa', *Urban Forum*, 8: 231–6.

— (2004) 'Inequality and urbanisation in the Johannesburg region, 1946–1996', in J. Gugler (ed.), *World Cities beyond the West: Globalisation, Development and Inequality*, Cambridge: Cambridge University Press, pp. 348–70.

Cross, J. (1998) *Informal Politics: Street Vendors and the State in Mexico City*, Palo Alto, CA: Stanford University Press.

Cruz, J. M. (2007) 'Factors associated with juvenile gangs in Central America', in J. M. Cruz (ed.), *Street Gangs in Central America*, San Salvador: UCA Editores, pp. 13–65.

CSS (1985) *Population Census 80: Geographical distribution of the population with a review for 1951–1980*, Report no. 02-80-13, Pretoria: Central Statistical Service.

— (1986) *Population Census 1985: Geographical distribution of the population*, Report no. 02-85-01, Pretoria: Central Statistical Service.

— (1987) *Labour Markets in South Africa During Apartheid*, Pretoria: Central Statistical Service.

— (1992) *Population Census 1991: Geographical distribution of the population with a review for 1970–1991*, Report no. 03-01-02, Pretoria: Central Statistical Service.

— (1993) *South African Labour Statistics 1993*, Pretoria: Central Statistical Service.

DAC (2001) *Guidelines on Poverty Reduction*, Paris: OECD/DAC.

Davis, D. (2005) 'Cities in global context: a brief intellectual history', *International Journal of Urban and Regional Research*, 29(1): 92–109.

— (2006) 'Beyond the quality of democracy: public insecurity and the collapse of Enlightenment political ideals in contemporary Mexico', Paper presented at the Latin American Studies Association International Conference, San Juan, March.

Davis, M. (1990) *City of Quartz, Excavating the Future in Los Angeles*, London and New York: Verso.

— (2004) 'Planet of slums: urban involution and the informal proletariat', *New Left Review*, 26: 5–24, March–April.

— (2006) *Planet of Slums*, London: Verso.

DBSA (2008) Unpublished memo on economic development, Midrand.

D'Cruz, C. and D. Satterthwaite (2005) *Building Homes, Changing Official Approaches: The work of Urban Poor Organizations and their Federations and their contributions to meeting the Millennium Development Goals in urban areas*, London: International Institute for Environment and Development (Poverty Reduction in Urban Areas series, working paper 16).

De Soto, H. (1986) *El Otro Sendero: La Revolución Informal*, Lima: El Barranco.

De Souza, J. A. (2002) *Sociabilidades Emergentes – Implicações da Dominação de Matadors na Periferie e Traficantes nas Favelas*, Unpublished PhD thesis, Rio de Janeiro: Universidade Federal do Rio de Janeiro.

Delta Business Service International/ Khattab and Associates (1981) *Analysis of Registered Private Voluntary Associations in Cairo and Alexandria*, Cairo: Agency for International Development, 21 June.

Department of Statistics (1976) *Population Census 1970: Geographical distribution of the population*, Report no. 02-05-10, Pretoria: Department of Statistics.

Dowdney, L. (2003) *Children of the Drug Trade*, Rio de Janeiro: 7Letras.

— (2008) *Neither War nor Peace. International Comparisons of Children and Youth in Organised Armed Violence*, Rio de Janeiro: COAV, VIVA RIO, ISER and IANSA.

DPLG (2005) 'Provincial growth and development strategy guidelines', Unpublished memo, Pretoria.

Durning, A. (1989) 'People, power and development', *Foreign Policy*, 76: 66–82.

Dyson, T. (2001) 'A partial theory of world development: the neglected role of the demographic transition in the shaping of modern society', *International Journal of Population Geography*, 7(2): 67–90.

Earle, L. O. (2009) *Occupying the Illegal City: Urban Social Movements and Transgressive Citizenship in São Paulo*, Unpublished PhD thesis, London: Development Studies Institute, London School of Economics and Political Science.

Ebtekar, M. (1998) 'Women's NGOs and poverty alleviation: the Iranian experience', *Farzaneh*, 4 (in English).

Eckstein, S. (2001) 'Epilogue. Where have all the movements gone? Latin American social movements at the new millennium', in S. Eckstein (ed.), *Power and Popular Protest. Latin American Social Movements*, 2nd revised edn, Berkeley and Los Angeles: University of California Press, pp. 351–406.

Economic Perspectives (1993) 11.

Eid, M. M. (1998) *Informal Economy in Madinat al-Nahda: Resistance and Accommodation among the Urban Poor*, Unpublished MA thesis, Cairo: American University in Cairo.

El-Karanshawy, S. (1998) 'Governance, local communities and international development in urban Egypt', Unpublished report, Cairo.

El-Sayyid, M. (1995) 'Is there a civil society in the Arab world?', in A. R. Norton (ed.), *Civil Society in the Middle East*, Leiden: E. J. Brill.

Escobar, A. and S. Alvarez (eds) (1992) *The Making of Social Movements in Latin America*, Boulder, CO: Westview Press.

Esser, D. (2007) 'Target Kabul: human insecurity in the Afghan capital', in *Human Security for an Urban Century, Local Challenges, Global Perspectives*, Ottawa: humansecurity-cities.org.

Evertzen, A. (2001) *Gender and Local Governance*, Amsterdam: Netherlands Development Organisation (SNV), April.

Fajnzylber, P., D. Lederman and N. Loayza (2002) 'Inequality and violent crime', *Journal of Law and Economics*, 45(1): 1–40.

Farag, F. (2000) 'Labour on the fence', *Al-Ahram Weekly*, 11–17 May.

Federation of Community Development Associations (1990) Fact sheet, Cairo, 14 March.

Financial Times (2003) 31 October.

Fraser, N. (2007) 'Reframing justice in a globalizing world', in D. Held and A. Kaya (eds), *Global Inequality*, Cambridge: Polity Press, pp. 252–72.

Frayne, B. (2004) 'Migration and urban survival strategies in Windhoek, Namibia', *Geoforum*, 35: 489–505.

Friedmann, J. (2003) 'China's urbanization', *International Journal of Urban and Regional Research*, 27(3): 745–58.

Gamile, D. A. (2000) *The Working Class of Shubra al-Khaima*, Unpublished MA thesis, Cairo: American University in Cairo.

Gay, R. (1994) *Popular Organization and Democracy in Rio de Janeiro: A Tale of Two Favelas*, Philadelphia, PA: Temple University Press.

— (2005) *Lucia: Testimonies of a Brazilian Drug Dealer's Woman*, Philadelphia, PA: Temple University Press.

Geffray, C. (2002) 'Social, economic and political impacts of drug trafficking in the state of Rondônia, in the Brazilian Amazon', in *Globalisation, Drugs and Criminalisation*, Paris: MOST/UNESCO, pp. 90–109.

Ghabra, S. (1991) 'Voluntary associations in Kuwait', *Middle East Journal*, 45(2): 199–215.

Gilbert, A. (1994) *The Latin American City*, Nottingham: Russell Press.

Godoy, A. S. (2006) *Popular Injustice: Violence, Community, and Law in Latin America*, Stanford, CA: Stanford University Press.

Goldstein, D. (2003) *Laughter out of Place: Race, Class, Violence, and Sexuality in a Rio Shantytown*, Berkeley: University of California Press.

— (2004) *The Spectacular City. Violence and Performance in Urban Bolivia*, Durham, NC: Duke University Press.

González de la Rocha, M. and A. Grinspun (2001) 'Private adjustments: household responses to the erosion of work', in N. Middleton, P. O'Keefe and R. Visser (eds), *Negotiating Poverty: New Directions, Renewed Debate*, London: Pluto Press, pp. 89–134.

González de la Rocha, M. et al. (2004) 'From the marginality of the 1960s to the "new poverty" of today: a LASA research forum', *Latin American Research Review*, 39(1): 183–203.

Graham, S. (2004a) 'Introduction: cities, warfare, and states of emergency', in S. Graham (ed.), *Cities, War and Terrorism: Towards an Urban Geopolitics*, Oxford: Blackwell, pp. 1–26.

— (2004b) 'Cities as strategic sites: place annihilation and urban geopolitics', in S. Graham (ed.), *Cities, War and Terrorism: Towards an Urban Geopolitics*, Oxford: Blackwell, pp. 31–53.

Gugler, J. (2003) 'World cities in poor countries: conclusions from case studies of the principal regional and global players', *International Journal of Urban and Regional Research*, 27(3): 707–12.

— (2004) *World Cities beyond the West: Globalization, Development and Inequality*, Cambridge: Cambridge University Press.

Halawi, J. (1994) 'Mosque stairs spark Shubra riots', *Al-Ahram Weekly*, 18–24 August.

Hammami, R. (1995) 'NGOs: the professionalization of politics', *Race and Class*, 37(2): 51–63.

Harb el-Kak, M. (1999) 'Participation practices in Beirut's suburb municipalities: a comparison between Islamic and "developmentalist" approaches', Paper presented at the 4th International Other Connections Conference, Sites of Recovery, Beirut, 25–28 October.

Harrison, P. (1983) *Inside the Inner City*, London: Penguin.

— (2006) 'Integrated development plans and Third Way politics', in U. Pillay, R. Tomlinson and J. du Toit (eds), *Democracy and Delivery: Urban Policy in South Africa*, Pretoria: HSRC Press.

Harrison, P. and A. Todes (2002) 'The use of spatial frameworks in regional development in South Africa', *Regional Studies*, 35: 65–72.

Harriss, J., K. Stokke and O. Tornquist (eds) (2005) *Politicising Democracy: The New Local Politics of Democratisation*, London: Palgrave Macmillan.

Hart, K. (1973) 'Informal income opportunities and urban employment in

Ghana', *Journal of Modern African Studies*, 11: 61–89.

Harvey, D. (2003) 'The right to the city', *International Journal of Urban and Regional Research*, 27(4): 939–41.

Heathcote, E. (2006) 'Slum prospect', *Financial Times*, 6 May.

Heller, P. (2001) 'Moving the state: the politics of decentralization in Kerala, South Africa and Porto Alegre', *Politics and Society*, 29(1): 131–63.

Henderson, V. J. (2003) 'The urbanization process and economic growth: the so-what question', *Journal of Economic Growth*, 8(1): 47–71.

Henry-Lee, A. (2005) 'The nature of poverty in the Garisson constituencies in Jamaica', *Environment and Urbanization*, 17(2): 83–99.

Hills, A. (2004) 'Continuity and discontinuity: the grammar of urban military operations', in S. Graham (ed.), *Cities, War and Terrorism: Towards an Urban Geopolitics*, Oxford: Blackwell, pp. 231–46.

Hiltermann, J. (1991) *Behind the Intifada*, Princeton, NJ: Princeton University Press.

Hinnebusch, R. (1996) 'Democratization in the Middle East: the evidence from the Syrian case', in G. Honneman (ed.), *Political and Economic Liberalization*, Boulder, CO: Lynne Rienner.

Hochstetler, K. (2000) 'Democratizing pressures from below? Social movements in the new Brazilian democracy', in P. R. Kingstone and T. J. Power (eds), *Democratic Brazil: Actors, Institutions and Processes*, Pittsburgh, PA: University of Pittsburgh Press, 167–82.

Holston, J. (2008) *Insurgent Citizenship. Disjunctions of Democracy and Modernity in Brazil*, Princeton, NJ: Princeton University Press.

Holston, J. and A. Appadurai (1993) 'Cities and citizenship', in J. Holston (ed.), *Cities and Citzenship*, Durham, NC: Duke University Press.

Holston, J. and T. Caldeira (1998) 'Democracy, law and violence:

disjunctions of Brazilian citizenship', in F. Aguero and J. Stark (eds), *Faultlines of Democracy in Latin America*, Princeton, NJ: Princeton University Press.

Hood, C. (1991) 'A public management for all seasons?', *Public Administration*, 69(1): 3–19.

Hoodfar, H. (1997) *From Marriage to Market*, Berkeley: University of California Press.

— (1998) *Volunteer Health Workers in Iran as Social Activists?*, Paris: WLUML Occasional Paper no. 10.

Hopkins, N. et al. (1998) *Social Response to Environmental Change and Pollution in Egypt*, Cairo: American University in Cairo (Social Research Centre).

Houtzager, P. (2003) From polycentrism to the polity', in P. Houtzager and M. Moore (eds), *Changing Paths: International Development and the New Politics of Inclusion*, Ann Arbor: University of Michigan Press.

Huggins, M. (1998) *Political Policing: The United States and Latin America*, Durham, NC: Duke University Press.

Human Rights Watch (1997) *Police Brutality in Urban Brazil*, New York: Human Rights Watch.

Human Rights Watch/Americas Final Justice (1994) *Police and Death Squad Homicides of Adolescents in Brazil*, New York: Human Rights Watch.

Huntington, S. P. (1991) *The Third Wave: Democratization in the Late Twentieth Century*, Oklahoma: University of Oklahoma Press.

Ibrahim, S. E. (1996a) *Egyptian Law 32 on Egypt's Private Sector Organizations*, Cairo: Ibn Khaldoun Centre for Developmental Studies (Working Paper no. 3).

— (1996b) 'Grassroots participation in Egyptian development', *Cairo Papers in Social Science*, 19(3).

— (1998) 'The troubled triangle: populism, Islam, and civil society in the Arab world', *International Political Science Review*, 19(4): 373–85.

ILO (2005) *Panorama Laboral 2004*, Lima:

Organización Internacional de Trabajo – Oficina Regional para América Latina y el Caribe.

Independent (2007) 15 May.

International Monetary Fund (1996) *IMF International Financial Statistics Yearbook, 1994, 1996*, Washington, DC: IMF Publications.

IPEA (Instituto de Pesquisa Econômico Aplicada) (2005) *Brasil: O Estado de uma Nação*, Rio de Janeiro: IPEA.

Ismail, A. M. (1998) *The Liberalization of Egypt's Agriculture Sector and Peasants' Movement*, Cairo: Land Centre for Human Rights.

Ismail, S. (2000) 'The popular movement dimensions of contemporary militant Islamism', *Comparative Studies in Society and History*, 42(2): 363–93.

Istanbuli, D. (1993) *The Future Role of Palestinian NGOs in an Emerging Palestinian Self-Government*, Middle East Working Group Seminar, Jerusalem, 21–22 June.

Jacobs, J. (1984) *Cities and the Wealth of Nations, Principles of Economic Life*, New York: Random House.

Jensen, S. and D. Rodgers (2009) 'Revolutionaries, barbarians or war machines? Gangs in Nicaragua and South Africa', in L. Panitch and C. Leys (eds), *2009 Socialist Register, Violence Today: Actually Existing Barbarism*, forthcoming.

Jones, G. A. and D. Rodgers (forthcoming) (eds) *Youth Violence in Latin America. Gangs and Juvenile Justice in Perspective*, New York: Palgrave Macmillan.

Jornal do Brasil (2001) 16 April.

— (2002) 13 March, 16 June, 6 and 9 August, 6 September, 26 November.

— (2003) 15 January, 20, 23 and 28 March, 8 May, 19 November.

— (2004) 18 January, 5, 9 and 10 March, 26 April, 1 June, 2 and 18 July, 20 and 24 August, 3 September, 28 November.

— (2005) 20 January, 27 March, 1 and 3 June, 19 December.

— (2007) 30 March, 1 April, 9 and 13 May, 14 August.

Jornal do Brasil Online (2006) www.jb.com.br/destaques/ 1006tortura/ tortura.html, accessed 7 February 2006.

Kawthar, D. (2000) 'Labour market in Lebanon: evolution, constraints, and the role of unionism', Paper presented at the Workshop on Changing Labour and Restructuring Unionism, First Mediterranean Social and Political Meeting, Florence, 22–26 March.

Kepel, G. (1986) *Muslim Extremism in Egypt*, Berkeley: University of California Press.

Kfoury, A. (1996) 'Hizb Allah and the Lebanese state', in J. Beinin and J. Stork (eds), *Political Islam*, Berkeley: University of California Press, pp. 136–43.

Khafagy, F. (1992) *Needs Assessment Survey of NGOs in Egypt*, Cairo: African Women's Development and Communications Networks, August.

Khosrowkhavar, F. (1992) 'Nouvelle banlieue et marginalité: la cité Taleghani à Khak-e Sefid', in C. Adle and B. Hourcade (eds), *Teheran: Capitale Bicentenaire*, Tehran: Institut Français de Recherche en Iran.

Koonings, K. (2004) 'Strengthening citizenship in Brazil's democracy: local participatory governance in Porto Alegre', *Bulletin of Latin American Research*, 23(1): 79–99.

— (2009) 'Surviving regime change? Participatory democracy and the politics of citizenship in Porto Alegre, Brazil', in P. Silva and H. Cleuren (eds), *Widening Democracy: Citizens and Participatory Schemes in Brazil and Chile*, Leiden: Brill (CEDLA Latin American Series [CLAS] no. 97), forthcoming.

Koonings, K. and D. Kruijt (eds) (2004) *Armed Actors: Organized Violence and State Failure in Latin America*, London: Zed Books.

— (2007) *Fractured Cities. Social Exclusion, Urban Violence and Contested Spaces in Latin America*, London: Zed Books.

Koonings, K. and S. Veenstra (2007) 'Exclusión social, actores armados y violencia urbana en Rio de Janeiro', *Foro Internacional*, 47(3): 616–36.

Kruijt, D. (2008a) 'Divided cities: urban informality, exclusion, and violence', in L. Boer (ed.), *A Rich Menu for the Poor. Food for Thought on Effective Aid Policies*, The Hague: Ministry of Foreign Affairs – DGIS, pp. 323–32.

— (2008b) 'Class structure in modern Latin America', in J. Kinsbruner and E. D. Langer (eds), *Encyclopedia of Latin American History and Culture*, 2nd edn, Detroit: Gale/MacMillan, vol. II, pp. 443–53.

Kruijt, D. and K. Koonings (1999) 'Violence and fear in Latin America', in K. Koonings and D. Kruijt (eds), *Societies of Fear. The Legacy of Civil War, Violence and Terror in Latin America*, London: Zed Books, pp. 1–31.

Kruijt, D., C. Sojo and R. Grynspan (2002) *Informal Citizens. Poverty, Informality and Social Exclusion in Latin America*, Amsterdam: Rozenberg Publishers (Thela Latin America Series).

Land Centre for Human Rights (1998) *Egypt's Labour Conditions during 1998: The Year of Strikes and Protests*, Cairo: Land Centre for Human Rights.

Landman, K. (2003) 'Crime, political transition and urban transformation in South Africa and Brazil', *SIIA Reports*, 36, Braamfontein: South African Institute of International Affairs.

Lapidus, I. (1967) *Muslim Cities in the Later Middle Ages*, Cambridge: Cambridge University Press.

LaTowsky, R. (1994) *Financial Profile of Egypt's PVO Sector*, Report prepared for the World Bank, June.

Laurent, B. and S. Galal (1995) *PVO Development Project Evaluation Report*, Report prepared for USAID/Egypt, Cairo, December.

Leeds, E. (1996) 'Cocaine and parallel polities in the Brazilian urban periphery: constraints on local-level democratization', *Latin American Research Review*, 31(3): 47–83.

— (2007) 'Rio de Janeiro', in K. Koonings and D. Kruijt (eds), *Fractured Cities: Social Exclusion, Urban Violence and Contested Spaces in Latin America*, London: Zed Books, 23–35.

Lemanski, C. (2004) 'A new apartheid? The spatial implications of fear of crime in Cape Town, South Africa', *Environment and Urbanization*, 16(2): 101–12.

— (2007) 'Global cities in the South: deepening social and spatial polarisation in Cape Town', *Cities*, 24(6): 448–61.

Lembruger, J., L. Musemeci and I. Cano (2003) *Quem Vigia os Vigias? Um Estudo sobre Controle Externo da Polícia no Brasil*, Rio de Janeiro: Record.

Leymarie, P. (2009) 'Comment les armées se préparent au combat urbain', *Le Monde Diplomatique*, March, pp. 4–5.

Lind, A. and M. Farmelo (1996) *Gender and Urban Social Movements: Women's Community Responses to Restructuring and Urban Poverty*, Geneva: United Nations Research Institute for Social Development (UNRISD).

Lindberg, S. et al. (eds) (1995) *Globalization, Democratization, and Social Movements in the Third World*, Research Report 35, Lund: University of Lund.

Loor, K., L. Aldas and F. López (n.d.) *Pandillas y Naciones de Ecuador. Alarmante Realidad, Tarea Desafiante: De Víctimas a Victimarios*, COAV (Children in Organized Armed Violence), www.coav.org.br.

Lubeck, P. and B. Britts (2001) 'Muslim civil society in urban public spaces', in J. Eade and C. Mele (eds), *Urban Studies: Contemporary and Future Perspectives*, Oxford: Blackwell.

Lund, F. and C. Skinner (2004) 'Integrating the informal economy in urban planning and governance: a case study of the process of policy development in Durban, South Africa',

International Development Planning Review, 26(4): 431–56.

Mahfouz, M. (1992) *Community Development in Egypt: The Case of CDAs*, Unpublished MA thesis, Cairo: American University in Cairo.

Majdalani, R. (1999a) 'Bridging the gap between the development agendas and the needs of the grassroots: the experience of Jordanian NGOs', Unpublished paper, Beirut.

— (1999b) 'Governance and NGOs in Lebanon', Unpublished paper, Beirut.

— (1999c) 'NGOs as power-brokers in the rebuilding of a fragmented state: the case of Lebanon', Unpublished paper, Beirut.

Manor, J. (1999) *The Political Economy of Democratic Decentralization*, Washington, DC: World Bank.

Marchetti, A. (2005) *The Characteristics of Brazilian Cities with Participatory Budgeting*, Porto Alegre: PUC-RS, unpublished article (mimeo).

Margulies, R. and E. Yildizoglu (1996) 'The resurgence of Islam and the Welfare Party in Turkey', in J. Beinin and J. Stork (eds), *Political Islam*, Berkeley: University of California Press.

Marques, E. and R. Bichir (2003) 'Public policies, political cleavages and urban space: state infrastructure policies in Sãn Paulo', *International Journal of Urban and Regional Research*, 27(4): 811–27.

Marshall, A. (1920) *Principles of Economics*, 8th edn, London: Macmillan and Co.

Mayer, M. (2006) 'Manuel Castells' *The City and the Grassroots*', *International Journal of Urban and Regional Research*, 30(1): 202–6.

McIlwaine, C. and C. Moser (2007) 'Living in fear: how the urban poor perceive violence, fear and insecurity', in K. Koonings and D. Kruijt (eds), *Fractured Cities: Social Exclusion, Urban Violence and Contested Spaces in Latin America*, London: Zed Books, pp. 117–37.

Mejía, T. (2007) 'In Tegucigalpa, the iron fist fails', *NACLA Report on the Americas*, 40(4).

Melo, M. A. and G. Baiocchi (2006) 'Deliberative domocracy and local governance: towards a new agenda', *International Journal of Urban and Regional Research*, 30: 587–600.

Memorandum on Post-Conflict Reconstruction (2005) The Hague: Ministries of Foreign Affairs, Defence and Economic Affairs.

Merrifield, A. (2002) *Dialectical Urbanism*, New York: Monthly Review Press.

Middle East Economic Digest (1991) 21 February.

Middle East Report (1999) 'Existing political vessels cannot contain the reform movement', *Middle East Report*, 212.

Miller, B. (2006) 'Castells' *The City and the Grassroots*: 1983 and today', *International Journal of Urban and Regional Research*, 30(1): 207–11.

Mingardi, G. and S. Goulart (2002) 'Drug trafficking in an urban area: the case of São Paulo', in *Globalisation, Drugs and Criminalisation*, Paris: MOST/UNESCO, pp. 92–118.

Mitlin, D. (2004) 'Civil society organisations: do they make a difference to urban poverty?', in N. Devas et al., *Urban Governance, Voice and Poverty in the Developing World*, London: Earthscan, pp. 123–44.

— (2005) 'Chronic poverty in urban areas', *Environment and Urbanization*, 17(2): 3–10.

Mitlin, D. and D. Satterthwaite (eds) (2004) *Empowering Squatter Citizen. Local Government, Civil Society and Urban Poverty Reduction*, London: Earthscan.

Moghadam, V. (1997) 'Women's NGOs in the Middle East and North Africa: constraints, opportunities, and priorities', in D. Chatty and A. Rabo (eds), *Organizing Women: Formal and Informal Women's Groups in the Middle East*, Oxford: Berg.

Moser, C. (1982) 'A home of one's own: squatter housing strategies in

Guayaquil, Ecuador', in A. Gilbert, J. E. Hardoy and R. Ramirez (eds), *Urbanization in Contemporary Latin America: Critical Approaches to the Analysis of Urban Issues*, London: Wiley.

— (1996) *Confronting Crisis: A Comparative Study of Household Responses to Poverty and Vulnerability in Four Poor Urban Communities*, Environmentally Sustainable Development Studies and Monograph Series no. 8, Washington, DC: World Bank.

— (1997) *Household Responses to Poverty and Vulnerability*, vol. 1: *Confronting Crisis in Cisne Dos, Guayaquil, Ecuador*, Urban Management Program Policy Paper no. 21, Washington, DC: World Bank.

— (1998) 'The asset vulnerability framework: reassessing urban poverty reduction strategies', *World Development*, 26(1): 1–19.

— (2004) 'Urban violence and insecurity: an introductory roadmap', *Environment and Urbanization*, 16(2): 3–16.

— (2009) *Ordinary Families: Extraordinary Lives: Asset accumulation and poverty reduction in Guayaquil, Ecuador, 1978–2004*, Washington, DC: Brookings Press.

Moser, C. and A. Felton (2007a) 'Intergenerational asset accumulation and poverty reduction in Guayaquil, Ecuador (1978–2004)', in C. Moser (ed.), *Reducing Global Poverty: The Case for Asset Accumulation*, Washington, DC: Brookings Press.

— (2007b) 'The construction of an asset index: measuring asset accumulation in Ecuador', CPRC Working Paper 76, Manchester: University of Manchester.

Moser, C. and C. McIlwaine (2004) *Encounters with Violence in Latin America: Urban poor perceptions from Colombia and Guatemala*, London and New York: Routledge.

Mubarak, H. (1995) *Al-Erhabiyoun Qademoun*, Cairo: Dal Al-Mahrousa.

Nakhleh, K. (1991) *Indigenous Organizations in Palestine*, Jerusalem: Arab Thought Forum.

Namazi, B. (2000) *Iranian NGOs: Situational Analysis*, Tehran.

Neary, M and A. Dinerstein (1998) 'Class struggle and the Communist Manifesto', Conference to Celebrate 150 Years of the Communist Manifesto, Paris, May.

Nelson, J. (1988) *The Politics of Pro-Poor Adjustment Policies*, Washington, DC: World Bank (Country Economics Department).

NEPAD and CLAVES (2000) *Estudo Global sobre o Mercado Ilegal de Drogas no Rio de Janeiro*, Rio de Janeiro: UERJ/FIOCRUZ.

Neto, P. M. (1999) 'Violência policial no Brasil: abordagens teóricas e práticas de controle', in D. C. Pandolfi, J. M. de Carvalho, L. Carneiro and M. Grynszpan (eds), *Cidadania, Justiça e Violência*, Rio de Janeiro: Editora Fundação Getúlio Vargas, pp. 130–48.

Neuwirth, R. (2005) *Shadow Cities: A Billion Squatters; a New Urban World*, New York and London: Routledge.

New York Times (2003) 8 June.

Norton, A. R. (ed.) (1995) *Civil Society in the Middle East*, Leiden: E. J. Brill.

Nun, J. (1989) *La rebelión del coro*, Buenos Aires: Ediciones Nueva Visión.

O Globo (2004) 1 May, 5, 19 and 22 August, 16 and 26 October.

— (2005) 20 February, 18 and 21 March, 10 and 11 April, 3 and 29 May.

— (2006) 3 February, 29 July, 6 August, 17 September, 5 November.

— (2007) 14 January, 16 March, 23 May, 30 June, 1, 3, 5 and 30 July, 5 and 19 August.

Ostrom, E., L. Schroeder and S. Wynne (1993) *Institutional Incentives and Sustainable Development: Infrastructure Policies in Perspective*, Boulder, CO: Westview Press.

Painter, J. (2000) 'State and governance', in E. Sheppard and T. Barnes (eds), *A Companion to Economic Geography*, Oxford: Blackwell, pp. 359–76.

Pandolfi, D. C. (1999) 'Percepção dos direitos e participação social', in

D. C. Pandolfi, J. M. de Carvalho, L. Carneiro and M. Grynszpan (eds), *Cidadania, Justiça e Violência*, Rio de Janeiro: Editora Fundação Getúlio Vargas, pp. 45–58.

Pandolfi, D. C. and M. Grynszpan (eds) (2003) *A Favela Fala*, Rio de Janeiro: Editora Fundação Getúlio Vargas.

Paris, R. and T. D. Risk (eds) (2009) *The Dilemmas of Statebuilding*, London: Routledge.

Parnell, S. (2005) 'Constructing a developmental nation – the challenge of including the poor in the post-apartheid city', *Transformation*, 58: 20–44.

Peace Building, a Development Perspective (2004) *A Strategic Framework*, Oslo: Norwegian Ministry of Foreign Affairs, August.

Perlman, J. (1976) *The Myth of Marginality. Urban Poverty and Politics in Rio de Janeiro*, Berkeley and Los Angeles: University of California Press.

— (2004) 'The metamorphosis of marginality in Rio de Janeiro', in M. González de la Rocha et al., 'From the marginality of the 1960s to the new poverty of today: a LARR Research Forum', *Latin American Research Review*, 39(1): 189–92.

— (2007) 'Globalization and the urban poor', Wider Research Paper 2007/76, Helsinki: WIDER.

— (2009) *FAVELA: Four Decades of Living on the Edge in Rio de Janeiro*, New York and London: Oxford University Press.

Pieterse, E. (2004) 'Recasting urban integration and fragmentation in post-apartheid South Africa', *Development Update*, 5: 81–104.

Pillay, U., R. Tomlinson and J. du Toit (eds) (2006) *Democracy and Delivery: Urban Policy in South Africa*, Pretoria: HSRC Press.

Pinheiro P. S. (2000) 'Democratic governance, violence, and the (un)rule of law', *Daedalus*, 129(2): 119–44.

Pochmann, M. (2001) *A década dos mitos*, São Paulo: Contexto.

Popple, K. and M. Shaw (1997) 'Editorial introduction: social movements: re-asserting "community"', *Community Development Journal*, 32(3): 191–8.

Portes, A. (1985) 'Latin American class structures: their composition and change during the last decades', *Latin American Research Review*, 20(3): 7–39.

— (1989) 'Latin American urbanization in the years of the crisis', *Latin American Research Review*, 24(3): 7–49.

— (1998) 'Social capital: its origins and applications in modern sociology', *Annual Review of Sociology*, 24: 1–24.

Portes, A. and K. Hoffman (2003) 'Latin American class structures: their composition and change during the neoliberal era', *Latin American Research Review*, 38(1): 41–82.

Posusney, M. P. (1997) *Labor and the State in Egypt*, New York: Columbia University Press.

Potts, D. (2003) '"Restoring order"? Operation Murambatsvina and the urban crisis in Zimbabwe', *Journal of Southern African Studies*, 32(2): 273–91.

Prefeitura Municipal de Porto Alegre (2005) 'Smic promove diálogo com camêlos do Centro', 26 June, www.portoalegre.rs.gov.br/noticias/ver_imprimir.asp?m1=31121, accessed 17 September 2007.

Project Municipal Innovations (forthcoming) Research reports of the Project Municipal Innovations, coordinated by J. Pearce, Bradford: University of Bradford.

Pugh, D. (1994) 'The street vendors of Minia', Ford Foundation Report.

Putnam, R. D. (1993a) 'The prosperous community: social capital and public life', *American Prospect*, 4(13).

— (1993b) *Making Democracy Work: Civic Traditions in Modern Italy*, Princeton, NJ: Princeton University Press.

Qandil, A. (1993a) 'The role of Islamic PVOs in social welfare policy: the case of Egypt', Paper presented at the conference 'The role of NGOs in national development strategy', Cairo, 28–31 March.

— (1993b) *Taqdim Adaa al-Islamiyya*

fi-Niqabat al-Mihniyya, Cairo: CEDEJ/ Cairo University.

— (1998) 'The nonprofit sector in Egypt', in H. K. Anheier and L. M. Salamon (eds), *The Nonprofit Sector in the Developing World*, Manchester: Manchester University Press, pp. 145-6.

Rahman, A. (1993) *People's Self-Development*, London: Zed Books.

Rao, V. (2006) 'Slum as theory: the South/ Asian city and globalization', *International Journal of Urban and Regional Research*, 30(1): 225-32.

Rekik, F. (2000) 'Mobilité sociale et flexibilité de l'emploi [Tunisia]', Paper presented at the Workshop on Changing Labour and Restructuring Unionism, First Mediterranean Social and Political Meeting, Florence, 22-26 March.

Ribeiro, R. J. (2007) *Democracia Petista, Republicanismo Tucano, 2002*, www.renatojanine.pro.br/Brasil/ democracia petista.html, accessed 3 March.

Richards, A. and J. Waterbury (1990) *A Political Economy of the Middle East*, Boulder, CO: Westview Press.

Rivero, P. S. (2000) *The Value of the Illegal Firearms Market in the City of Rio de Janeiro: Prices and Symbolism of Guns in Crime*, Rio de Janeiro: Viva Rio.

Roberts, B. (1996) 'The social context of citizenship in Latin America', *International Journal of Urban and Regional Research*, 20(1): 38-65.

— (2005) 'Globalization and Latin American cities', *International Journal of Urban and Regional Research*, 29(10): 110-23.

Robinson, J. (2002) 'Global and world cities: a view from off the map', *International Journal of Urban and Regional Research*, 26(3): 531-54.

Rodgers, D. (2009) 'Slum wars of the 21st century: gangs, *Mano Dura*, and the new urban geography of conflict in Central America', *Development and Change*, 40, forthcoming.

Rogerson, C. (1996) 'Dispersion within concentration: the changing location of corporate headquarter offices in South Africa', *Development Southern Africa*, 13(4): 567-79.

— (2009) 'Review of National Urban Development Frameworks', Paper prepared for the South African Cities Network, Johannesburg.

Rogerson, C. and J. M. Rogerson (1999) 'Industrial change in a developing metropolis: the Witwatersrand 1980-1994', *Geoforum*, 30: 85-99.

Rose, K. (1992) 'Where women are leaders; the SEWA movement in India', London: Zed Books.

Rotker, S. (ed.) (2002) *Citizens of Fear. Urban Violence in Latin America*, New Brunswick, NJ: Rutgers University Press.

Rozema, R. (2008) 'Urban DDR processes: paramilitaries and criminal networks in Medellín, Colombia', *Journal of Latin American Studies*, 40: 423-52.

Ru'ya (Cairo) (1996) 8 and 9, Summer.

SACN (2008) *Inclusive Cities 2008*, Braamfontein: South African Cities Network.

SA Office of Census and Statistics (1922) *Third Census of the Population of the Union of South Africa, Enumerated 3rd May 1921: Population, organisation and enumeration, number, sex, and distribution (all races)*, Part 1, *UG15-'23*, Pretoria: South Africa Office of Census and Statistics.

— (1949) *Population Census, 7th May 1946*, vol. I, *Geographical distribution of the population of the Union of South Africa (UG51-1949)*, Pretoria: South Africa Office of Census and Statistics.

Santos, B. de Souza (1998) 'Participatory budgeting in Porto Alegre: towards a redistributive democracy', *Politics and Society*, 26(4).

— (2002) *Produzir para viver. Os caminhos da produção não capitalista*, Rio de Janeiro: Civilização Brasileira.

— (2005a) 'Two democracies, two legalities: participatory budgeting in Porto Alegre, Brazil', in B. de Souza Santos and C. A. Rodríguez-Garavito (eds), *Law and Counter-Hegemonic Globalization: Toward a subaltern cosmopolitan legality*, Cambridge: Cambridge University Press.

— (2005b) 'Beyond neoliberal governance: the World Social Forum as subaltern cosmopolitan politics and legality', in B. de Souza Santos and C. Rodríguez-Garavito (eds), *Law and Counter-Hegemonic Globalization: Toward a subaltern cosmopolitan legality*, Cambridge: Cambridge University Press.

Sarvestani, R. S. (1997) *Barrasi-ye Jame-shenakhti-ye Ravabet-e Hamsayegui dar Tehran*, Tehran: Tehran University, Institute of Social Studies and Research.

Sassen, S. (1991) *The Global City: New York, London, Tokyo*, Princeton, NJ: Princeton University Press.

— (2000) *Cities in a World Economy*, Thousand Oaks, CA: Pine Forge Press.

— (2001) *The Global City: Strategic Site/ New Frontier. Seminar Globalization*, July 2001, www.india-seminar.com/ 2001/503/503%20saskia%20 sassen. htm.

— (2002) *Global Networks, Linked Cities*, New York: Routledge.

Satterthwaite, D. (2006) 'Book review: *Planet of Slums* by Mike Davis and *Shadow Cities* by Robert Neuwirth', *Environment and Urbanization*, 18(2): 543–6.

— (2008) 'Editorial: the social and political basis for citizen action on urban poverty reduction', *Environment and Urbanization*, 20(2): 307–18.

Sayyah, G. (1993) 'Potential constraints upon NGOs in Lebanon', Paper presented at the workshop 'Reconstruction, rehabilitation, and reconciliation in the Middle East: a view from civil society', Ottawa, 21 June.

Schaefer Davis, S. (1995) *Advocacy-Oriented Non-Governmental Organization in Egypt: Structure, Activities, Constraints, and Needs*, Cairo: USAID/ Egypt.

Scheper-Hughes, N. (1992) *Death without Weeping: The Violence of Everyday Life in Brazil*, Berkeley, Los Angeles and London: University of California Press.

Shatkin, G. (2007) 'Global cities of the South: emerging perspectives on growth and inequality', *Cities*, 24(1): 1–15.

Singerman, D. (1995) *Avenues of Participation: Family, Network, and Politics in Cairo's Quarters*, Princeton, NJ: Princeton University Press.

Skinner, C. (2007) 'Synchronicities and mismatches: urban planning, policy and practice towards street traders in Durban', Paper presented at the conference 'Living on the margins', 26–28 March.

Smulovitz, C. (2004) 'Citizen insecurity and fear: public and private responses in Argentina', in H. Fruhling and J. Tulchin (eds), *Crime and Violence in Latin America. Citizen Security, Democracy and the State*, Washington, DC: Woodrow Wilson Center Press and John Hopkins University Press, pp. 125–52.

Soares, L. E. (2001) *Notícias de Porto Alegre*, Porto Alegre: PMPA.

Soja, E. (2000) *Postmetropolis: Critical Studies of Cities and Regions*, Oxford: Blackwell.

South Africa (1994) *Reconstruction and Development Programme*, Pretoria: Government Printers.

— (2003a) *The Ten Year Review*, Pretoria: Government Printers.

— (2003b) *National Spatial Development Perspective*, Pretoria: Government Printers.

— (2006) *National Spatial Development Perspective Update*, Pretoria: Government Printers.

— (2008a) *National Spatial Trends Overview*, Unpublished report and annexures.

— (2008b) *Towards a Fifteen Year Review*, Pretoria: Government Printers.

— (2008c) *Regional Industrial Development Strategy*, Pretoria: Department of Trade and Industry.

Souza, C. (2001) 'Participatory budgeting in Brazilian cities: limits and possibilities in building democratic institutions', *Environment and Urbanization*, 13(1): 159–84.

Staeheli, L. A. (2006) 'Re-reading Castells: indifference or irrelevance twenty years on?', *International Journal of Urban and Regional Research*, 30(1): 198–201.

StatsSA (2007) *Labour Force Survey September 2007: Statistical Release P0210*, Pretoria: Statistics South Africa.

Sullivan, D. (1994) *Private Voluntary Associations in Egypt*, Bloomington: University Press of Florida.

Tajbakhsh, K. (2002) *The Promise of the City: Space, Identity and Politics in Contemporary Social Thought*, Berkeley, Los Angeles and London: University of California Press.

Tanada, H. (1996) 'Survey of migrant associations in Cairo metropolitan society (Egypt), 1955–1990: quantitative and qualitative data', *Social Science Review*, 42(1).

Tawfiq, I. (1995) *Community Participation and Environmental Change: Mobilization in a Cairo Neighborhood*, Unpublished MA thesis, Cairo: American University in Cairo.

Telles, V. (2007) 'Transitando na linha de sombra, tecendo as tramas da cidade', in F. de Oliveira and C. Rizek (eds), *A era da indeterminação*, São Paulo: Boitempo.

Tendler, J. (1997) *Good Government in the Tropics*, Baltimore, MD, and London: Johns Hopkins University Press.

Thompson, A. (2004) *An Introduction to African Politics*, Abingdon: Routledge.

Tibaijuka, A. (2000) 'A revitalized habitat committed to fighting the urbanization of poverty', *United Nations Chronicle*, 37(4): 54.

— (2005) *Report of the Fact-Finding Mission to Zimbabwe to Assess the Scope and Impact of Operation Murambatsvina by the UN Special Envoy on Human Settlements Issues in Zimbabwe*, Nairobi: UN-Habitat, July, www.unhabitat.org/documents/ZimbabweReport.pdf.

Tilly, C. (1998) *Durable Inequality*, Berkeley: University of California Press.

Tinker, I. (1993) *Evaluation of the Organization for Development and Support of Street Food Vendors in the City of Minia: model for empowering the working poor*, Cairo: SPAAC, August.

Turok, I. and S. Parnell (2009) 'Reshaping cities, rebuilding nations: the role of national urban policies', *Urban Forum*, 20, forthcoming.

UN (2008a) *World Urbanization Prospects. The Revision 2007. Executive Summary*, New York: United Nations, Department of Economic and Social Affairs – Population Division, February (ESA/P/WP/205).

— (2008b) *World Urbanization Prospects. The Revision 2007. Highlights*, New York: United Nations, Department of Economic and Social Affairs – Population Division, February (ESA/P/WP/205).

UNDP (1994) *Human Development Report 1994*, New York: United Nations Development Programme.

— (2004) *La democracia en América Latina. Hacia una democracia de ciudadanas y ciudadanos: Argentina, Bolivia, Brasil, Chile, Colombia, Costa Rica, Ecuador, El Salvador, Guatemala, Honduras, Méjico, Nicaragua, Panamá, Paraguay, Perú, República Dominicana, Uruguay*, www.democracia.UNDP.org.

UNESCO (2005) *Deaths by Gun Fire in Brazil from 1979–2003*, Paris: UNESCO.

UN-Habitat (United Nations Human Settlement Programme) (2006) *The State of the World's Cities Report 2006/2007. The Millennium Development Goals and Urban Sustainability: 30 Years of Shaping the Habitat Agenda*, London: Earthscan and UN-Habitat.

— (2007) *Enhancing Urban Safety and Security: Global Report on Human Settlements 2007*, London: Earthscan.

— (2008) *State of the World's Cities 2008–2009*, London: Earthscan.

USAID/Cairo/EAS (1993) *Report on Eco-*

nomic Conditions in Egypt, 1991–1992, Cairo: USAID.

Van Huyssteen, E. O., M. Robinson and E. Makoni (2009) 'South Africa's city regions: a call for contemplation ... and action', *Urban Forum*, 20, forthcoming.

Varshney, A. (2003) *Ethnic Conflict and Civic Life. Hindus and Muslims in India*, New Haven, CT, and London: Yale University Press.

Veja (2002) 18 September.

Venables, A. (2005) 'Spatial disparities in developing countries: cities, regions and international trade', *Journal of Economic Geography*, 5(1): 3–21.

Vendors in the City of Minia (1993) New York: Ford Foundation.

Ventura, Z. (1994) *Cidade Partida*, São Paulo: Schwartz.

Verges, M. (1996) 'Genesis of a mobilization: the young activists of Algeria's Islamic Salvation Front', in J. Beinin and J. Stork (eds), *Political Islam*, Berkeley: University of California Press, pp. 292–308.

Vertovec, S. and R. Cohen (eds) (2002) *Conceiving Cosmopolitanism: Theory, Context and Practice*, Oxford: Oxford University Press.

Vidal, D. (2005) 'Casser l'apartheid à la française', *Le Monde Diplomatique*, December.

Villavicencio, G. (2001) *El Costo Social del Delito en el Ecuador y Guayaquil*, Guayaquil: Instituto Superior de Criminología y Ciencias Penalistas, Universidad de Guayaquil.

— (2003) 'Eje: defensa de los derechos. Mesa: informalidad y economía subterránea', Paper presented at Diálogo Nacional por la Unidad y el Desarrollo, Capítulo Guayas, Guayaquil, 19–20 March.

— (2004) *Diagnósticos y Propuestas para la Seguridad Ciudadana de Guayaquil*, Seminario Internacional sobre 'Política Pública de Seguridad y Convivencia Ciudadana', Quito, 24–26 March.

Wacquant, L. (2003) 'Toward a dictatorship over the poor? Notes on the penalization of poverty in Brazil', *Punishment and Society*, 5(2): 197–205.

— (2004) *Los Condenados de la Ciudad. Gueto, Periferias y Estado*, Buenos Aires: Siglo Veintiuno Editores.

— (2007) *Urban Outcasts*, Cambridge: Polity Press.

Waiselfisz, J. (2007) *Mapa da Violência dos Municípios Brasileiros*, Brasilia: Organização dos Estados Ibero-Americanos para a Educação, a Ciência e a Cultura.

Walton, J. (1998) 'Urban conflict and social movements in poor countries: theory and evidence of collective action', *International Journal of Urban and Regional Research*, 22(3): 460–81.

Walton, J. and D. Seddon (1994) *Free Markets and Food Riots*, London: Blackwell.

Wampler, B. (2007) *Participatory Budgeting in Brazil. Contestation, Cooperation, and Accountability*, University Park, PA: Pennsylvania State University Press.

Ward, K. and E. J. McCann (2006) 'The new path to a new city? Introduction to a debate on urban politics, social movements and the legacies of Manuel Castells' *The City and the Grassroots*', *International Journal of Urban and Regional Research*, 30(1): 189–93.

Warren, R. (2002) 'Situating the city and September 11th: military urban doctrine, "pop-up" armies and spatial chess', *International Journal of Urban and Regional Research*, 26(3): 614–19.

WCPG (Western Cape Provincial Government) (2006) *iKapa Elihlumayo: Provincial Growth and Development Strategy*, Green Paper, Cape Town: WCPG.

Webster, N. (1995) 'The role of NGDOs in Indian rural development: some lessons from West Bengal and Karnataka', *European Journal of Development Research*, 7(2): 407–33.

Weinstein, L. (2008) 'Mumbai's development mafias: globalization, organized crime and land development',

Bibliography

International Journal of Urban and Regional Research, 32(1): 22–39.

Weizman, E. (2004) 'Strategic points, flexible lines, tense surfaces, and political volumes: Ariel Sharon and the geometry of occupation', in S. Graham (ed.), *Cities, War and Terrorism: Towards an Urban Geopolitics*, Oxford: Blackwell, pp. 172–91.

Westley, J. (1998) 'Change in Egyptian economy, 1977–1997', *Cairo Papers in Social Science*, 21(3).

Wickham, C. R. (1996) 'Islamic mobilization and political change: the Islamist trend in Egypt's professional associations', in J. Beinin and J. Stork (eds), *Political Islam*, Berkeley: University of California Press, pp. 120–35.

Wikan, U. (1997) *Tomorrow, God Willing*, Chicago, IL: University of Chicago Press.

Wirth, L. (1938) 'Urbanism as a way of life', *American Journal of Sociology*, 44(1): 1–24.

Wood, E. (2000) *Forging Democracy from Below: Insurgent Transitions in South Africa and El Salvador*, Cambridge: Cambridge University Press.

Woolcock, M. (2007) *Towards an Economic Sociology of Chronic Poverty: Enhancing the Rigour and Relevance of Social Theory*, CPRC Working Paper 104, Manchester: University of Manchester.

World Bank (1991) *Urban Policy and Economic Development: An Agenda for the 1990s*, Washington, DC: World Bank.

— (1997) *World Development Report: The State in a Changing World*, Washington, DC: World Bank.

— (2009) *Reshaping Economic Geography. World Development Report 2009*, Washington, DC: World Bank.

Young, C. (2004) 'The end of the post-colonial state in Africa? Reflections on changing African political dynamics', *African Affairs*, 103: 23–49.

Zaluar, A. (1994) *Condomínio do Diablo*, Rio de Janeiro: Editora Revan.

— (2004a) *Integração Perversa: Pobreza e Tráfico de Drogas*, Rio de Janeiro: Editora Fundação Getúlio Vargas.

— (2004b) 'Urban violence and drug warfare in Brazil', in K. Koonings and D. Kruijt (eds), *Armed Actors: Organized Violence and State Failure in Latin America*, London: Zed Books, pp. 139–54.

Zaverucha, J. (1999) 'Military justice in the state of Pernambuco after the Brazilian military regime: an authoritarian legacy', *Latin American Research Review*, 34(2): 43–74.

Zhang, L. (2001) *Strangers in the City: Reconfigurations of Space, Power, and Social Networks within China's Floating Population*, Stanford, CA: Stanford University Press.

Index

Index